Sociology for Business

Sociology for Business

A Practical Approach

MARTIN JOSEPH

Polity Press

Copyright © Martin Joseph 1989

First published 1989 by Polity Press
in association with Basil Blackwell
Reprinted 1990

Editorial Office:
65 Bridge Street
Cambridge CB2 1UR, UK

Basil Blackwell Ltd
108 Cowley Road, Oxford OX4 1JF, UK

Basil Blackwell Inc.
3 Cambridge Center,
Cambridge, MA 02142, USA

British Library Cataloguing in Publication Data

A CIP catalogue record for this book is available from the British Library.

ISBN 0–7456–0433–1
ISBN 0–7456–0434–X Pbk

Library of Congress Cataloging in Publication Data

Joseph, Martin.
  Sociology for business : a practical approach / Martin Joseph.
    p. cm.
  Includes index.
  ISBN 0–7456–0433–1 (Blackwell)
  ISBN 0–7456–0434–X (Blackwell : pbk.)
    1. Industrial sociology. 2. Sociology. I. Title.
HD6955.J67   1989   89–837
306'.36—dc19   CIP

Typeset in 9½ on 12 pt Plantin
by Photographics, Honiton, Devon
Printed in Great Britain by T.J. Press Ltd, Padstow

Contents

Detailed Chapter Contents

Acknowledgements

I would like to thank all my colleagues at Oxford Polytechnic, including Alastair Neilson, Peter George, John Astley and especially Frank Webster and Keith Lambe. I am grateful too for the help I received from Ian Glover and Michael Kelly of Dundee College of Technology and Professor Roderick Martin of Imperial College. I must also thank David Held, Sue Vice, Harriet Barry and the staff of Polity Press for all their care. I should like to thank my two typists, Ines Slay and Jacqui Smithson for their accurate work. My college, Oxford Polytechnic, has always been most helpful.

Finally I must thank my family for making allowances for me.

The author and publishers are grateful to the following for permission to reproduce material which originally appeared elsewhere:

Collins Publishers Ltd for two diagrams from S. Hughes, *The Structure of Industry*, 1986. *Fortune* © 1987 Time Inc., all rights reserved, for an extract from the listing 'Fifty largest industrial companies in the world', August 1987. Hodder & Stoughton Ltd and Times Books for a table from Anthony Sampson, *The Changing Anatomy of Britain*. Routledge & Kegan Paul for extracts from J. Fidler, *British Business Elite* and T. J. Watson, *Sociology, Work and Industry*. A. Neilson, Oxford Polytechnic, for extracts from *A Short Course for Managers Concerned with Personnel*. McGraw-Hill for a table from J. D. Thompson, *Organizations in Action*, copyright © 1967. Longman for extracts from G. Salaman, *Work Organizations*. Jonathan Cape Ltd for an extract from A. Jay, *Corporation Man*. The *Guardian* for an article by N. Foster, 19 August 1987. Hutchinson Ltd for an extract from R. Lee and P. Lawrence, *Organizational Behaviour*. Pergamon Press for an extract from J. Chilver, *People, Communication and Organization*, and K. K. Tse, *Marks and Spencer: Anatomy of Britain's Most Efficiently Run Company*. ICI Group for extracts from the *Annual*

Report 1986. HMSO Books for extracts from the *Employment Gazette*, and from *Social Trends* 1986, 1987. OPCS for unpublished data from the General Household Survey 1985. Macmillan for an extract from R. Hyman, *Strikes* 1984. John Wiley and Sons Inc. for a diagram from F. Herzberg, *The Motivation to Work*. EOC for a table from *Women and Men in Britain*, 1986. Piatkus Books for extracts from M. Davidson, *Reach for the Top*, 1985. Gower for an extract from B. Wilkinson, *The Shop Floor Politics of New Technology*. Penguin Books Ltd for an extract from M. Whitehead, *Inequalities in Health*, copyright © Margaret Whitehead 1988.

1   Introduction

1   Aims of the Book

This book assumes no previous knowledge of sociology by the
student, tutor, practitioner or general reader. The aim of the book
is to make sociology available to a very wide audience, particularly
business and management students. To achieve this it seeks to be
practical, relevant to the business world, jargon-free, easily understood
at first reading, and generally interesting! Learning sociology should
teach you to question, analyse and think about what is really going
on, to help you make informed decisions – though it may not make
those decisions easier.

What is sociology?

Sociology, as the name suggests, is about relationships between people
– social relations. This covers all interaction between individuals and
groups of people. You may think social relationships aren't important
to the real business of getting things done – running a factory,
managing a shop, and so on. But such things depend on people, and
the way they co-operate (or otherwise) with each other can have a
fundamental impact on the success (or otherwise) of the organization.

Social relationships are important at all levels in society, from the
personal to the governmental. We all have assumptions about the
way society is organized and the way people should and do behave
within it. Sociology questions these assumptions about what is
'normal', 'true' and 'obvious'. The fact that different societies and
cultures have different ideas about what is normal (for example, about
marriage customs or truth-telling) indicates that these are shared
assumptions, rather than facts.

Sociology is not easy. We need to be alert to our own bias – so, if you are cynical about sociology's value, think about your cynicism in the light of what you read in the rest of this book.

Sociology and work

Among other things, this book seeks to show the social nature of work. Work involves a way of life, entrenched habits which are hard to change. The motivation to work is complex; work organizations – factories, offices, hospitals – do not always function in a rational way; industrial relations are in some cases a constant struggle between management and employees based on differing ways of seeing the social world (or *ideologies*).

Sociology and business studies

Certain problems arise in writing a book of this kind. First, some sociologists may see the emphasis on practicality and relevance as somehow compromising the 'purity' of the discipline – believing that sociology, with its emphasis on describing and analysing the real world of people, can't be put to the service of particular powerful groups in society, for example employers! (They are right, of course; sociology does not intend to serve any particular group, but to enlighten everyone who shares it.)

Secondly, there are serious constraints on sociology in business studies; for example, the attitudes and values of some lecturers in Business Studies departments, 'who seem untroubled by the basis and uses of the knowledge they seek to pass on'[1] (whereas sociology stresses the need to question everything). Business studies is about learning specific skills and facts; sociology is about analysis.

Thirdly, and similarly, the technical and vocational orientation of many Business Studies students may mean that they just want to learn something 'useful' without questioning it. Sociology *is* useful, though not if you want prescribed rules. It will help you to understand the situations you find yourself in, and thus deal with them more effectively.

2 What Does Sociology Do?

Finding out what is really going on

Sociology helps to illuminate what is really going on in any situation, such as in the family, school or hospital. In the world of business and industrial relations sociologists seek to understand what goes on in specific situations such as a meeting of company executives, a selection interview or a promotions board. Sociologists want to know the 'unofficial' view of what is going on; they might, for instance, explain what is going on in an office from the viewpoint of a junior; they will investigate the strikers' viewpoints more closely than the managers'. The reason for this is that the 'official view' is already well known through the media, and taken for granted. Sociologists frequently find the unofficial view gives useful insights into the situation. Not surprisingly, this is one of the reasons why sociology can be unpopular with some of those in authority, who would prefer us not to question the assumptions behind all our actions.

Sociology also takes a wide view, looking at society as a whole – what are the common views of most people in society? It asks whether most people assume financial success is important, that profitability should be the goal of the firm, that most of the unemployed are scroungers, that most old people are 'past it', that it is right for women or black people to do lower-status work. *If* people hold such views, why should this be so, and how are these views sustained? Thus sociology also seeks to show how individuals are affected by the society of which they are part, and how individuals, especially in powerful and elite groupings, can themselves influence the beliefs that people hold.

Sociology stresses that we are what we have learnt rather than what we have inherited. To a large extent a person *learns* the role of, say, personnel manager, skilled worker, accountant or secretary. But we also learn and come to accept that these different positions carry more or less power, status and reward. Again, why should this be so? Why should there be considerable variations in the status attached to a particular occupation from one society to another? For example, in Germany engineers of all sorts usually have more status than their British counterparts. Such differences cannot be explained by theories of instinct or genetic inheritance.

Debate and criticism

I have attempted above to indicate some of the areas of interest in the world of work. But sociology is a wider subject. Some sociologists see the real problem of sociology as explaining how order is maintained in society. Sociology first developed as a reaction to problems of disorder caused by the Industrial Revolution and the French Revolution (1789).[2] People sought an explanation for major upheavals. Later sociologists, following Karl Marx (1818–83), have stressed the class struggle in society, seeing the government in a capitalist society as an instrument of the ruling class, and seeing the dominant ideas in society as the ideas of that class. Debates between different sociologists of this type contribute enormously to sociology in general and to our understanding of industrialization and organization. The subject makes progress through criticism and debate, and the text will introduce some of these debates in an easily understandable way.

A sociological view

Everyday common-sense views

The 'official' or commonly held view of society and its organizations is probably right; there's no need to question it.

We are what we are because of what we have inherited from our parents.

You cannot change human nature. There will always be ruthless selfish people just as there will always be lazy people. Trust your instincts!

Some behaviour seems pointless, for example some strikes, or violence on the picket line.

Individuals are seen as responsible for their own actions, as knowing right from wrong, as having a free will.

A sociological view

The 'official' or commonly held view should normally be questioned. The unofficial views (of those at the bottom of organizations) should always be considered and examined.

We are what we are because of what we have learnt, especially in early childhood.

Sociologists stress learning rather than inheritance or instincts. We are what we have learnt to be (hence it is possible to change); though of course there are individual variations.

No adult behaviour is pointless or senseless. The sociologist must try to find out why certain behaviour is taking place; to explain the apparently inexplicable.

No two people are exactly the same, but individuals are seen as influenced by the society from which they sprang. Thus sociologists stress the importance of class, race and religion, because this seems to explain a lot of individual and group behaviour. Our society is within us, so to speak.

3 The Individual, the Organization and the Wider World

Throughout your study of this book, it is important to keep two points firmly in mind. Firstly, as already emphasized, we are very largely what we have learnt. Secondly, business takes place in a *cultural* setting. Perhaps the diagram will help to explain this.[3]

'Culture' means the body of ways of thinking and acting commonly accepted in society. Culture includes *norms* and *values*. Norms in turn are the accepted means of achieving values or goals. 'Organization' here means any work organization, including the factory, office, hospital, town hall, small firm, school and so on, each of which will have its own formal or informal organizational goals.

The beliefs (culture) of a particular society will affect the behaviour of individuals in that society. For example, Max Weber, an important early German sociologist, argued that industrialization first took place in Protestant areas of Europe for cultural reasons. (Many historians agree with this view.) Protestants, unlike Catholics, could not be sure of salvation. However, hard work and thrift in this life was seen as a sign of election in the next world, this belief helped to stimulate industrial capitalism. In other words the culture of that society stressed the need to work hard and to achieve. Hard work and saving are the norms; success (such as for example establishing a factory or mill) is the goal. These same norms and values permeate any work organization in Western society today by being accepted by the individuals comprising that organization. Individual people during the Industrial Revolution were *socialized* by society to accept that culture; they were taught norms and values based on Protestant beliefs from their cradles, so that they seemed 'natural'. Thus they were *socialized* (taught informally by society) to their proper 'roles' in society, to become hard-working factory owners, diligent workers and responsible parents, passing on to their children the morality of Christian stewardship and so handing on the culture, the heritage, to the next generation. Weber's view of the rise of capitalism can be criticized on many grounds (for example, that many aspects of traditional Catholic teaching were equally compatible with capitalism), but this example does indicate how the culture of a society affects its ultimate forms and actions; its norms and values vitally affect its individual members and the organizations in which they live and work.

The influence of culture can be a two-way affair. Society and its organization affect the individual; but the individual is not *solely* a product of socialization. He or she can influence the organization. Where two cultures meet, one or both must adapt. This is often how change comes about. Thus a Japanese factory in Britain may have to adjust to British work norms. In some Japanese factories workers are not allowed to talk to each other during working hours, but in Britain this rule may have to be relaxed, as British people are not used to it. Again, many multinational enterprises (or transnationals) may have to adjust to the work norms and values of the host country rather than trying to enforce the work norms of the home country ('head office') (see chapter 2).

It should also be realized that the prevailing culture affects, for example, the selection of new staff (the organization will tend to select people similar to those already employed).

4   Can Sociology Help the Manager?

At this point the sceptical reader may be thinking 'but I still don't see how this helps the manager. In fact, I cannot see the *practical* use of sociology.' The main practical use of sociology is to alert the reader, student, manager or lay person to unexamined common assumptions that may be influencing their decision-making. The key question is 'what is going on here?' – not 'what do managers or subordinates *think* is going on?', but 'what is *really* happening?'. The rest of the book shows in detail how to find this out, by:

- describing difficulties and challenges that arise at work, for example strikes, attempts to achieve higher productivity, lack of enthusiasm, etc.;

- showing how various experts, including psychologists, industrial relations consultants, managers and especially personnel managers, explain these situations, and describing their theories and practical recommendations;
- showing how sociologists approach these difficulties at work, and what criticisms they would make of the theories of others;
- showing how the insights gained from the sociological approach can be utilized to improve work situations.

If this sounds too theoretical, remember that theories are only ways of looking at 'real' situations, designed to help us think more clearly. No one would argue that they are better off *not* thinking clearly! Most people would agree that as a general rule it is useful to examine the assumptions we are making before rushing into action. What is the real problem? Is it simply finding a way to break the strike or to stop the pilfering, or are these problems symptoms of some deeper malaise that we could deal with or at least minimize? Is the idea we first had to solve the problem going to cause a worse one (e.g. searching the staff as they leave may lead to a strike and will certainly destroy co-operation between management and workforce)? Take, for example, power and control at work. Managers assume they have the right to manage (and at first sight this seems a reasonable assumption). But is there a problem here? What does it imply about the workers' role? To the sociologist the problem may be that of too much control, too much management, which leads to employee dissatisfaction or, deeper still, the real problem may be that industrial workers are alienated (this is explained in chapter 6). Workers may feel they are over-supervised, over-controlled, and not really trusted. Their reaction to this may be to behave accordingly, to *be* untrustworthy.[4] Thus attempts to impose tighter control, to penalize absenteeism, shorten tea breaks, or quicken the production line may be self-defeating.

But surely managers know all this, says the sceptic. Unfortunately, they often behave as if they don't. As chapter 6 shows, they are influenced by a managerial culture that stresses their 'right' to manage and control. This claim can be confirmed by listening to what managers actually say during disputes; by reading managers' biographies (for example Sir Michael Edwardes' book *Back from the Brink*), and by working through the case studies in this book which involve problems arising in real work situations.[5]

In summary, then, sociology can be of practical use in the following ways:

- It alerts managers and others to the common assumptions we make.
- It helps to show what is really going on rather than what those in authority may say is happening.

- It shows up different viewpoints about what is going on; what is good for one group may be bad for another.
- It develops a questioning and critical view which in the long run improves the quality of decision-making.

5 Working Through the Book

As you will have gathered, there are two main themes to this book. First, a constant emphasis on seeing beyond the obvious, of questioning what is taken for granted, of making sense of the 'senseless'. The second theme is the emphasis on active practical sociology.

Examining what is really going on

A sociologist must investigate everything, even (or especially) the obvious, the familiar, the self-evident. The 'obvious stubbornness' of a union leader, the 'obvious unreasonableness' of management; the sociologist must look behind all this.

The main sociological tool used in this quest is the concept of 'ideology'.

Ideology

This concept is difficult to define, but here are some pointers.

- Different beliefs, attitudes and opinions are held by different groups of people in society, for example there are 'professional' ideologies and 'managerial' ideologies.

- These ideologies become ways of looking at the social world which favour dominant social groups, for example men over women (the ideology of sexism), whites over blacks (racism), professional over client. (Can you think of others?)

- 'So far as the world of work is concerned, it seems that many people tend to view the world through occupational spectacles'. Thus it has been argued that the medical profession tends to concentrate on 'cures' and sometimes overlooks other approaches to health, such as preventative medicine.[6]

- The task of the sociologist is not to say whether ideologies are good or bad; true or false; but rather to show that they do exist and that they distort our view of the social world.

Let us take one example, that will come up again throughout this book, the ideology of 'scientific management' or 'Taylorism' (after the author of *The Principles of Scientific Management*[7]). Scientific management stresses management's right to manage, to control every stage of the work, and to say not only what must be done but how it is to be done. This is an exaggeration and distortion of the obvious fact that the management of an organization must have ultimate responsibility and control. Thus, during most strikes management seems to be emphasizing the importance of managerial prerogative and management's right to manage, no matter what the issue was that caused the strike – how often do you hear this view in the news? Ideologies are all around us: look out for them!

Active practical sociology

Case studies   Case studies are provided as exercises throughout the book. I suggest that, to get the most from them, the student group be divided into subgroups of, say, three. Each subgroup works through the problem and puts together some sort of report, perhaps an informal one. Each subgroup should have a chairperson who tries to ensure that everyone speaks, and a spokesperson. There could then be a session at the end, when each spokesperson tells the main group what their subgroup thought, and a general discussion might ensue.

Project work   In case-study work the material required is usually provided within the case study itself. In project work, the student must often seek the information required. Any reports should usually be addressed to the managing director, or the personnel director, so as to give a real-life feel to the exercise. Naturally the student should go beyond the obvious, and should make the report sociological, always questioning what is happening.

Role play, essays, criticism   The exercises set here also include role play, essay-type questions, quotations to be criticized, and so on. Often there is no one correct answer, but the student should demonstrate clearly an ability to analyse problems in a sociological manner, rather than just describe situations. Students should always try to get beyond what every person knows.

The book is intended for a wide variety of students, including those on B/TEC, BA Business Studies, Business Management and Administration, Institute of Personnel Management etc. courses.

Some questions are more suited for one group than another. Thus a B/TEC student should normally go for the more practical questions.

It will be more useful to work through the questions, case studies and other exercises than just passively to try and 'learn' the subject. But, of course, reading is important, and most chapters have a Further Reading section at the end. It is seldom necessary to read a book from cover to cover; rather you should try to extract the 'meat' as efficiently as possible. Always adopt a critical attitude to what you read.

Various sociological concepts and terms will be used and explained in this book. Many are familiar words used in a rather specific way. The glossary at the end of the book (pp. 234–8) is designed to give you reminders of the meaning of terms.

Exercises

Self-examination question

(This question can be answered from the text of this chapter.)
What is meant by:

* technical and vocational orientation
* ideology
* role
* culture – of a society
* culture – of an organization
* norms

Project

Take an item of current business news such as a take-over bid or a strike, and treat it as a case study. Describe and understand the background, analysing what is happening, and show clearly the viewpoints of all the parties, including the likely views of those *not* described in the newspapers.

Further Reading

T.F. Honour and R.M. Mainwaring, *Business and Sociology* (Croom Helm, London, 1982)

D.S. Pugh et al. (eds), *Writers on Organisations* (Penguin, Harmondsworth, 1983), especially sections on Weber and Taylor

T.J. Watson, *Management Organisation and Employment Strategy* (Routledge and Kegan Paul, London, 1986)

D. Weeks and C. Inns, *Business Organization, Work and Society* (Holt, London, 1981).

Notes

1. T.F. Honour and R.M. Mainwaring, *Business and Sociology* (Croom Helm, London, 1982), Preface.
2. See, for example, E. Durkheim, *The Division of Labor in Society* (Free Press, New York, 1964).
3. D. Weeks and C. Inns, *Business Organisation, Work and Society* (Holt, London, 1981), p. 7.
4. A. Fox, *Man Mismanagement* (Hutchinson, London, 1985).
5. M. Edwardes, *Back from the Brink* (Collins, London, 1983).
6. E. Freidson, *Professional Powers* (University of Chicago Press, Chicago, 1986).
7. F.W. Taylor, *Scientific Management* (Harper and Row, New York, 1964).

2 Business and Society

1 Introduction

The aim of this chapter is to illuminate the nature of business by examining business attitudes in four types of society: the USA, Japan, Britain and the underdeveloped countries. Two facts emerge.

- There are important cultural differences between these societies, resulting from their different histories and place in the world.
- As a result of the requirements of industrial capitalism, these societies have more in common than at first appears.

Why do some countries succeed in the international economy, and why do others slip behind? Can sociology shed some light on this? One approach might be to look at the culture, the values, of successful societies and compare them with those of the less successful. Some sociologists might condemn this as crude 'culturalism', the idea that the culture *determines*, say, the rate of industrialization. Another objection is that there is probably not much to be gained by looking for 'causes'. Rather it would be more useful to look for similarities (a theme of this chapter); for example, what are the similarities between American and Japanese capitalism? Certain characteristics are shared by all capitalist countries, but some may be better placed with the world capitalist system to do well.

2 Business Values in the USA

Independence and success

Despite a relative decline in recent years, the United States' economy is still regarded as an outstanding example of free enterprise. Why?

Capitalism

Capitalism implies the private ownership of capital including goods and the means to produce them (factories), profit, and a free market economy in which goods, services and labour can be freely bought and sold. In nineteenth-century Britain and the USA in particular there was a large number of small firms owned and controlled by individuals and their families, and a free market. There was a generally accepted doctrine of *laissez-faire*, implying the government did not intervene.

Throughout the twentieth century Britain, the USA and Japan have moved away from this earlier model of capitalism to what could be called 'monopoly capitalism', characterized by large firms which dominate their markets. There has also been a big increase in the size and power of financial institutions like banks, insurance companies, holding companies and pension funds. The term 'finance capitalism' is used to denote the increasing power of these financial institutions.

The United States has traditionally been seen as the land of opportunity, of the 'open frontier', where hard work brings its own reward. Many migrants from Europe were driven to America by poverty or persecution (the 'push' theory of immigration) at home; others were attracted there to build a new life free from state interference (the 'pull' theory of immigration).[1] On their way to a new life in a new land many would have passed the Statue of Liberty at the entrance to New York Harbour. Its inscription epitomizes the hopes of many immigrants.

> Give me your tired, your poor,
> Your huddled masses yearning to breathe free
> The wretched refuse of your teeming shore,
> Send these, the homeless, tempest-tossed to me:
> I lift my lamp beside the golden door.[2]

Such sentiments appear to lie deep in the American culture. They are attractive today to the hopeful Hispanic immigrant, who by a cruel irony is then barred from admission to the promised land (or land of promise). They are sought by (and denied to) blacks.

The stress on individualism is attractive to many American managers. Rugged independence, with a stress on action (getting things done) seems to be exemplified in the image of the cowboy, often the lonely cowboy who makes up his own mind and is only guided by his own values. Finally, associated with this vision of independence in an open society is the ideal of the free market, with many buyers and sellers, freedom of choice, no state interference, contracts freely entered into, and no barriers to foreign trade.

Independence is a strong value in the business culture of the USA. It is shown in the widespread suspicion of government interference in business and in the belief in competition. It is summarized in the concept of *laissez-faire*, in which government stands back and does not try to regulate business – leave it all to market forces (supply and demand), could be the motto. It is expected that any shortages of commodities will lead to a rise in the price, thus stimulating higher production.

The second belief taken here as epitomizing the business culture of the USA is the desire for success. American culture stresses the need to strive for one goal (which is thought to be open to all) – *success*. Apparent failure is just a setback on the road to ultimate success. The only genuine failure lies in being a quitter, giving up the struggle. Succss is normally defined in terms of money, power and status.

Many examples could be given of the importance of the success ideology in the USA. The biography of almost every businessman, businesswoman and politician testifies to the importance of striving for, and achieving success; so too do the life histories of millions who did not make it from 'bell boy to President', but perhaps the following example will suffice. It comes from Dale Carnegie's famous best-selling book *How to Win Friends and Influence People*. The book is full of home-spun philosophy and good advice – nothing wrong in that, yet underlying this is the constant emphasis on competing and succeeding. Here is an example:

> 'The way to get things done', says Schwab (an industrialist) 'is to stimulate competition. I do not mean in a sordid, money-getting way, but in the desire to excel'. The challenge! Throwing down the gauntlet! An infallible way of appealing to men of spirit.[3]

Robert Merton, a leading American sociologist, comments that Americans always seem to say 'I need just that 25 per cent more' – and of course the desire is never satisfied; there is always more to strive for. The family, the school and the workplace seem to unite in providing the intensive disciplining required to keep individuals well motivated to achieve success.[4]

A criticism of American business beliefs

So far it has been suggested that there are two fundamental business beliefs in the USA: a belief in *independence* (including individualism and *laissez-faire*), and a belief in *success*.

Taking the belief in independence first; there is in fact strong government regulation of business in the USA, and the belief in

---

Concentration

Concentration of industry in fewer and fewer hands is a feature of modern capitalism. Monopoly through concentration steadily increased in Britain from the 1870s until the Second World War. It occurs when few and increasingly fewer large corporations occupy the major part of the economy or dominate a particular market. In 1980 the top 100 companies contributed 40 per cent of net output in Britain, while in the USA it is near 35 per cent.[6]

Increased concentration may come about through the merger of firms in a similar area of activity, for example, two airlines. Alternatively, one firm may buy another even though the two firms have no intrinsic economic connection, leading to the growth of conglomerates (such as the Hanson Trust in the UK).

Diversification, the practice of producing different goods for a different market, often leads to the formation of conglomerates; for example, a firm wanting to introduce new products may acquire another firm already in that field, rather than starting production from scratch.

---

laissez-faire may hide what is really going on. In fact US industry is highly concentrated in the largest firms, who tend to buy up competitors. The strong American 'anti-trust' laws (laws against monopolies) are testimony to the existence of this problem.[5] Why then do Americans strongly believe in the free market when concentration and monopoly are so strong in the USA and have been considerably interfered with by governments? As mentioned, *laissez-faire* implies little government intervention, a belief that governments should not direct or support industry; American governments intervene to prevent excesses, but they don't plan or direct industry. Supportive policies by governments would cost money – taxpayers' money – and usually this means the money of the more wealthy in society. Hence it could be argued that the doctrine of *laissez-faire* protects the interests of the wealthy in society. It can also be argued that the wealthy tend to own the firms, and they do not want their profit-making interfered with.

The idea that *only* in a free market can industry grow is perhaps an ideology rather than a fact (although Britain and America seem to have developed in this way in earlier days). In fact most industrialized countries really developed through state intervention, state control and state encouragement. The three main examples of this occurred in the late nineteenth century in Germany, Japan and Tsarist Russia. In all three cases the reasons were probably military and transport needs, and a desire for prestige.

I said that the success ideology is strong in American society, but what of those who do not achieve success? There are various reactions to failure, which can roughly be categorized. The *conformist* is the person who approves of society's goal (success), and who uses approved means towards achieving this goal, such as hard work, even when they evidently aren't going to get there. The *innovator* approves of the goal, but sees that hard work won't get him or her to it, and may take short cuts, such as stealing. In a country like the USA which prizes success so highly but in which there is great inequality of opportunity (in the inner-city ghettos, for instance), it is perhaps not so surprising that crime rates are high.[7] The ideology of success causes major problems, as the excluded become more sharply aware of their lack of success, and lack of opportunity to achieve it.

The following example may help to bring together the main points made in this section – that there is a strong emphasis on success and individualism in the business culture of the USA, but that they have become ideologies which hide what is really happening.

An investigation into successful companies in the USA showed that top companies insisted on top quality, fawned on customers, listened to employees and treated them like adults. The authors mentioned eight attributes that seemed to characterize 'go-ahead' management.[8]

- *A bias for action*. They have a bias towards getting on with things, however uncertain the outcome.
- *Close to the customer*. They listen to the customer. Many of the best product ideas come this way, said an IBM executive.
- *Autonomy and entrepreneurship*. Contrary to conventional ideas about big corporations the 3M Corporation is run 'like a loose network of laboratories and cubby holes populated by feverish inventors and dauntless entrepreneurs who let their imaginations fly in all directions'. (Note the stress on individualism.)
- *Productivity through people*. Well-managed companies treat rank and file employees as a source of quality and productivity (IBM and Texas Instruments). Another example is Delta Airlines which operates an 'open door management' policy, under which management tries to talk to employees as often as possible.
- *Hands on, value driven*. Some executives, for example at Hewlett Packard, are legendary for walking the plant floors visiting stores, checking quality, etc. The firm's managers pay strict attention to the firm's values. Probably the best example in Britain would be Marks and Spencer plc (see chapter 4).
- *Stick to the knitting*. A Procter and Gamble chief executive commented: 'This company has never left its base. We seek to be anything but a conglomerate.' (Contrast this with the activities of Hanson Trust, where Chairman Lord Hanson said 'everything is for sale'.)

- *Simple forms, lean staff.* Many successful American companies have a simple organizational structure. Often the stress is on 'flat' rather than 'tall' hierarchical organizations. (A flat organization is where there are few layers of hierarchy and a short chain of command.)
- *Autonomy at all levels.* Often successful companies have pushed autonomy down to the shop floor. (Note the stress on individualism again.)

These eight management practices are found in the many successful American companies, according to the authors, and may be seen as typifying the 'best' American management styles, or at least what many managements aspire to. (Many other American companies are seen as over-planned and too bureaucratic.)

A sociological critique

A sociologist might make some criticisms of these eight attributes of go-ahead management. They may describe how the managers of the organizations concerned like to see themselves. Further, these organizations may expect (or demand that) their individual employees adjust to the corporate image and support it. The structure of the organization, its ideology, is seen as given; if any change is necessary to make employees and management get along, it is the individual employer who must change, not the organization. This has been called *psychologism.*[9] (This is covered in more detail in chapter 4.)

The corporation may strive to be open and democratic, yet the employee may still feel frustated or unhappy – why is this? The following three subsections try to answer this question.

US business values emphasize individualism, but in fact, many American writers have noted the unimaginative overcentralization of their large corporations. There is a conflict between organization to fulfil management's aims and the aims of individual members of staff. The ponderous organization may crush democratic participation; managers want to manage without interference from the staff. The aims of autocratic and democratic organization are in conflict.

US business values emphasize success, but success may be bought at a heavy price. Far from being liberating, success can be stressful, making the successful person fearful and watchful. In the following quotation a successful executive speaks of his fears.

> The danger starts as soon as you become a district manager. You have men working for you and you have a boss above. You're caught in a squeeze. The squeeze progresses from station to station. I'll tell you what a squeeze is. You have the guys working for you that are shooting

for your job. The guy you're working for is scared stiff you're gonna shove him out of his job. Everybody goes around and says, 'The test of the true executive is that you have men working for you that can replace you, so you can move up.' That's a lot of boloney. The manager is afraid of the bright young guy coming up.[10]

What is the importance of *individual* values?   Many writers have argued that what is important is not the values of individual executives but rather the requirements of the economy as a whole (sometimes called 'the system'), in which corporations must compete in order to survive. However much a corporation would like to be a good employer, pay good wages and adopt an open, democratic style of management, it is constrained by the competition of other corporations bent on undercutting rivals. The following two quotations illustrate this.

> The need to maximize profit has direct repercussions on internal organisation and company decision-making. It results in the need constantly to monitor and improve the efficiency of the work process. This requires expert attention to the design of work with a view to reducing the time taken to produce a unit of production. This entails attention to technology, work design, payment systems, work flow, the 'rational' fragmentation and co-ordination of the labour process. The efficiency of these processes for profit is constantly under inspection by expert managers and technicians.[11]

> Managers' thinking may be ideological, in that they assume capitalism is a 'natural' system, is necessarily here to stay. But what others call their 'ideology' managers call 'common sense'. And 'common sense' tells them that they must not forfeit control; that the business of business is profit; and that, whatever ideas they might have in their heads, and whatever enriching or participatory ventures they may institute, there are limits – not of their making – to what they can 'sensibly' do.[12]

3   Japanese Business Values

How did Japan become the economic superpower it is today? It may be helpful first to investigate this in order to gain some understanding of Japanese business values.

The modern history of Japan could be seen as one of humiliation by foreign powers. In the first half of the nineteenth century the Western powers had repeatedly sent expeditions to Japan to persuade it to open its ports to trade. But Japan, which could be described as then a feudal country, resisted. However, in 1853 Admiral Perry entered Tokyo Bay and delivered a note from the President of the

United States demanding the inauguration of trade relations. Under the threat of superior military power Japan was forced to accede, a humiliation that was long remembered. However, this event could also be seen as the start of the modernization of Japan, which brought with it comparative prosperity, and a desire to challenge and overtake the West economically.[13] This was made easier by a hard-working labour-force and an accumulation of capital.

The second great humiliation of Japan was its defeat in the Second World War. In the West this is usually seen in purely military terms, but it is important to mention the economic aspects from a Japanese viewpoint. Japan was expanding into South East Asia, but in July 1940 the USA imposed a partial trade embargo, in the hope of stopping its further expansion. Withdrawal from this area hit Japanese trade, causing her to look elsewhere in order to break the tightening economic blockade. Japan's long-term economic aim was then to achieve what it called a 'Greater East Asia Co-Prosperity Sphere', a kind of empire.[14] The crushing defeat of Japan in 1945 destroyed this hope.

Economic pressure on Japan, and the military defeat itself, *could* be seen as (at least partially) leading to Japan's desire to excel economically. This line of thinking suggests that this desire is an important part of Japanese culture. But how deep is this desire? Is it really a lasting part of the culture of Japan? It has been argued that as Japan becomes more fully integrated into the world economy she may develop new and different goals and ambitions. Commercial success may no longer be the dominant value, and she may no longer be the industrial giant she is today.[15]

Values and goals can change, then. Moreover, the same values may not apply uniformly to the whole of society. Japan is an economic superpower today, with strong commercial ambitions, but society contains many elements of traditional ways of thinking and organizing. For example, on the one hand six Japanese companies are in the fifty largest companies in the world; on the other hand the majority of Japanese firms are very small, as table 2.1 shows (p. 20).

Another important value in Japanese society is the importance of the group, and here the legacy of Japanese Confucianism may be important. In the Confucian's world-view subordinates were seen as human beings responsive to moral influence rather than donkeys responsive only to stick and carrot.[16] Japanese Confucianism seemed to assume original virtue rather than original sin. This may have led Japanese management to believe that employees would be useful and co-operative, and to make unremitting efforts through ritual and ceremony to promote a sense of common enterprise in the group, including company slogans and insignia. It is the sense of common

Table 2.1   *International comparison of size of establishment by numbers of employees (percentages)*

	Number of employees in establishment			
	1–99	*100–499*	*500–999*	*1000+*
Japan (1979)	58.3	21.3	7.0	13.4
USA (1977)	25.4	18.0	29.0	27.5
West Germany (1979)	18.9	30.0	13.2	37.9

Source: Nichon Kokusei Zue 1982, p. 326. Reprinted in T. Fukutake, *The Japanese Social Structure*.

enterprise that visiting managers find so striking; the shared goal rather than conflict between management and labour. In many companies the concept of lifetime commitment binds employer and employee together. People believe the company ought to be the community, caring for its employees. (This has been called *paternalism* by some sociologists; see chapter 4.)

So far a number of Japanese business values have been highlighted, including the need to catch up and surpass rivals, the importance of the group, and paternalism and the tradition of life-long employment in some big firms. But are these a remnant of pre-capitalist, traditional Japanese qualities, or are they essentially aspects of a particular kind of capitalist society? Some sociologists researching Japanese culture have challenged the idea that practices such as life-long employment with one company have been embedded in the culture of Japanese society from feudal times.[17] Might not these so-called 'traditions' really hide strong managerial control? The West may simply be less successful at hiding the real conflict of interests that exists between management and workers; it may have a less effective *ideology*.

It might be helpful here to reconsider what has been said about Japanese business values.

- There may be historical and cultural reasons for the Japanese economic drive – a desire to catch up with the West and wipe out past defeats. But this is not necessarily an unchanging phenomenon.
- Japanese culture stresses commitment to the groups; in industrial terms, this means to the company.
- Rather than being a specifically Japanese miracle, Japanese economic development could be seen as that of another country that has industrialized more successfully than many other capitalist countries. The real reason for the economic success of Japan could be the successful adoption of Western capitalism. The Japanese economy

contained all the necessary pre-requisites for industrial capitalism, including a pliant labour force, and available venture capital.

4 British Business Values

The 'British Disease': economists', historians' and sociologists' views

Britain was the first country to industrialize, and from the middle of the eighteenth century until the First World War it was a leader in most areas of production, including coal, steel, ship-building, and cotton. Many economists and historians have sought the reasons why the first 'industrial revolution' in the world took place in Britain. These reasons include the presence of cheap energy (coal), an empire to trade with, inventions that speeded up production, a modern financial system, and so on.

Economic historians argue that the changes that justify the use of the term 'revolution' in Britain included, first, a shift from the self-sufficient family as the unit of production to impersonal production units – the factory, mill or mine.[18] Secondly, there was the evolution of a nationwide market into an international market for British goods.

The engine of growth was the expansion of demand (due in part to the initial production of cheaper goods) which led to the rise of specialist institutions (banks, corporate enterprises, etc.). This in turn led to more efficient production through improved availability of capital. The combination of these factors guaranteed growth.

Earlier expansion had been rather slow, affecting limited areas of the economy. Although other countries developed, their industries did not have access to technological improvement that Britain did, through her inventors and entrepreneurs.

This line of argument goes further, claiming that the capitalist industrial state which emerged from the English Industrial Revolution had reached what was essentially its modern form well before the end of the nineteenth century.

> By 1880 the population of Great Britain had more than trebled in less than a century, and four out of every five of these people were living in large towns; agriculture accounted for only about a tenth of the gross national product; and more than a third of the nation's expenditure went on imports, largely in purchasing essential food-stuffs and industrial raw materials. The share of agriculture in gross national product was to fall a little more; the structure of manufacturing output was to alter considerably; and the economy was to become a little less open, and its growth rate more erratic, as the spread of the industrial

revolution in the rest of the world forced the original country to adopt more defensive commercial policies. But in its most characteristic aspects the economic system which had taken shape by the fourth quarter of the nineteenth century was still in existence at the middle of the twentieth century.[19]

Sociologists have a different approach to explaining the Industrial Revolution. One influential sociologist who has commented on the industrialization of parts of Europe is Max Weber (1864–1920). He showed that industrialization took place in Protestant parts of Europe, where the work ethic was very strong. In Britain it is noticeable that the early entrepreneurs and innovators tended to be members of nonconformist churches. In other words, sociologists emphasize cultural factors in explaining Britain's rise.

From its position as a leading industrial power throughout the eighteenth and much of the nineteenth centuries Britain has experienced a gradual decline (see figures 2.1 and 2.2), a process sometimes known as *de-industrialization*.

How can we account for this? As with explaining Britain's rise, economists and sociologists have different ideas. One economic explanation, that of Andrew Gamble,[20] will be followed by the sociological view.

The decline is long term, lasting over a hundred years. Two aspects stand out: the absolute decline of the British imperial state and the relative decline of the British economy as measured against the

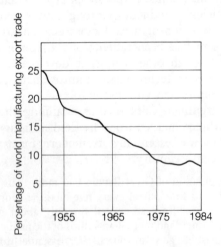

Figure 2.1 *Britain's share of world export trade in manufactures (percentages)*

Source: S. Hughes, *The Structure of Industry* (Collins, London, 1986), p. 6.

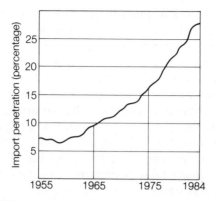

Figure 2.2 *UK import penetration ratio for manufactured goods (percentages)*

Source: S. Hughes, *The Structure of Industry* (Collins, London, 1986), p. 6.

performance of rivals; the two may be linked. The most common diagnosis is that Britain is living beyond its means, that we have been paid more than the sales of our goods can justify. However, Gamble thinks that the real problem lies in the weakness of British capital and the failure of political attempts to overcome it.[21] Gamble believes the British decline can only be understood when it is related to the world economy which Britain once dominated and to which it is now chained.[22] Thus he rejects such notions as excessive imports, weak governments, heavy public expenditure and lazy workers. In this context Labour governments in the past have proved more financially orthodox than Conservative governments, so the cause of failure cannot be located in socialism.

What happens to British governments, Gamble argues, depends on the international economy, and it has long lain outside the power of the British government to influence it to any great extent. It will be seen, therefore, that in accounting for Britain's rise and decline as an industrial power, Gamble has drawn on economic theories and particularly on the concept of the international economy. But are these explanations adequate, or are there deep social reasons for Britain's industrial decline?

In trying to answer these questions M.J. Wiener has put forward the view that the idealization of material growth and innovation were pushed back by the contrary ideals of stability, tranquillity, closeness to the past and non-materialism. An English way of life was accepted which stressed non-material qualities. There was a sort of countryside of the mind that was everything industrial society was not – ancient, slow-moving, stable, cosy and 'spiritual'.[23] Wiener calls the industrial revolution 'the revolution that never was', and argues that the transition was mild and incomplete, whereas in other industrializing countries traditional social patterns were fundamentally disrupted by change. Again, there was no absolute antagonism between the old aristocracy and the new bourgeoisie or middle class in Britain. Consequently there was no bourgeois revolution giving rise to a modern, industrializing elite to replace the old aristocracy.

In a similar vein, Hobsbawm, a historian, traces the relative decline of the British economy. Was it due to the decline of enterprise among businessmen? Or to the conservatism of British society, or to the desire of the British capitalist to become a gentleman or aristocrat and to be accepted as such?

> The aristocratic scale of values, which included amateur status and not apparently trying too hard among the criteria of the 'gentleman', and inculcated them in the 'public schools' which indoctrinated the sons of the risen middle class, was indeed dominant. Being 'in trade' was indeed an awful social stigma; though 'trade' in this sense meant small scale shopkeeping much more than any activity in which really big money – and therefore social acceptance – could be gained.[24]

It seems that an aversion to things industrial lies deep in British thinking, and needs to be understood. Indeed, it seems that the country is best at pre-industrial activities; farming, banking and finance, insurance and merchanting. Industry does not seem to have status and therefore does not attract high-status people.

Another cultural argument that has been advanced is that Britain, being the first country to industrialize, may be the first country to de-industrialize. There has been a decline in the work ethic, some have suggested.

Does this discussion of culture and status in the past really help us to understand Britain's industrial decline today? Perhaps it is impossible to divorce the question of managers' incentives from the climate of society which surrounded them.[25] The climate has been a chilly one for English economic enterprise and business pride. As will be seen in chapter 3, managers of industrial firms in England come from homes of lower status than managers of financial institutions. Finally, by contrast, on the Continent an engineer is frequently addressed as an engineer much as a medical person is addressed as a doctor; i.e. to be an engineer is to have high status.

Today, despite the policies of British governments, these attitudes still exist.

> At the end of the day, it may be that Margaret Thatcher will find her most fundamental challenge not in holding down the money supply or

inhibiting government spending, or even in fighting the shop stewards, but in changing this frame of mind. English history in the eighties may turn less on traditional political struggles than on a cultural contest between the two faces of the middle class (forward looking and backward looking).[26]

5   The Underdeveloped Countries

Why do the developed countries of the North forge ahead? Why do most of the underdeveloped countries of the South remain poor? Why do these poorer countries apparently fail to acquire technical expertise, fail to develop their natural resources, and cannot repay international loans? An interesting way of tackling these questions is to look at the activities of large multinational (transnational) enterprises.

The box gives a brief view of the internationalization of capital, while the rest of this section shows the effects of the work of multinational corporations. Finally the project and role play at the end of this chapter should give the reader a wider awareness of the problem of underdevelopment.

The Internationalization of Capital

Scott shows that the growth of multinational enterprises can be seen as part of the internationalization of capital – capital does not stay in the country in which it was generated, but goes to the country which offers the biggest return. Thus, for example, throughout the nineteenth century there was a large export of British capital, rising in 1914 to a massive (in those days) £4,000m. In earlier days, British capital was invested directly in overseas enterprises such as railways, but later portfolio investment, the ownership of shares in foreign companies, became more usual. American investment on the other hand tended to be direct. Generally this direct investment in overseas enterprises goes to where the prospects of profit are greatest (not necessarily to where the local needs are greatest). These direct investors are usually multinational enterprises whose headquarters are in the advanced countries (the North), but whose operations are to a large extent in the underdeveloped countries (the South).[27] Capital is highly mobile and flows to the countries offering the highest returns – rather than the country in greatest need of capital.[28]

The multinational enterprise

The multinational enterprise is a corporation that has its roots in one country but carries out a large part of its activities in other countries. Multinational enterprises are important partly because they are so large, as table 2.2 shows. They appear to be a force for good in the world in that they provide goods and employment in many countries, and this is especially important in the underdeveloped countries of the 'Third World'. Many large corporations such as car manufacturers can only function if their activities are international. The costs of manufacturing cars by mass production are such that an enormous market is needed, across many countries. There are many advantages, too, in manufacturing in more than one country; for example, they can sometimes avoid the effects of a strike in one country by switching production to factories in other countries (though sometimes trouble in one country stops all the plants in the others, as they are all dependent on each other), and they can get past import barriers by setting up their activities inside that country. They can also avoid taxes through transfer pricing (charging different prices in different countries in order to make low profits in a high-tax country and vice versa).

The main case *against* these multinational enterprises is that investment decisions are determined not by what is best for the countries but what is best for the multinational corporation. Secondly, there is a lack of accountability to the host nation. General Motors makes its strategic decisions regarding operations in, say, Latin America, behind boardroom doors in Detroit. Thirdly, it follows from this that there is a lack of control by the host nation over the activities of the multinational, which controls the technology, the flow of capital, wages and so on. Many multinationals are based in the USA (as table 2.2 shows), and their power and influence have risen alongside that of the USA, particularly since the Second World War.

It is in the home country that vital policy decisions are made. It is in the home country that specialized training is carried out, where technical and business courses exist in high-status colleges (for example the Harvard Business School and the Harvard Law School). It is in the home country that rising young executives were groomed for top posts, finance is raised, and specialized financial institutions exist.

Thus the multinational enterprise benefits the 'headquarters' country in many subtle ways. The profits are returned home; the home banks are rewarded with interest; and the education system at home expands to provide the technologists and other qualified staff, some of whom go overseas to manage the affairs of the multinational enterprise.

Table 2.2 *The world's 25 biggest multinational enterprises*

Rank	Company	Headquarters	Industry	Sales ($000)	Net income ($000)
1	General Motors	Detroit	Motor vehicles and parts	102,813,700	2,944,700
2	Exxon	New York	Petroleum refining	69,888,000	5,360,000
3	Royal Dutch/Shell Group	The Hague/London	Petroleum refining	64,843,217	3,725,779
4	Ford Motor	Dearborn, Mich.	Motor vehicles and parts	62,715,800	3,285,100
5	International Business Machines	Armonk, NY	Computers	51,250,000	4,789,000
6	Mobil	New York	Petroleum refining	44,866,000	1,407,000
7	British Petroleum	London	Petroleum refining	39,855,564	731,954
8	General Electric	Fairfield, Conn.	Electronics	35,211,000	2,492,000
9	American Tel. & Tel.	New York	Electronics	34,087,000	139,000
10	Texaco	White Plains, NY	Petroleum refining	31,613,000	725,000
11	IRI	Rome	Metals	31,561,709	197,118
12	Toyota Motor	Toyota City (Japan)	Motor vehicles and parts	31,553,827	1,717,733
13	Daimler-Benz	Stuttgart	Motor vehicles and parts	30,168,550	831,600
14	E.I. du Pont de Nemours	Wilmington, Del.	Chemicals	27,148,000	1,538,000
15	Matsushita Electric Industrial	Osaka	Electronics	26,459,539	946,571
16	Unilever	Rotterdam/London	Food	25,141,672	973,983
17	Chevron	San Francisco	Petroleum refining	24,351,000	715,000
18	Volkswagen	Wolfsburg (W. Germany)	Motor vehicles and parts	24,317,154	286,133
19	Hitachi	Tokyo	Electronics	22,668,085	679,609
20	ENI	Rome	Petroleum refining	22,549,921	342,275
21	Chrysler	Highland Park, Mich.	Motor vehicles and parts	22,513,500	1,403,600
22	Phillips Gloeilampenfabrieken	Eindhoven (Netherlands)	Electronics	22,471,263	414,418
23	Nestlé	Vevey (Switzerland)	Food	21,153,285	994,566
24	Philip Morris	New York	Tobacco	20,681,000	1,478,000
25	Siemens	Munich	Electronics	20,307,037	629,353

Source: Fortune Magazine, 3 Aug. 1987.

It might seem at least that the multinational enterprise is doing some good by providing high wages in the poorer countries, but really this is not as good as it appears. Often these enterprises pay higher wages than local companies can afford, so taking all the best talent. Their wages are still lower than those paid to staff in the headquarters country, however. Their activities, which are often involved in exporting, attract labour from indigenous activities such as subsistence agriculture, with the result that a country may become unable to feed itself. The development of these countries is therefore distorted to suit the needs of the multinationals.

Finally, in the past Britain and now the USA often intervenes as the world's policeman to ensure peace or a particular political regime favourable to them in areas where their corporations have economic interests. Aid to poorer countries may be given selectively, according to political considerations.

This section may be summarized as follows.

- Although the activities of multinational enterprises appear to be beneficial to poorer countries, they can sometimes inhibit their development. Interest and profits flow to the prosperous 'head-quarters countries', while the economies of the poorer countries remain distorted (growing cash crops rather than food for themselves, etc.).
- The governments of prosperous countries look after their multi-national enterprises and may intervene in a 'police' role if they are threatened – hence there is political control too to ensure governments friendly to the West. Aid to poorer countries may be used to prop up authoritarian regimes or destabilize regimes considered unfriendly to the developed countries.
- Loans are based on the highest return rather than the best overall interests of the borrowing industry.
- The policies of the West often cause and perpetuate distortions in the poorer country's economy.

Question

This section is controversial. Of course one could quote many instances of genuine aid and concern for Third World problems. The problems of the Third World are constantly in the news (famines, coups, etc.). Assess what has been said in this section in the light of current events in the Third World.

Note: many world events appear to have no sociological significance: for example, floods and droughts. In fact, the sociology of disasters shows that these occurrences often affect the poorest people tending the lowest priced land much more than they affect the rich.

6 Conclusion

Appearances	*Possible realities*
There appear to be great diversities between the commercial institutions within a country and especially between different countries, for example the small Japanese family business, the large US corporation, etc. Surely you cannot make general statements governing all these varied examples.	These diversities are more apparent than real. The requirements of capitalism especially the need to maximize profits in the long run (in order to compete) ensures that these commercial institutions are fundamentally similar throughout the world (even though this logic is played out in varied cultural contexts).
The governments in advanced countries appear to adopt a variety of policies ranging from *laissez-faire* to state planning.	In fact three general trends may be discerned in most advanced economies: • concentration (fewer and larger corporations) • increased state intervention; • the internationalization of capital.
American values stress freedom and independence, taking the image of the rugged cowboy as an ideal.	There is much bureaucracy and control in American commercial life. Most Americans work in large, often impersonal organizations. Many factory and office workers find their work unsatisfying.
American culture stresses success – this cannot be bad!	Success as measured by high status, wealth and power is in limited supply. Many at the bottom of the heap never make it, so a few try short cuts because they are denied the opportunity to succeed. Hence perhaps the higher crime rates. Success-seeking is also stressful.
The typical Japanese enterprise is large and efficient.	By comparison with most Western countries Japan has a much higher proportion of small and family businesses.

The successful way in which Japanese industry and commerce has developed is due to the peculiar qualities of the Japanese culture which stresses Confucianism – respect for all, high or low; the importance of the group; and the need to surpass the other advanced economies in order to wipe out past humiliations.

The success of the Japanese economy can be seen as an aspect of capitalism. Deference to the manager, integrated work groups, hard work and so on may be the trappings which hide the reality of strict managerial control of the sort which prevails in most industrialized societies.

The reasons for Britain's comparative decline as an industrial power are obvious. Compared with the USA and Japan there seems to be a lack of drive. Industry needs modernizing. Trade unions with old-fashioned ideas impede progress; industrial relations are poor.

Britain's decline has a long history. There seems to be an anti-industrial culture in the country. As soon as the early industrialist made his pile he would usually retire to the country, instead of building up the firm. He wanted to be accepted as a country gentleman. The social malaise lies deep in the English culture – it is not just (or mainly) a matter of economics.

Prosperity in the advanced countries should eventually benefit poorer countries which will then have bigger markets and receive more (and cheaper) capital.

It does not work like this. The poorer countries remain poor. Taking transnationals as an example, profits are returned to the home (advanced country) where the headquarters office resides while the economies of the poorer countries are distorted.

Exercises

Self-examination question

What is meant by:

- Concentration
- state intervention
- the internationalization of capital

- multinational enterprises (or transnationals)
- *laissez-faire*
- the free market
- independence and success in American culture
- the British Disease
- the Protestant ethic
- capitalism.

Essay or discussion questions

1   Compare conventional views of the commercial success of Japan or the USA with views a sociologist might put forward.
    Suggestions: avoid generalizations; keep the answer specific, e.g. quote specific writers and commentators. Use books written by leading historians and compare their views with those of sociologists Weber, Merton, Worsley, Scott. Use the Further Reading list and the notes to this chapter. Several books have been written comparing the USA and Japan.

2   Taking Britain as an example, attempt a sociological account of the relationship between a society's values and the success of its economy.
    Suggestions: you could compare the views of economists Gamble, Weiner and historian Hobsbawm as shown in the text. Treating the question historically, you could discuss on the one hand the views of economic historians and on the other the views of influential early sociologists such as Max Weber and Emile Durkheim.

3   'The rich get richer and the poor get poorer.' Discuss in relation to the Third World.
    Suggestions: The discussion here of the operation of multinational enterprises indicates how the inequality between richer and poorer nations persists. Take this further, using books such as Manley and Brandt, *The Global Challenge*, and news items in the present and recent past. Here *Keesing's Record of World Events* (in most big libraries) might help. Use also general and specialist magazines and journals (*The Economist, Fortune, New Internationalist, New Statesman and Society*, etc.). Apart from the question of the multinationals, another important topic is the burden of debt. You could investigate this for yourself using the Further Reading list and magazines and journals. Try to quote actual examples.

Project

The multinational enterprise has been the focus of attention here because this book examines, among other things, the problems of business. However, looking at these multinationals in a wider context — of the Third World underdevelopment and distorted development — the following recommendations, from Manley and Brandt, *Global Challenge*, are of interest.

- The domination of the world economy by a handful of giant transnational corporations must be challenged.
- There should be stronger co-operation among the countries of the South.
- The International Monetary Fund which lends to poorer countries often imposes harsh terms for its loans, including high rates of interest and a requirement that the countries adopt stringent economy measures. Alternative ways of raising capital must be sought.
- One third of the gross domestic product of poorer countries goes in armament, much of them purchased from the North. This too must stop.
- The present imbalance is due partly to the fact that the North has its own problems, but uses the South to try to solve them, e.g. through the transmission 'home' of overseas profits. There must be multilateral solutions to multilateral problems.

(a) Using newspapers, journals and such magazines as *Fortune*, *Encounter*, *The Economist* and *Keesing's Record of World Events*, find and examine examples of some of the problems mentioned in this section, e.g.
- The multinational whose operations benefit the home country more than the host country.
- The debt problem of poorer countries.
- The policy of the International Monetary Fund.
- Britain or the USA playing the world policeman role.

(b) As a director of the International Monetary Fund, what proposals would you advance to help the poorer countries of the world and generally narrow the gap between rich and poor? Why might richer countries object? Set our your views in the form of a report to your fellow directors.

Role play

It might be interesting to use the preceding project as the basis for a role play, with the following parts:

- A director of the International Monetary Fund.
- Two directors of named multinational enterprises.
- Two prime ministers of named Third World countries.
- A prime minister of an industrial country.
- A sociologist/commentator.

Further Reading

G.W. Domhoff, *Who Rules America?* (Prentice Hall, Englewood Cliffs, 1983).
Emile Durkheim, *The Division of Labour in Society* (Free Press, New York, 1964).

E.J. Hobsbawm, *Industry and Empire* (Weidenfeld and Nicolson, London, 1968).

M. Manley and W. Brandt, *The Global Challenge: From Crisis to Co-operation: Breaking the North–South Stalemate* (Pan, London, 1985).

B. Mintz and M. Schwartz, *The Power Structure of American Business* (University of Chicago Press, Chicago, 1985).

T.J. Peters and R.H. Waterman, *In Search of Excellence: Lessons from America's Best Run Companies* (Harper and Row, London, 1982).

A.M. Rugman, *Inside the Multi-Nationals* (Croom Helm, London, 1981).

J. Scott, *Corporations, Classes and Capitalism* (Hutchinson, London, 1985).

M. White and M. Trevor, *Under Japanese Management* (Heinemann, London, 1983).

Max Weber, *The Protestant Ethic and the Spirit of Capitalism* (Allen and Unwin, London, 1930).

M.J. Wiener, *English Culture and the Decline of the Industrial Spirit, 1850–1980* (Penguin, Harmondsworth, 1985).

P. Worsley, *The Three Worlds* (Weidenfeld and Nicolson, London, 1984).

Notes

1. A classic: sociological work on immigration to the United States is W.I. Thomas and F. Znaniecki, *The Polish Peasant in Europe and America* (Octagon Books, New York, 1974).
2. Emma Lazarus, 'The New Colossus', Inscription for the Statue of Liberty, New York Harbour.
3. D. Carnegie, *How to Win Friends and Influence People* (The World's Work, Kingswood, 1956).
4. R. Merton, *Social Theory and Social Structure* (Collier Macmillan, London, 1968), pp. 189 ff.
5. E.S. Herman, *Corporate Control, Corporate Power* (Cambridge University Press, Cambridge, 1981).
6. D. Jeffreys, *Monopoly* (Collins, London, 1985), p. 9; J. Scott, *Corporations, Classes and Capitalism* (Hutchinson, London, 1985), p. 201.
7. Merton, *Social Theory*.
8. T.S. Peters and R.H. Waterman, *In Search of Excellence: Lessons from America's Best Run Companies* (Harper and Row, London, 1982).
9. G. Salaman, *Work Organisations, Resistance and Control* (Longman, London, 1979), p. 202.
10. S. Terkel, *Working* (Wildwood House, London, 1975), p. 335.
11. G. Salaman, *Class and the Corporation* (Fontana, London, 1981), p. 245.
12. G. Esland and G. Salaman, *The Politics of Work and Occupations* (Open University, Milton Keynes, 1980), p. 300.
13. E.O. Reischauer, *Japan Past and Present* (Duckworth, London, 1964).
14. Ibid., pp. 208 ff.
15. G.C. Allen, *The Japanese Economy* (Weidenfeld and Nicolson, London, 1981).
16. R.P. Dore, *Japanese Society: Tradition and Change* (Sussex Publications, Devizes, 1973).

17. M. White and M. Trevor, *Under Japanese Management* (Heinemann, London, 1983), p. 4.
18. P. Deane, 'The Industrial Revolution in Britain', in C.M. Cipolla (ed.), *The Emergence of Industrial Societies*, vol. 4 (Harvester Press, Hassocks, 1976), pp. 161 ff.
19. Ibid., pp. 223–4.
20. A. Gamble, *Britain in Decline* (Macmillan, London, 1985).
21. Ibid., p. xviii.
22. Ibid., pp. 12 ff.
23. M.J. Weiner, *English Culture and the Decline of the Industrial Spirit* (Penguin, Harmondsworth, 1985), ch. 1.
24. E.J. Hobsbawm, *Industry and Empire* (Weidenfeld and Nicolson, London, 1968), p. 154.
25. A. Sampson, *The Changing Anatomy of Britain* (Hodder and Stoughton, London, 1981), p. 338.
26. Weiner, *English Culture*, p. 166.
27. Scott, *Corporations*, pp. 205–14.
28. M. Manley and W. Brandt, *The Global Challenge* (Pan, London, 1985), p. 75.

3 The Social Nature of Work

'A man's work is as good a clue as any to the course of his life, and to his social being and identity.'

(Everett Hughes, *Men and their Work*, 1981)

1 Introduction

Why investigate the social aspects of work? Surely people are just people, whatever they are doing? The sociological view is that people are influenced by their social environment; work is not just a way of earning money; it is a major part of a way of life. Occupations are indicators of social class, which often denotes a person's life chances (likelihood of illness, early death, etc.) and life-styles. Any individual manual labourer will probably share with others a distinctive way of life, recognizable as that of a working-class area in terms of housing, diet, education, dress, attitudes and leisure pursuits. (Of course there are individual differences, but the general characteristics are common.) Nor does the manual worker cease to be working class when his wages rise. Class positions are not so much a matter of money as of occupation. Some manual workers earn more than white-collar workers (clerical workers are sometimes also known as black-coated workers, or clerks), yet their way of life remains working class; many do not want to become middle class, nor would many middle-class people happily accept such affluent workers in their clubs, pubs and families.[1] Examples would be teachers, who are poorly paid but middle class, and oil-rig workers, highly paid working class.

This chapter is largely an explanation of the nature of occupations and professions, as seen by sociologists researching them. It should be seen as providing essential background knowledge rather than giving direct advice to the manager or personnel officer (or business student). The implications of sociological insights and research for actual practice will be discussed later in this chapter. For now, just becoming aware of what is involved in being a doctor, manager, clerk, salesperson, or semi-skilled manual worker is the aim. It should broaden the mind, lead to a wider awareness, help one to see what is really going on in particular situations, and in the long run lead to better decision-making.

The aims of this chapter can be summarized as follows:

- to emphasize the social nature of the work people do, showing that work is not just a way of earning money, but part of a way of life;
- to demonstrate the social nature of a profession, to show that, for instance, a profession is like a community of equals;
- to show that the most senior managers are drawn from an elite whose members have a similar background (as shown for example by the attendance at similar elite schools and universities);
- to show that members of occupations, especially managers and professionals, have ideologies which support what they are doing but which may give a distorted view of the world;
- to describe the nature of routine clerical and manual work, and its supporting ideologies;
- to analyse the ways in which people adjust to routine alienating work and how this affects their lives;
- to compare the life-styles of different types of manual workers, for example, craftspeople, 'affluent workers', workers in traditional industries, the 'deferential worker';
- to demonstrate the nature of the *labour process*, that is to say the process by which labour is transformed into commodities – to show that this process reflects the type of society we live in, in which the process is inevitable, alienating and exploitative, and that it involves managers maintaining full control of the work situation, assisted by the ideology of scientific management.

This is a long list so perhaps it is worth mentioning two themes which underlie this chapter. They are:

- identifying occupational ideologies;
- demonstrating the social nature of work.

2   The Professions

To the ordinary person what constitutes a 'profession' seems clear. We all know roughly what kind of work a lawyer, doctor, architect or accountant does. Generally professional people are seen as conscientious, and having a strong moral code; one which stresses that the professional's first duty is to the client. Many professionals are self-employed or are partners in a firm, and the image of the *independent* professional is important (even though most professionals actually work in large organizations).

In the past sociologists have spent a lot of effort defining what is meant by a profession and identifying the significant *traits*.[2] One researcher, Millerson, analysed the work of 21 writers on the professions and showed the key elements in table 3.1 to have been included in their various definitions.

The *trait* approach outlined here would probably have the widest appeal to a lay public, and perhaps few readers would disagree with the table except possibly to alter the order of the traits. However, there are some objections to this approach; in particular it seems to take professionals on their own opinions. This is what professionals might like to believe about themselves, and there may indeed be much truth in these beliefs. However, these beliefs may get exaggerated so that they become *ideologies* – professional ideologies justifying for example the power of the professional over the client (if clients believe professionals have these desirable traits they will defer to and obey

Table 3.1   *The traits of professionalism: the number of times a particular trait was mentioned in 21 works on the subject*

Traits	Number of mentions
Professionals adhere to a professional code of ethics	13
Professions are organized occupations	13
Professional skills are based on theoretical knowledge	12
A profession requires training and education	9
Competence is tested	8
Professions stress altruistic service	8
Skills are applied to the affairs of others	5
Professionals provide indispensable public services	2
Professions are licensed or registered	2
There is a definite professional–client relationship	2
The best impartial service is given	2
There is a definite fee	2
Professionals have strong loyalty to colleagues	1

Source: C. Millerson, *The Qualifying Associations* (Routledge and Kegan Paul, London, 1964), p. 5.

the professionals). The danger is that general or just desirable characteristics become assumed to be *facts* about the whole profession.

Here is an example of a professional ideology. According to sociological researchers, the medical profession has a 'cure' ideology. It emphasizes the importance of cures at the expense of, say, preventative medicine, a better standard of living, etc. Here is one analysis.[3]

The unmasking of medicine

Ian Kennedy makes the following points about the nature of the medical profession and its ideologies.

Medical viewpoints	*Comment*
● Medicine as it is taught and practised now is scientific.	Doctors therefore see themselves as scientists. Medicine is concerned with the ills that ail the patient rather than the causes and origins of ills and the means of preventing them.
● Modern medicine is thought of as dispensing cures. The image of the doctor is that of the mechanic curing a sick engine.	Many illnesses that kill us before our time are not amenable to cure; therefore the emphasis on 'cure' is inappropriate.
● Doctors are encouraged to adopt the mentality of problem-solvers.	The more we look for problems the more we shall find. This is a mentality that converts medical care into crisis care. Waiting for a problem to arise and then responding to it is not a good way of providing health care.
● Medicine is perceived as dealing with specific diseases and medical specialisms.	If illness is seen only in terms of diseases this gives rise to a sort of tunnel vision and may cause the doctor to lose sight of the whole person involved.
● Modern medicine teaches that the appropriate reaction to a complaint is to *do* something.	Again this ignores the origins of the complaints. What are the long-term effects of the response? Should anything be done at all?

- Increasing medical care is a good thing, e.g. more hospitals.

Hospitals are the epitome of the problem-solving, disease-oriented scientific engineer approach to medicine. 'Heroic forms of intervention in which the only hero is the patient become the order of the day.'

Professionalization as a process

Instead of seeing professions as static and fixed, with definite unchanging traits, sociologists prefer a *dynamic* (changing) model, showing how professionalization has increased, why some occupations become professions (and others do not), how some professions cease to be seen as such and how the power of the professions has increased.

Some researchers have suggested that in Western societies sociologists have concentrated too much on individual social mobility, how an *individual* moves to a higher-status career than that of his or her parents.[4] They think it would be more useful to concentrate on *collective* mobility – the process through which whole occupations become professions and achieve a higher status. Professionalization is the most important strategy for occupations in achieving this collective upward mobility.

Historians have shown that the professions in the early nineteenth century and before were rather like clubs, companies of equals, and that the qualification for admission was that the applicant was a gentleman; in other words, it was a matter of status. Certain occupations were thought suitable for gentlemen; these became professions, while other skilled work, *not* done by gentlemen, did not. In time the work of particular professions became more defined, as did their formal organization. The big step forward in Britain in this formalization process came with a government *Report on the Organization of the Permanent Civil Service*, in 1854, and its aftermath. The report recommended competitive entry into the civil service, and this was implemented. Its effect was felt not only in the public sector but also throughout the professions, who followed suit. In particular, entry to professions by examination replaced the old ways of patronage, purchase and nepotism. With examinations, knowledge became compartmentalized, and access to it was guarded by the appropriate professional bodies.[5] The idea that a professional is middle or upper class persisted.

As to the future, it has been said that an industrializing society is a professionalizing society, and this may be even more true of post-industrial societies, with their emphasis on the generation and transfer of knowledge through new information technology.[6] Professionals have a leading role here, for example in computerizing of information.

Professional socialization

This may be seen as the process by which the entrant to a profession acquires the 'correct' professional attitudes during training. Consider what happens at a military academy like Sandhurst or West Point, or a seminary ordaining priests. These examples could be seen as extreme instances of professional socialization.

Professional socialization happens to some extent in all professions. Through learning the ideology, values, norms – the culture of the profession – members become bound to their chosen field and to each other.

The power of the professions

There are two chief aspects to this: first, a profession's power over its own members – internal organization and control; secondly, the professions' power and influence throughout society.

As a profession grows there is increasing internal control over the membership. This is depicted in the box. Professions also exert power over their clients and over the public at large (for example by trying to influence government decisions). One reason for the power of the

---

Internal control in a profession

From emerging profession	*To established profession*
• The early profession can be likened to a club; a company of equals.	The later profession can be likened to a formal organization with a hierarchical structure.
• Decisions are taken informally by an elite group.	Decisions are taken by the organization's council and appropriate committees.
• Admission procedures are informal.	Admission procedures are formal – based for example on school-leaving qualifications.
• Little formal training.	Formal curriculum.
• Informal examination.	Formal examination.
• Professional knowledge not fully developed.	There is a body of formal knowledge, both practical and theoretical.

professions is that they control the knowledge they profess. Lawyers and accountants, etc., practise as members of their respective professions possessing a distinctive body of knowledge.[7] It has been argued that the power of the professions by virtue of the knowledge they possess is 'disabling'. The professional has power, while the client, having no expert knowledge, is powerless.

> The Age of Professions will be remembered as the time when politics withered, when voters, guided by professors, entrusted to technocrats the power to legislate needs, renounced the authority to decide who needs what and suffered monopolistic oligarchies to determine the means by which these needs shall be met. It will be remembered as the age of schooling, when people for one-third of their lives had their learning needs prescribed and were trained how to accumulate further needs and for the other two-thirds became clients of prestigious pushers who managed their habits. It will be remembered as the age when recreational travel meant a packaged gawk at strangers, and intimacy meant following the sexual rules laid down by Masters and Johnson and their kin; when formed opinion was a replay of last night's TV talk-show, and voting the approval of persuaders and salesmen for more of the same.[8]

Question

How far (if at all) do you consider the above quotation to be an exaggerated view?

Suggestion: Ask yourself: can modern society exist without professionals – doctors, engineers, accountants, lawyers etc.? Is the professional that powerful? (Many patients sue their doctors in the USA.) Is this writer imagining a 'golden age' in the past – without experts?

Summary

It may be helpful here to outline a sociological view of the professions.

- A profession is more than just an occupation; it is also a claim to high social status, and to a particular life-style.
- Professions should be seen as the outcome of professionalization – that is to say the process by which an occupation is able to acquire the attributes of a profession.
- A profession is like a community. Its members share similar norms and values; it can also be likened to a club.
- Professions have supporting ideologies. The ideologies (unintentionally perhaps) distort their view of the work and act in support of the professional.

- Professionals are socialized to their roles. In the transition from lay person to professional the student acquires more than just technical skills. More importantly, the professional student acquires the 'correct' norms and values, the correct professional personality (e.g. the doctor's bedside manner).
- The professional is in a strong position when meeting the client. He or she has the knowledge sought by the client, and usually controls the interview.
- Professions control access to the knowledge they profess.

3   Management

Higher management

Higher management is, or should be, open to the best brains in the land. Surely the leaders of industry and commerce, and leaders in the public sector, should be of the highest calibre? In many cases they probably are, but the fact is that they are selected from a rather narrow band of people. This means that able people outside this tiny elite group do not even get considered for these top positions.

Who are these top people, and what are their social characteristics? It seems safe to say that education is a very good indicator of social background. Thus, while it may be possible to quote examples of the sons and daughters of dustmen having attended a prestigious school, or Oxford or Cambridge universities, it will normally be the children of higher-status parents who attend these elite institutions. It seems a good idea, therefore, to find out who are the leaders in industry, commerce and the public sector, including the directors, of, say, the important industrial companies, banks and insurance companies, the highest grade civil servants, members of important public boards, and then see what schools and universities they attended. One researcher has produced detailed evidence to show the relatively narrow social class base of leading managers, as table 3.2 indicates. Of course, this was a small sample. Is it truly representative of the country as a whole? There is ample evidence to show that it is a fair representation. Take, for instance, the information given in table 3.3 (p. 44), which shows the social background of leading industrialists in the country in the early eighties. The proportions are slightly lower here, reflecting the slightly lower status of industrialists in relation to leaders of financial institutions, but the general trend is clear.

It is interesting to note that *all* of the eighteen governors of the Bank of England in 1982 went either to a major public school, or

Table 3.2   *Education of leading UK managers, as indicated by a sample of 130 individuals*

Schools attended	Percentage
Eton	12
Other public schools	45
Other independent schools	5
State schools	32
Foreign schools	5
Higher education	
Oxford/Cambridge	38
All other universities	15
Other colleges	5
No higher education	43

Source: J. Fidler, *The British Business Elite* (Routledge and Kegan Paul, London, 1981), pp. 84–5.

Oxford or Cambridge or both. Dirctors of banks, insurance companies and other financial institutions also come in higher proportions from elite educational backgrounds. Here are a few examples:

Clearing banks	Six chairmen – five were from major public schools and/or Oxbridge, or the Guards.
Accepting houses	Seventeen chairmen – fourteen were from major public schools and/or Oxbridge.
Major life insurance companies	Twelve chairmen – eight were from major public schools and/or Oxbridge.[9]

But, assuming it is true, does all this matter? Does it affect Britain's performance as a country? It is arguable that it does matter, on a number of grounds. First, it shows that there is a firm basis for a 'them' and 'us' view of society; a fairly rigid class division still exists, which is unfair. Second, some of these people are not effective, and share anti-industrial values (see chapter 2, section 4, 'The British Disease'). The country may not be being led by the most able people. Third, these two elements combine to make the British economy less efficient and active than those of its competitors.

It may be objected that managers need, above all, leadership qualities. They need to inspire their employees; they need charisma.

Table 3.3 *The leaders of the top 30 British industrial companies*

Company	Main activity	Chairman or chief executive	Education	Turnover (£000)	Number of Employees
1 British Petroleum	Oil	Peter Walters	Birmingham University	25,347,000	118,200
2 Shell Transport and Trading	Oil	Sir Peter Baxendell	London University	15,846,000	—
3 BAT Industries	Tobacco	Sir Peter Macadam	Stonyhurst School	7,497,000	177,000
4 Imperial Chemical Industries	Chemicals	Sir John Harvey-Jones	Dartmouth	5,715,000	143,200
5 Unilever	Food, detergents	Kenneth Durham	Manchester University	4,345,800	79,148
6 Imperial Group	Tobacco	Geoffrey Kent	Grammar school, RAF	3,929,000	127,300
7 Shell UK	Oil	John Raisman	Dragon School/Oxford University	3,263,100	20,150
8 Esso Petroleum	Oil	Archibald Forster	London University	3,219,400	8,614
9 General Electric	Electrical engineering	Lord Weinstock	Cambridge University	3,004,800	188,000
10 Ford Motor Company	Motor cars	S. E. G. Toy	Winchester/Cambridge University	2,924,000	76,000
11 Rio Tinto Zinc	Mining	Sir Anthony Tuke		2,795,800	65,799
12 Grand Metropolitan	Hotels, breweries	Sir Maxwell Joseph		2,582,600	106,565
13 Czarnikow	Commodity brokers	Richard Liddiard	Oundle/Oxford University	2,567,451	717
14 S. & W. Berisford	Merchant commodity trading	E. S. Margolies		2,452,539	4,607

15 Allied Suppliers	Food, drink, tobacco	James Gulliver	Glasgow Grammar School	2,310,290	63,300
16 Rothmans International	Tobacco	Sir David Nicholson		2,271,198	24,700
17 Allied-Lyons	Brewers, vintners, hotels	Sir Derrick Holden-Brown	FCA Grammar School	2,267,700	83,971
18 P. and O.	Shipowners	Earl of Inchcape	Eton/Cambridge University	2,240,269	14,599
19 George Weston Holdings	(Associated British Foods)	Garry Weston	Oxford University	2,157,375	72,601
20 Guest, Keen & Nettlefold	Steel and engineering	Trevor Holdsworth	FCA Grammar School	1,922,700	101,605
21 Texaco	Oil	Thomas Cottrell	Hamilton University, NY	1,883,000	4,373
22 Dalgety	Merchants	David Donne	Stowe/Oxford University	1,876,000	28,567
23 Marks & Spencer	Shops	Lord Sieff	Grammar School	1,872,900	44,646
24 Gallaher	Tobacco, opticians	Stuart Cameron	Grammar School	1,835,781	27,536
25 Bowater	Paper	Lord Erroll	Oundle/Cambridge University	1,760,000	34,500
26 Lonrho	Mining	'Tiny' Rowland	Marlborough/Oxford University	1,744,990	140,000
27 Courtaulds	Textiles	Christopher Hogg	University	1,709,900	88,000
28 Thomas Tilling	Industrial holdings	Sir Robert Taylor	Exeter University	1,696,600	45,700
29 Thorn EMI	Electronics	Sir Richard Cave	Tonbridge/Cambridge University	1,620,900	125,458
30 Great Universal Stores	Shops, mail order	Lord Wolfson		1,580,554	34,649

Source: A. Sampson, *The Changing Anatomy of Britain* (Hodder and Stoughton, London, 1982), pp. 343-4; updated.

These are social rather than technical qualities. Here we leave the rational world of technical qualifications and training and enter the world of beliefs, values and attitudes – we need to examine what managers think in order to understand what they do.

Scientific management

When discussing the nature of the professions it was suggested that professionals tend to view the world through their ideological spectacles. The same may be true of managers. Managerial ideology seems to centre around the concept of 'scientific management', though many managers have never heard of them. The idea has a long history, but is usually associated with the name of Frederick ('Speedy') Taylor, who at the turn of the century codified a system of management which became highly popular.[10] Other management ideologies are discussed in chapter 4 on organizations.

It follows from Taylor's views that managers are required first to know the functions of the organization (personnel, production, marketing, etc.), and then to forecast, plan, allocate and make decisions: 'Workers are not to be left with esoteric knowledge. The emphasis is on the key role of management thinking; management has the monopoly of thought.'[11]

Scientific management entails a breaking down of the work into smaller and smaller parts so that each worker's job is reduced to a single task if possible – a process of fragmentation of the work and de-skilling (this can apply to offices as well as factories). Further, de-skilled labour should be cheap to hire. This process gives management more power, since it has to co-ordinate these separate tasks; the management role gains increased legitimacy.

Scientific management

- The first principle of scientific management, according to Taylor, is that each stage of the work must be controlled by management, including the labour process itself – the workers are not to control output levels.

- The labour process must be dissociated from the skills of the worker; the labour process is to be rendered independent from the craft tradition, i.e. the worker becomes less skilled, less in control.

- The third principle is the separation of conception from execution. All brainwork should be removed from the shop floor and centred in the management/planning department – a separation of hand and brain.

Although Taylor's main work on *Scientific Management* first appeared in 1911, the ideology of scientific management does appear to influence management decision-making today. It applies to work measurement and work study – the idea that it is possible to measure output scientifically. The concept of managerial prerogative, management's right to manage, is derived partly from the ideology of scientific management, and with it comes the non-participation of workers in decision-making and the strong line – staff demarcation which typifies many firms.

Some may wonder how we can avoid scientific management, if it leads to profit, which is after all the aim of firms in a capitalist system. Surely it is justifiable on those grounds? Many sociologists have argued that scientific management relies on wrong assumptions about individuals' motivation and what really constitutes efficiency, and is believed, in the face of obvious contrary evidence, because it supports and justifies desire for power and control. A concentration on measuring production ignores other relevant factors – absenteeism, stress and ill health constitute 'hidden' costs (either to the firm or to society in general). How efficient a system is depends on how you choose to measure it.

Central to management is the need for the power to control and change. Unless workers have powerful unions or, perhaps, are in short supply, management is very powerful. An example is the introduction of new technology at British Leyland's Longbridge plant. While management wanted technological change (i.e. changes in working practices), it was unable to offer anything to the workers in return.[12] The unions were unable to challenge management's power, because of worsening employment prospects. (For further discussion of managerial power, see chapter 5 on industrial relations.)

Criticism

This chapter seems rather harsh on managers who are trying to do an honest job to the best of their ability. They do not all practise scientific management (seeing their staff as just commodities, and to be kept from using their intelligence); they are not all hard on their staff. Perhaps readers would like to check on this for themselves from their own experience, from the news, from the writings of managers. See also projects set in chapter 5.

The labour process

The 'labour process' is the process by which labour power is applied to raw material and machinery to produce goods, commodities. As mentioned above, in the pursuit of profit this increasingly means de-skilling and the fragmentation of the task to enable management to control the staff more easily. Unskilled labour is seen as more controllable than skilled labour, while machinery (which replaces workers) is the most controllable of all.

Historians and sociologists have come to the conclusion that early mills and factories were established not so much for technological reasons as for reasons of control; management wanted to control what the worker actually did in the firm's time,[13] and set targets, be able to predict output, etc. Previously, workers had been in effect self-employed, regulating their own pace of work, hours and output, and selling the product to merchants.

The title of Harry Braverman's book *Labor and Monopoly Capitalism: The Degradation of Labor in the Twentieth Century* gives a further clue as to what has happened in the 'labour process' over the last 200 years. According to Braverman, it is not the technology that determined the way in which work is done. Rather the way work is done in factories and offices is a reflection of the exploitation of labour by capital. Because labour is alienated (not motivated; see chapter 4) managers seek to control it, hence the need for 'scientific management' as described here. Further, in order to maximize profits managers seek to keep labour costs down, and this is (apparently) achieved through de-skilling work and fragmenting work tasks. Maximizing profit is the ultimate goal – control of labour is seen as the best means of achieving it.

However, this account ignores various factors, for example labour's resistance to de-skilling, to lowering (or not raising) wages, and to management's attempt to exercise close control at work. Indeed most of chapter 5 on industrial relations could be seen as an account of this continuous struggle.

In addition to scientific management or 'Taylorism', another possible and similar managerial approach commented on by many writers is 'Fordism', based on the flow-line principles of assembly work. The flow of work, is achieved by conveyor belts moving continuously past workers who must stay at their work positions. This enables closer supervision and control over the pace of work by supervisors. 'Fordism' could be seen as an extreme version of scientific management. It is scientific management applied to both labour and technical processes (the line of machinery). It heightens scientific management's stress on managers as monopolists of information and knowledge.

Questions

Does the labour process have to work to labour's disadvantage?
What other factors, not mentioned here, may help to support the ideology of scientific management?

Management as the balancing of interests

There are many more managerial beliefs and ideologies than have been so far mentioned here (several are discussed in chapter 4). Managers often see themselves as balancing the interests of all concerned in an organization.

> The ideology of 'balancing interests' maintains that in the long term the interests of all groups concerned with the firm – shareholders, employees, customers and the public at large – are served by the success of the company. The pursuit of profit thus serves the interests of all. Those who run the company are in the position of balancing the interests of all groups connected with it – but they do so only in the short term. If the interests of all are correctly balanced, then in the long term the firm will prosper.[14]

Question

In your view, how accurate is the idea that managers act in the interest of all parties? Are some parties more important than others?

Lower levels of management

What is the role of lower-level managers, of supervisors? How do the ideologies of management and workers apply to their roles?

Supervisors used to be very important in the past, managers often left much of the day-to-day management, including hiring and firing, discipline, output targets and achievement, and interpretation of results, to such people, who knew the details of the work being done far better than they did. With unionization, central wage-bargaining and the introduction of new technology, the supervisor's position has weakened. More of the day-to-day decisions have to be agreed with unions or are regulated by agreements; monitoring of output and targets etc. is much more sophisticated. Where does the future lie for such people? There are two possible directions, one downwards to the shop floor, the other upwards towards management or the professions.[15] In the past, the foreman could be seen as a kind of self-made man, someone able by his own efforts to climb out of the working class. Today such a status may derive from becoming a professional, and many supervisory roles are becoming professionalized. One example of this in Britain is the professionalization of personnel management. The need for this was felt by a number of pioneering employers in Britain before the First World War, including Rowntree, Salt, Cadbury, Lever and Boot. They were motivated both by profit and by conscience. Jesse Boot (of Boots the Chemist) was a Wesleyan who felt a strong attachment to the working class, and the values he represented permeate the now well-established Institute of Personnel Management. Personnel managers, it holds, must pay attention both to profit and to the welfare of employees and their aspirations. Personnel officers see their commitment to their profession and to their employing organization as complementary.[16] They tend to see both management (of which they are part) and the employees as their masters.

Question

Do personnel managers have an ideology? What are the problems of combining the two allegiances?

Many supervisory jobs have become professionalized, with all that this entails socially (in terms of the background of people doing the jobs). Others have come to be seen as part of middle management, with access to promotion further up. Alternatively, they may become unionized, joining such unions as MSF (the Manufacturing, Science and Finance Union). Where a job has risen in status, it usually comes to be done by people with a middle-class background; where it falls, the working class continue to occupy it.

Final points on management

- Management as a career stresses competitiveness, striving and organizational hierarchy, as shown also in chapter 2 in the discussion of American business values.
- The people who make it to the top tend to have been to public school and Oxford or Cambridge universities.
- Management is tending to become more professionalized, with a profusion of business degrees both in Britain and the USA. Supervisors are tending to be absorbed into lower management. Professional institutions like the Institute of Personnel Management are growing.
- Managerial ideologies evolve to justify what managers do. One of the most important of these ideologies was discussed in this chapter – Taylorism, or 'scientific management', which stresses managers' right to manage.

4 White-Collar Occupations

This section looks at white-collar occupations such as sales and clerical work. The usual sociological questions are considered: what is really going on in the shop or office? How do people give meaning to their lives? How do people maintain status? (rather than 'how can management raise the productivity of the clerk', for example). Firstly, then, consider the question . . .

What qualities does sales work require?

Few people would disagree strongly with the view that sales work requires verve and pep and an outgoing personality. Yet some sociologists see sales work and similar jobs as middle-class equivalents to routine working-class jobs: de-motivating or alienating (see chapter 6).[17] The smile of the salesperson is hard and calculating, not a spontaneous expression of friendliness. Salespeople sell their pleasant personality by the hour. One salesgirl said: 'You are working among lovely things you can't buy. But when you go home (with your low pay) you do not feel genteel or anything, but humiliated.' Selling has always had its positive and negative side, but in modern times centralization has meant the loss of creativity and personal freedom. Today's commercial traveller is only a unit of a big organization, following procedures laid down by the company.

Much of what has been said here is even more true of the clerk, the next occupation to be considered.

Has the status of the clerk declined?

There would seem to be plenty of evidence to support the view that the status of the clerk has declined. With universal secondary education, clerical workers (sometimes referred to as 'white-collar' or 'black-coated' workers) were no longer in a monopoly position. In the field of white-collar employment clerks are now more numerous and perhaps therefore less valued. In Britain in 1911 clerical workers constituted 19 per cent of the working population, but by 1971 this proportion had risen to 43 per cent.[18] Most significantly of all, the pay of clerks in Britain had fallen from an index of 122 in 1913 to 93 in 1978 (taking a mean of 100 for all occupations). In the same period, the pay of unskilled manual workers rose from 78 to 86.[19]

Another possible indicator of the loss of status by clerical workers is the unionization of clerks. In 1911 12 per cent of white-collar workers were in unions, but by 1978 the proportion had risen to 43 per cent.[20] This and other changes in the occupational structure are discussed more fully in chapter 8. Table 3.4 updates these figures.

Table 3.4 *British average earning index: (selected occupations)*

	Mechanical engineering (manual workers)	Banking, finance and insurance
1980	107	113
1986	192	218

Source: Adapted from *Employment Gazette*, March 1987.

Question

Taking the figures mentioned in this section so far, what 'story' do they tell?
Suggestion: Throughout most of the century the clerk in Britain has probably lost status, as the figures indicate. The recent catching up is probably to the decline in engineering, and in industry generally in Britain.

The status of the clerk also appears to have declined through the routinization of many office tasks. With increasing centralization and new office technology (an adaptation of the ideology of scientific management) many office jobs are becoming 'rationalized' and de-skilled, and this of course lowers the status of routine white-collar work. In the past clerks could borrow prestige from their close relations with their employers, but this is less likely now because these relationships are becoming increasingly impersonal. Within the office there are many petty hierarchies which cut out the possibility of comradeship (the authoritarian treatment of many office juniors is an example in point). Management's efforts to create job enthusiasm reflects the unhappy unwillingness of employees to work spontaneously at their routinized tasks.[21]

False consciousness

This is a term used by Marxists to describe workers like clerks who are not aware of their true class position. Thus the proletariate, who do not own the means of production, do not see what is in their best interests. There may be many reasons for this; for example they may identify with management and accept their views – perhaps because they want promotion or even, in recession, to hold on to their (lowly?) jobs.

Question

Does the above overstate the factory-like nature of the office? What differences remain? Are there ways in which office modernization may have reduced workers' feelings of alienation?

One sociologist, David Lockwood, compared clerks with manual workers in three situations, in the employment market, at work, and in status.[22]

- In the market, the clerk normally has a higher income, job security, a chance of rising to a managerial role, and a pension (and various 'perks').
- At work, the social relations between clerical workers and management are normally based on co-operation, whereas there is estrangement between manual workers and management.
- In status the clerk has lost ground because of universal literacy and, particularly, increasing centralization and bureaucratization in the office. Increasingly clerks are becoming unionized, and this in the long run *may* make their status nearer to that of manual workers.

What effect will computerization have on the social structure of the office? Will it lead to increasing control by management, increasing centralization, with higher management controlling the flow of information? Or will it lead to more autonomy and responsibility for the clerks? See the projects at the end of this chapter.

I suggested above that increasing unionization would perhaps be taken as an indicator of loss of status by clerical workers, but against this others have suggested that white-collar workers join unions not because they reject their own middle-class values but because they see the unionization as a better way of supporting these values. In other words they look on the union as a means of obtaining dignity, prestige and control over the work environment, things which are denied them in the modern office system. Middle-class attitudes towards white-collar trade unions may be changing, as the figures indicate.

What of the future of the clerk? The obvious tendencies are: an increasing proportion of white-collar workers in the workforce, greater unionization, more centralization and larger work units, and the computerization of office work. Much office work is alienating, and, as mentioned, petty hierarchies in the office persist. On the other hand, white-collar workers are associated with management. This and a new kind of unionization which stresses medium-term planning

---

Proletarianization

The term refers to the process by which sections of the middle class become absorbed into the working class. Here are a few examples:

- A once highly respected profession that has lost status. A possible example of this is school teachers.
- A craft whose skill has become outdated, for example, typesetters, locomotive drivers, welders. De-skilling and the fragmentation of the task leads to proletarianization.
- Clerks who formerly identified with management but have now joined a trade union in order to protect their interests.

Responses to proletarianization may be militancy, unionization or increased attempts to identify with management.

(rather than instant reaction to events) may help to maintain the clerk's social status in the future.[23]

5   Manual Occupations

This section looks at the way manual workers view their work. How do those in crafts compare their work to others? What about those doing boring hard manual work – how do they put up with it? Are manual workers becoming more middle class because many are earning more money than the clerical workers?

What is a craft?

At first sight the answer seems obvious. Yet when the professions were discussed earlier it was shown that an understanding of attitudes and values is important in understanding the true nature of professionalism. The same is true of craftsmanship. Some argue that members of a craft tend to see the world through their own occupational spectacles: every social phenomenon is seen from a limited perspective.[24]

Researchers have found that technical students tend to look down on craft students, whereas craft students see technical students as 'stuck up'.[25] It is interesting then to contrast the social position of the technician (for example the laboratory technician) with that of the craftsperson (for example the printer or the carpenter). In the social hierarchy they are not far apart, yet they take particular care to differentiate themselves. On the one hand there is the semi-professionalism of technical education and the progression of some technical occupations to the status of profession. On the other hand, many older skilled occupations (such as printing) are becoming de-skilled, partly as a result of new technology. The rise of the one group and decline of the other is reflected even in the training stage; further education keeps the two groups apart and sustains rather than challenges the social relationships which separate young workers from one another. These differences between craft and technical students are also a reflection of differences that have persisted historically, that is to say that crafts were traditionally working-class, and technical jobs middle-class.

What is likely to be the future of the skill divide in an era of depression and technological change?[26] Some believe that skilled workers will continue to resist new technologies which reduce their status and earning power, but new technologies also, it can be argued, offer opportunities for development of new skills.

A few points on the social aspects of craftsmanship can now be made.

- Craftspersons, like professionals, form a distinct social group.
- Like professionals, the craft group tends to view the world through its own 'occupational spectacles'.
- The group defines what constitutes a good job. However, the group is less self-referring than a profession, since in the last resort it is the employer who really decides what standard is required.
- The craft position is constantly being undermined through new technology, which results in de-skilling and fragmenting of the task and an increase in managerial control.

Well-paid manual workers

Question

Are well-paid manual workers likely to have middle-class attitudes and life-styles (the 'embourgeoisement thesis')?

One of the best-known studies of this question was by four researchers who surveyed three firms in the Luton area: the Vauxhall car factory, Skefco Ball Bearings, and La Porte Chemicals. The choice of subjects was deliberate – the workers were involved in three different types of technology. Luton was a prosperous area; many workers were geographically and socially mobile and owned their own homes.[27]

Embourgeoisement

This is the opposite tendency to proletarianization – working-class people becoming like the middle class.

The researchers found that the Luton workers had an *instrumental* attitude to their work – that is, they regarded their work as just a means to an end. That end was money – they just worked for the money. There was no real sense of solidarity with the working class and little involvement with the firm. Their involvement with the union was also instrumental – will it get us more money? Similarly their involvement in politics was instrumental – which party will get us more money? Education was seen as a means of getting a highly paid job. This may be contrasted with the middle-class view of work, where career prospects, job satisfaction and social status are very important. Although this study was carried out in the late sixties, later studies tend to confirm its findings; for example, an analysis of the 1979, 1983 and 1987 general elections showed that many 'non-traditional' workers like Ford car workers voted Conservative because they feared a Labour government might introduce an incomes policy which could lower their earnings.[28] Some criticisms could be made of the earlier study – in particular it may be that when unemployment threatens, these affluent workers may again, like the more traditional worker, stress solidarity.

The traditional working class

The theme of this chapter is the *social* nature of work. I hope it has shown so far that all individuals' attitudes to work are influenced by social inheritance and that they tend to form self-contained groups, according to their type of work. This applies no less to the 'traditional' workers in industry and mining.

There is in Britain a common image of the working class, what could be called the *traditional* working class. Examples of this group would be miners, railwaymen, steel-workers and dockers. (Note that this is basically a male image.) In these groups there is a strong feeling of solidarity. Work is experienced not solely as a means to an end – money – but also as a group activity. Members would not indulge in activities that would threaten group solidarity or offend other members. The strong moral involvement with the group contrasts with the *lack* of group involvement of the 'affluent workers' in the studies mentioned above. While the involvement with the group is strong, the involvement with the employing organization is weak or negative; they are alienated, there is a 'them and us' feeling. Involvement in the work may be strong, work being experienced as a shared activity. This is particularly true where the work is dangerous, such as mining. Again, in comparison with the affluent worker, involvement in politics and trade union activity is much stronger, and is less likely to be solely instrumental (seen as a means to an end).

Finally, there is a strong feeling of community generally, binding not just the workers but their families. Examples are the mining village or the railwaymen's cottages. There is a distinctive occupational culture which ensures high group involvement generally.[29]

The deferential worker

There are several other groups of manual workers which are difficult to classify; for example people who work for small firms, older workers, especially if they are in some supervisory role, agricultural workers and so on. Research on these groups seems to show that their relationship with the employer is one in which the employer is often *paternalistic* (the employers usually look after their work people and take a personal interest in them). The workers on their part often have what is called a deferential attitude to the employer. Quite often this kind of worker is heavily dependent on the employer; for example he or she may not be able to get a job in a big firm, or in the case of agricultural work he or she may be living in the employer's accommodation. Apart from this, the employer and the employee work in close contact with each other, often doing similar work; employees cannot be considered as just so many units of output.

One study of farmworkers showed that many of them seemed to have fatalistic attitudes.[30] Most of them saw social class as largely inherited rather than achieved; saw their own class position as low; saw little hope of social mobility and, overwhelmingly, saw class difference as inevitable. It could of course be argued that on all these counts they were being realistic.

6   Individuals, Groups and Ideologies

Two sociologists who have studied work extensively have put forward a general categorization of attitudes to work which broadly agrees with the outline of types of worker given above.[31] Firstly, there is the *instrumental* or calculative orientation of the affluent unskilled worker (e.g. the Luton workers mentioned above). Secondly, there is the *bureaucratic* orientation of the 'faithful clerk' (like lower

---

Orientations to work

- *Instrumental*   This sees work as a means to an end – money. Work is therefore experienced as mere labour. The worker's involvement in work is calculative. A typical example would be assembly-line work.

- *Bureaucratic*   The primary meaning of work is as a service to the employing organization in return for good prospects – that is to say a 'proper career', for example in banking or insurance, etc.

- *Solidaristic*   While the money is important to this group, work is also seen as a group activity. Thus work represents a central life interest. Work and leisure are intimately related – in fact work implies a whole way of life. A typical example would be miners.

---

managers, supervisors, clerical workers and deferential workers). Thirdly, there is the *solidaristic* orientation of the traditional worker in one of the older industries. These three orientations are described in the box.

The chapter so far should have helped to identify certain *group* attitudes to work. But here the reader might be saying 'I am not like that', or 'I know someone who does not fit that description.' However, two points should be mentioned.

First, it is *group* attitudes that are being analysed here; clearly particular individuals may not share all the attitudes of fellow group members. We must look at how the *individual* views the organization and interprets what is happening. The individual who moves from one job to another may revise his or her outlook, may reject or take on a particular group attitude according to the circumstances. 'Group' attitudes are always approximations to any one individual's views.[32]

Secondly, even group attitudes can sometimes change. Earlier in this chapter the orientation of the 'deferential' worker was discussed, for example the farm worker or the worker in a small firm. It has been argued that perhaps the orientation depends on the situation of the workers, and that when this situation changes the corresponding orientation changes too.[33] One study showed that when 'deferential' workers were made redundant their deferential attitudes changed quite quickly. They went on strike and generally acted more like traditional workers. Another example might be a change in attitude of a group of 'professional' workers whose status is falling.

The concept of work ideologies may be a useful analytical tool here. As mentioned in chapter 1, many ideologies are beliefs which justify the interests of the powerful, for example the professional or the manager. The box is designed to show the importance of occupational ideologies and to give an overview of the chapter.

Occupational ideologies

Occupation	Ideological component
The professions	'The professional knows best'. Professional ideologies abound, for example in the medical profession could be seen as stressing the 'cure' ideal at the expense, say, of preventative medicine. Architects may stress creativity, yet design unpouplar tower blocks.
Management at all levels	Whether conscious or not, many managers tend to stress the following: • scientific management, controlling not only what is to be done but how it is to be done. • their role in the 'balancing of interests' for the benefit of all. • the manager as a good organization person but also a strong individual. Many American studies stress this 'individualism'.
Clerical and sales work	Identification with the employer. An ideological dimension justifies subordination, emphasizing the caring role of the paternalist employer. Often management ideology has been largely accepted.
The 'deferential worker'	Like clerks, they accept management's ideology.
Craftsperson	Like the professional, these people have their own standards and ways of working: they 'know best'.
Affluent manual workers	These have an *instrumental orientation* – just working for the money.
Traditional manual workers	These have a *solidaristic orientation* – work as part of a group activity as well as providing an income.

A sociology of occupation as outlined here is useful in showing the social nature of work; that work is not just the performance of a technical task, as many might tend to see it. It is important to remember that work gives individuals a sense of identity; many occupations give a sense of belonging.

It will be noted that the examples and discussion above concern men primarily; the position of women in the occupational structure is discussed in chapter 7.

Conclusion

One way of summarizing this chapter is to ask 'what is the usefulness of all this to the manager, in particular the personnel manager?' Here are some ideas.

- This chapter demonstrates the social nature of work; that work is not solely the performance of a technical task. It indicates the social nature of occupational choice; that, for example, higher management is recruited from a narrow section in society and is not really open to the 'best brains'.
- It is useful to know about the social significance of occupational groups; where they are recruited from; what the group members desire; what they believe; how their occupations give them a sense of identity and belonging.
- All this enables the manager to perceive occupational ideologies – beliefs which may sometimes be helpful in task performance but which may also distort reality – for example the ideology of 'scientific management', the belief that professionals know best.
- These insights into the social relations of different occupations should show the manager the alienating nature of a lot of work, both routine manual and non-manual. This is further demonstrated in chapters 5 and 6. Some work which is well paid but unpleasant in various ways will attract people with an 'instrumental orientation' to work. Thus while job enrichment may be desirable, it may not be what these groups are really interested in. They will put up with feeling alienated and still work hard if they are paid enough. An example could be oil-rig workers. Other alienated groups might become less so, if more consultation or more freedom were introduced.

Criticism

Regarding the above conclusions, particularly the last one, is it right that managers should pay higher wages to buy off feelings of alienation? A few people might argue that workers should be encouraged to respond to their feelings of alienation by taking control away from management. Which view would you choose and why?

Suggestion: Chapter 5 on industrial relations sets out clearly the differing viewpoints on this kind of issue. One section discusses the question 'Is industrial democracy possible?'

Exercises

Self-examination question

What is meant by:

- the social nature of work
- profession
- embourgeoisement
- traditional working class
- deferential worker
- the labour process
- false consciousness

- proletarianization
- ideology
- professional ideologies
- professionalization
- managerial ideologies
- paternalism
- scientific management?

Essay or discussion

1 Criticize and discuss the following statements
   (a) Work is a matter of performing a task.
   (b) The occupational structure is open. It is a matter of choosing a suitable career and striving hard to achieve success in it.
   (c) Higher occupations such as the professions select applicants on the basis of their merit rather than their social status.
   (d) Factory workers should be more involved in their work and put in a fair day's work for a fair day's pay.
   (e) Apart from the physical effort, manual work is not that dissimilar to clerical work nowadays.
   (f) The term 'occupational choice' is a misnomer, since for most young people (whether from middle-class or working-class homes), there is no choice.

Suggestion 1: See the books by W. M. Williams and P. Willis in the Further Reading list.

2 'Technological change has transformed the office worker into a white collared proletarian.' Do you agree with this assessment of the social class position of the office worker?

3   Referring to table 3.3, chart the development of the careers of some of
    the chairmen. This could easily be done from *Who's Who*, which will be
    in most libraries – it should not take long.

Project 1

Look at the following elements of a course for managers. What does it tell
us about managerial ideologies? Answer the questions at the end once
you've read the material.

*A short course for managers concerned with personnel: understanding the
recruitment and selection process*
Finding, and getting into, a good department, is a two-way process; one indicator
of a good department is certainly how it attracts, selects, retains and develops
staff – the most valuable resource. It is useful for the potential candidate to
understand the mechanisms which organizations use to recruit and select
appropriate staff. This paper provides a simple outline of approaches to
recruitment and selection.

1   Objectives of the recruitment and selection process
    (a) To obtain and maintain appropriate staff levels, both quantitatively and
        qualitatively.
    (b) To ensure that you get the right person in the right job at the right time.
    (c) To be effective in: attracting a sufficiently wide field of suitable
        candidates; sorting out the unsuitable, thereby avoiding errors, and
        selecting suitable candidates.
    (d) To be efficient in achieving (c) above within budgetary constraints (i.e.
        cost-effective methods).
    (e) To be fair: the employer has an image and reputation to uphold.
    (f) To observe those constraints imposed by the policies and procedures
        of the organization, and the law.
2   The recruitment and selection process
    This can easily be understood as a series of questions to which the
    organization/department must find appropriate answers:
    (a) What do we need/want?
        First, one must define requirements.
    (b) Who do we want?
        Next, we must attract suitable candidates.
    (c) How do we pick them?
        By choosing selection methods, criteria and weights: by applying these.
    (d) What do we do next?
        Placement, induction and follow up.
    (e) How do we know if it works?
        By monitoring and evaluating results.
3   Defining requirements: questions to be considered
    (a) Are these part of an agreed programme of human resource planning?
    (b) Are requests for staff:
                        justified/appropriate?
                        properly requisitioned?
                        approved?

(c) Are job descriptions accurate/updated/appropriate?
Are person (employee) specifications properly constructed?
(d) Are terms and conditions of employment properly defined? Agreed?

4 Recruitment and selection mechanisms

A. *Job descriptions*

These are essential: they provide an essential information set. They clarify:
(a) the purpose of the job;
(b) the position of the job in the structure;
(c) the key duties/responsibilities (key result areas);
(d) an outline of specific tasks;
(e) an explanation of working relationships in the job.

B. *Person (employee) specifications*

Whereas the job description defines the properties/tasks of the job, the person/employee specification defines those levels of intelligence, knowledge, skill and experience, plus attitudes/behaviour needed to perform the job successfully.

They specify what would be required of the 'ideal' job holder; however, it is usual to distinguish between:

Essential	– what the job holder *must* have
Desirable	– present in the ideal candidate
Contraindications	– what the candidate must *not* have

The 'Seven Point Plan'[34] was devised to cover the various types of attribute which might be required.

1 physical make-up (i.e. health, physique, appearance, bearing and speech);
2 attainments (i.e. education, training, experience and achievements);
3 general intelligence;
4 special aptitudes (e.g. mechanical, dexterity, mathematical);
5 interests (e.g. intellectual, practical, active, social);
6 disposition (e.g. acceptability, influence, steadiness, self-reliance);
7 circumstances (e.g. geographical mobility).

Questions

1 What managerial ideologies, if any, do you perceive in this programme?
2 Can aptitude, personality, motivation, character and mental abilities be measured?
3 What factors do you think are likely to influence the selection of candidates?

Suggestions:

• Sociologists believe that most occupations and professions have ideologies – look for them!
• In aptitude and similar tests it is not too difficult for many applicants to detect what the employer wants to hear, so they may answer accordingly. The sceptic may ask, for example, 'mental ability' for what? Most people

are very intelligent at what interests them, but *general* intelligence tests may not allow for this, so the results may not be helpful – assuming ability could be measured anyway.

- Show how difficult it is to prevant bias. (You may like to refer to chapter 7 on racial and sexual bias.)

Project 2

There are sometimes examples in the news of apparently irrational strikes – strikes over the exact number of minutes in a tea-break, cleaning-up-time strikes and so on. Read the following passage and answer the questions below.

> The management of a company designed and began to build a new factory in which it intended to move over a thousand employees. Planning and design was carried out without consulting the workforce and the official management position was that the change was a minor geographical one and that employee objections were unlikely, since the only implication for the workforce was an improvement in working conditions. But as awareness of the intended move increased, so the resistance of the workforce to it grew. Complaints were made about the likelihood of increased bus fares to the new site, the threat to health involved in working in a windowless factory, the arrogance of management's deciding what was best for the workforce, and the potential undermining of certain craft distinctions by the locating of the whole workforce under one roof. The issue which emerged as the main talking-point, and the item over which strike action was threatened, was the management's intention to encourage employees to make use of the newly purchased vending machines for tea and coffee by making illegal the 'mashing' of tea on the shop floor.
>
> The tea-making issue was initially regarded by the management as arising from shop-floor irrationality, and, had a strike in fact occurred, one can well imagine (on the evidence of rather similar cases) how the press would have handled it! *Yet the shop floor perceived the management's intention to interfere with their established break-time practices as a very serious infringement of their autonomy.* In my terms, the implicit contract was seriously threatened by the management's apparent intention to increase the sphere in which it exerted control over employee behaviour. As many employees explicitly stated, this was a matter of principle. Ultimately this issue was conceded by the company, and a number of other fairly costly concessions had to be made in the course of negotiations before union co-operation with the introduction of changes was secured. *The whole shop floor strategy was based on a sensible, rational and wisely sceptical approach to defending the implicit existing contracts of employees. Yet to many observers, especially those within management, this essential rationality was far from clear.*[35]

1   Does the passage demonstrate the sort of managerial ideologies referred to in this chapter? Which ideologies can you discover?
2   Comment in particular on the italic sections.
3   With the aid of insights you have gained, analyse one or two of the 'senseless' strikes that have been in the news.

Project 3

Read this passage and then answer the questions that follow.

The most dramatic application of scientific management principles in the office has occurred in clerical work. Clerks form the largest single, non-manual occupation (14 per cent of the total British labour force in 1971; 18 per cent of the total US labour force in 1970). Rationalization has followed the principles of decomposing multi-functional jobs with high discretion into simple and repetitive tasks, the introduction of time and motion study which established standardized work methods and times, and the removal of work planning from clerks to office managers. Indeed, management consultants over the last two decades have eroded the distinction between manual and clerical work, establishing the notion of the 'universal process' and the application of the same rules of work analysis in offices as on the shop floor.

Office rationalization has coincided with the mechanization and automation of office work, which further increases managerial direction of work processes and worker effort. The introduction of office machinery which simplifies tasks and makes them more routine also means that it is easier to subject them to a standard measure; thus managers are able more effectively to record and control the quality and quantity of worker output.

The advent of computers has had an even more startling impact, because their application has often involved structural change throughout the organisation. Weir, in a discussion of office computerisation, shows how organisations tend to be re-structured into departments organised by function, rather than departments continuing to handle the multiple functions associated with, say, a particular product or geographical area. Departments emerge which specialise in data preparation, output handling and queries, and such specialisation encourages task fragmentation. The number of hierarchical levels tends to be reduced because many intermediate jobs are eliminated by the computer. Banks and insurance companies provide the most notable examples of this process, and computerisation produces something approaching a two-tier structure of senior managers, who deal with policy issues, and clerical workers, who prepare data for the computer and deal with customers – the computer assumes most of the functions of checking transactions and controlling the work which used to be performed by senior clerks and middle managers. Because all information about work activities within the firm is centralised, senior managers have the knowledge to direct and co-ordinate these activities far more thoroughly than before and to deal with a wider range of issues than before.

In computerised offices, lower level jobs become more routine and the required levels of skill and discretion are reduced, while higher level jobs become more interesting and responsible. The computer contains all the knowledge necessary for the satisfactory performance of work and can make its own decisions, so that the co-ordination of the work process is carried out inside the computer without human intervention. As the result, clerical work in computerised offices mainly involves feeding information into the computer and then acting on its instructions. Even the collection of information is highly routinised because clerks must follow strict procedures which allow no discretion, in order to prepare data in the appropriate form. Higher level jobs gain; computers provide the designers of office systems and senior managers with more scope for decision-making and more power to influence the activities carried out in their firms.

Attempts have also been made to apply the techniques of rationalised management into other spheres, notably technical work. Engineering design has traditionally been a skilled occupation and designers have been free to organise their own work with the minimum of intervention, because employers have generally been content to accept occupational principles of organisation. However, several cases have been recorded of firms with large design staffs attempting to rationalise design work in order to increase managerial control. In the early 1970s, Rolls Royce in Britain wanted to impose work measurement techniques on design staff and divide jobs into their basic elements, in order to establish standard times which would then be used to control labour effort. Union resistance prevented Rolls Royce implementing this scheme. American firms have tried to break down design work into its elements, allocate these to different individuals, and use engineering managers to co-ordinate and integrate the work process. Such attempts are not yet widespread, but that they should occur at all indicates how managers are concerned to regulate all the activities carried out within their firms.[36]

1   What is the effect of more office rationalization and automation?
2   Does the introduction of computers raise or lower the levels of skill and discretion in office work? For workers? For managers?
3   Give one or more examples of the effects of computerization in the world of commerce and industry.
4   Does this passage illustrate the application of 'scientific management' and the concept of the 'labour process' as discussed in this chapter? In what ways?

Further Reading

As this is a long list, the more important works are indicated by an asterisk*.
*P. Armstrong, *White Collar Workers, Trade Unions and Class* (Croom Helm, London, 1986).
*H. Braverman, *Labor and Monopoly Capital* (Monthly Review Press, New York, 1974).
J. Child and B. Partridge, *Lost Managers: Supervision in Industry and Society* (Cambridge University Press, Cambridge, 1982).
R. Compton and G. Jones, *White Collar Proletariatim* (Macmillan, London, 1984).
R. Crompton and J. Gubbay, *Economy and Class Structures* (Macmillan, London, 1979).
G. Deem and G. Salaman (eds), *Work, Culture and Society* (Open University Press, Milton Keynes, 1985).
S. Dex, *The Sexual Division of Work* (Wheatsheaf, Brighton, 1985).
*R. Dingwall, *The Sociology of the Professions* (Macmillan, London, 1983).
P. Elliott, *The Sociology of the Professions* (Macmillan, London, 1972).
E. Freidson, *Professional Powers: A Study of the Institutionalization of Formal Knowledge* (Chicago, Chicago University Press, 1986).
*J. H. Goldthorpe, D. Lockwood, F. Bechofer and J. Platt, *The Affluent Worker: Industrial Attitudes and Behaviour* (Cambridge University Press, Cambridge, 1969).

S. Hill, *Competition and Control at Work* (Heinemann, London, 1981).

M. Holbok-Jones, *The Supremacy and Subordination of Labour* (Heinemann, London, 1982).

R. Hyman and R. Price (eds), *The New Working Class: White Collar Workers and their Organisations* (Macmillan, London, 1983).

I. Illich, *Disabling Professions* (Boyars, London, 1977).

T. J. Johnson, *Professions and Power* (Macmillan, London, 1972).

C. R. Littler, *The Experience of Work* (Gower, Aldershot, 1985).

D. Lockwood, *The Black Coated Worker* (Allen and Unwin, London, 1958).

C. W. Mills, *White Collar* (Oxford University Press, New York, 1956).

H. Newby, *The Deferential Worker* (Allen Lane, London, 1977).

*S. R. Parker, R. K. Brown, J. Child and M. A. Smith, *The Sociology of Industry* (Allen and Unwin, London, 1981).

S. R. Parker, *The Sociology of Leisure* (Allen and Unwin, London, 1981).

R. Penn, *Skilled Workers in the Class Structure* (Cambridge University Press, Cambridge, 1985).

K. Prandy, A. Stewart and R. M. Blackburn, *White Collar Work* (Macmillan, London, 1982).

J. Storey, *Managerial Prerogative and the Question of Control* (Routledge and Kegan Paul, London, 1983).

P. Thompson, *The Nature of Work* (Macmillan, London, 1983).

W. M. Williams (ed.), *Occupational Choice* (Allen and Unwin, London, 1974)

P. Willis, *Learning to Labour* (Saxon House, Farnborough, 1977).

Notes

1 J. H. Goldthorpe, D. Lockwood, F. Bechofer and J. Platt, *The Affluent Worker in the Class Structure* (Cambridge University Press, Cambridge, 1969).

2 A. M. Carr-Saunders and P. A. Wilson, *The Professions* (Cass, London, 1964); G. Millerson, *The Qualifying Associations* (Routledge and Kegan Paul, London, 1964).

3 I. Kennedy, *The Unmasking of Medicine* (Allen and Unwin, London, 1981), pp. 28 ff.

4 J. and J. Parry, *The Rise of the Medical Profession* (Croom Helm, London, 1976), p. 247.

5 W. J. Reader, *Professional Men* (Weidenfeld and Nicolson, London, 1966).

6 D. Bell, *The Coming of Post-Industrial Society* (Heinemann, London, 1974).

7 E. Freidson, *Professional Powers* (Chicago University Press, Chicago, 1986), p. 225.

8 I. Illich, *Disabling Professions* (Boyars, London, 1977), pp. 12–13.

9 A. Sampson, *The Changing Anatomy of Britain* (Hodder and Stoughton, London, 1982), p. 274.

10 F. W. Taylor, *Scientific Management* (Harper and Row, London, 1947).

11 H. Fayol, *General and Industrial Management* (Pitman, London, 1949).

12 P. Willman and G. Winch, *Innovation and Management Control* (Cambridge University Press, Cambridge, 1985).

13 S. A. Marglin, 'What Bosses Do', in A. Gorz (ed.), *The Division of Labour* (Harvester Press, Hassocks, 1976); E. P. Thompson, 'Time, Work–discipline and Industrial Capitalism', Past and Present, 36 (1967), 56–97.

14 J. Fidler, *The British Business Elite* (Routledge and Kegan Paul, London, 1981), pp. 264–5.

15 J. Child and B. Partridge, *Lost Managers* (Cambridge University Press, Cambridge, 1982).

16 T. J. Watson, *The Personnel Managers* (Routledge and Kegan Paul, London, 1977).

17 C. Wright Mills, *White Collar* (Oxford University Press, New York, 1956).

18 R. Hyman and P. Price (eds), *The New Working Class: White Collar Workers and their Organizations* (Macmillan, London, 1982), p. 6.

19 Ibid., p. 8.

20 Ibid., p. 151.

21 Mills, *White Collar*.

22 D. Lockwood, *The Black Coated Workers* (Allen and Unwin, London, 1958).

23 C. Jenkins and B. Sherman, *The Collapse of Work* (Eyre Methuen, London, 1979).

24 Bensman and Lillienfeld, 'Craft and Craft Consciousness', in G. Esland, G. Salaman and M. Speakman (eds), *People and Work* (Open University Press, Milton Keynes, 1975).

25 P. Gleeson and G. Mardale, *Further Education Training* (Routledge and Kegan Paul, London, 1980).

26 R. Penn, *Skilled Workers in the Class Structure* (Cambridge University Press, Cambridge, 1985), p. 190.

27 J. Goldthorpe et al., *Affluent Worker*.

28 I. Crewe, *Guardian*, 15 and 16 June 1987.

29 One of the best-known studies of this solidarity is M. Young and P. Willmott, *Family and Kinship in East London* (Penguin, London, 1957).

30 H. Newby, *The Deferential Worker* (Allen Lane, London, 1977).

31 Goldthorpe et al., *Affluent Worker*.

32 D. Silverman, *The Theory of Organisations* (Heinemann, London, 1970).

33 R. Martin and R. H. Fryer, *Redundancy in Paternalist Capitalism* (Allen and Unwin, London, 1973).

34 Equal Opportunities Commission, *Fair and Efficient Selection* (HMSO, London, 1986), p. 14.

35 T. J. Watson, *Sociology, Work and Industry* (Routledge and Kegan Paul, London, 1980), pp. 253–4.

36 S. Hill, *Competition and Control at Work* (Heinemann, London, 1981), pp. 37–9.

4 Sociological Insights into Organizations

1 Introduction

Organizations are of fundamental importance in all our lives. We all belong to or use organizations: the office, factory, college, club, trade union, political party, hospital, local authority, civil service, church, public transport and so on. As Amitai Etzioni, a distinguished writer on organizations, puts it:

> We are born in organisations, educated by organisations and most of us spend our lives working for organisations. We spend much of our leisure time paying, playing and praying in organisations. Most of us will die in an organisation and when the time comes for burial the largest organisation of all – the State – must grant official permission.[1]

The trouble with organizations is that most of us think we know all about them, or that the subject is dull, or too theoretical or too obvious. Take college, for example. It seems obvious that the college is there to teach, and it is a place where students go to learn. But sociologists want to know much more: who really runs the college? *How* is it run? What makes it work? Where does power reside? Who decides the curriculum? Who benefits? What is the effect of separating college-goers from non-college-goers? Does this separation increase or reflect class and status divisions in society? What are the beliefs and ideologies of different groups within the college? These are the sorts of question this chapter seeks to answer.

This chapter starts by comparing theories of organizations. It considers reasons for a sociological interest in organizations and the benefits of such a study. It introduces the key terms, such as power, authority, communications, and decision-making. The chapter also exposes some organizational ideologies, and shows how these cloud our judgement. All this is illustrated by reference to two actual organizations.

A key figure in the sociological investigation of organizations was the distinguished German sociologist Max Weber (1864–1920). He identified power and authority as important aspects of organizations, and put forward his idea of the most efficient kind of organization – bureaucracy. First, we'll consider power and authority.

Power in organizations

Power is the ability to get someone to do what you want, whether it is with their agreement or not. It is a *relationship*, usually exercised in a collectivity like an organization. It often involves *dependence*, one person or group depending on another. Dependence always exists in the hierarchies which comprise most organizations. Apart from their superior resources and their ability to hire, promote and fire, holders of high office also possess knowledge, which itself is a great source of power (without relevant knowledge you cannot act effectively). This fact is important in designing an organization. Each level should have the knowledge and information necessary for its task in the organization. To withhold information is to withhold power (this fact can lead to obsessive secrecy in organizations, as discussed later in this chapter).

Not all power is official, formal or strictly hierarchical. Sometimes the less powerful members of an organization try to gain power. One example of this is where a work group develops its own methods of work and tries to work at its own pace. A study of American medical students facing the problem of work overload showed how they, as a group, tried to find out in subtle ways what it was that the staff really wanted them to know, hence reducing the strain on themselves.[2] (There were three main stages in the group reaction to the stress of a heavy work load. First, to try to learn everything; secondly, a realization that 'you can't do it all'; thirdly, in time, the more calculative group response: 'What do they – the Faculty – actually want?') Trade unions are another instance of countervailing power (see chapter 5). In other cases, people low in the hierarchy can be powerful because of their access to information and to top people – the managing director's secretary or assistant, for example.

Authority

Authority can be looked upon as a special instance of power; one in which the powerless group accepts the commands of the powerful group because they accept their power as *legitimate*. The question that interested Weber was, 'how does power become authority?'

Weber distinguished between three types of authority: the first type is based on the qualities of the leader. He used the Greek word *charisma*, referring to the personal qualities that set the leader apart from ordinary people. Examples of charismatic leaders would be some political leaders, religious prophets, some founders of successful corporations. Often charismatic leaders come to the fore in times of turmoil; Hitler is an example. Some have argued that charismatic authority is revolutionary in the sense of not being bound to the existing order: 'don't follow the rules; follow me!'[3]

The second type of authority is *traditional*. It occurs in situations where the belief in everyday routine as an inviolable rule of conduct is strong. The bases of authority in traditional organizations are precedent and usage. The leader's authority is based on inherited status and custom. The feudal system in Western Europe could be taken as an example of traditional authority, monarchy today another; *custom* is largely sufficient justification for the way things are done.

The third type of authority according to Weber is the *rational-legal* type, and Weber sees this as the dominant form in Western society. This type of authority is called *rational* because the means are designed to meet specific ends, such as making a profit. It is called *legal* because authority in organizations is exercised according to definite rules and procedures – for example the rules of a corporation, hospital or school. This led Weber to advance his 'ideal type' bureaucracy.[4]

2   Max Weber's 'Ideal Type' Bureaucracy

In studying organizations most sociologists start with the important work of Max Weber and his concept of *bureaucracy*. He used four key concepts – power, authority, 'ideal type' and bureaucracy. So far Weber's view of power and authority have been outlined. Now his use of the concept of 'ideal type' will be examined. The aim of looking at these concepts is to understand more clearly how organizations really function.

An *ideal type* emphasizes certain aspects of behaviour that are *typical* of the institution you are observing. The term 'ideal' has nothing to do with evaluations of any sort. The aim is to produce a picture of the typical characteristics of the phenomenon studied. For analytical purposes one may construct 'ideal types' of prostitution as well as of religious leaders. They aid our understanding because they show what is the *typical* about that phenomenon, helping us sift out the non-typical or unusual elements.[5] Perhaps Weber's use of *bureaucracy* will help to explain this. *Bureaucracy* should not be confused with our everyday understanding of the term, denoting inefficiency and red tape. For Weber the bureaucratic organization is the most efficient form of organization possible. This is because the means (the structure of the organization) are especially designed to achieve the organizational ends, and because the organization is not disrupted by the whims of a charismatic leader or held back by traditional procedures which do not serve the ends of the organization.

An 'ideal type' of bureaucracy has the following characteristics.

1 The staff members are personally free, observing only the impersonal duties of their offices.
2 There is a clear hierarchy of offices.
3 The functions of the offices are clearly specified.
4 Officials are appointed on the basis of a contract.
5 They are selected on the basis of a professional qualification, ideally substantiated by a diploma gained through examination.
6 They have a money salary, and usually pension rights. The salary is graded according to position in the hierarchy. The official can always leave the post, and under certain circumstances the post may also be terminated.
7 The official's post is his or her sole or major occupation.
8 There is a career structure, and promotion is possible either by seniority or merit, and according to the judgement of superiors.
9 The official may appropriate (take over for his or her own profit) neither the post nor the resources which go with it.
10 The official is subject to a unified control and disciplinary system.[6]

Before reading on, the reader might like to consider and make a list of criticisms that could be made of Weber's ideal type bureaucracy. Do not read the next section until you have.

Some criticisms of Weber's 'ideal type' bureaucracy

• Weber's ideal type neglects the disadvantages (or 'dysfunctions') of bureaucracy, including especially 'goal displacement' – the idea that gradually the means may displace the ends, for example correct record-keeping to be seen as more important than doing the job.
• Weber's ideal type bureaucracy seems to underestimate conflict; for example, he failed to look at conflicts based on ambition that exist within organizations, assuming that people would be content with their defined roles.
• Weber neglected informal organizations such as work groups. These may be an important source of values, for example, or ideas about what is 'normal' in any job (see chapter 6).

- Weber's model of an ideal type bureaucracy may not be applicable to many organizations – even as a model. It seems to be more applicable to organizations in the public sector such as councils, or totalitarian regimes, rather than commercial enterprises.

Question

Why do you think Weber's ideal type bureaucracy seems more applicable to public sector organizations?

- Even within rational bureaucratic organizations, charismatic figures may emerge from time to time to rejuvenate the organization. For example, distinguished American universities have known periods of deterioration following the deaths of their original founders, but many have been revived by later charismatic leaders. (An example of how this might apply to a business is given in a case study on p. 112.)
- Organizations may change their character – the peace-time army may be a bureaucracy in Weber's sense of the term, but in war rules may be waived and personal leadership becomes vital (not only at the top, either). In other words, an organization adapts to the environment.

In short, Weber's idea neglects human characteristics, which are influential in all organizations. While it appears to be reasonable, closer examination shows that in practice organizations in general and specifically the business sector may be quite different. But to be fair to Weber, he was putting forward an ideal type – a model of organization which emphasizes the ideal characteristics of a *pure* organization (or 'bureaucracy') rather than an organization that actually existed.

3 Compliance in Organizations

Amitai Etzioni, an American sociologist, has asked some basic questions.[7] Why do organizations keep going? Why do members conform? How is social control exercised? In answering these questions Etzioni uses the term *compliance*. Compliance means that a member (or *actor*) in an organization behaves in accordance with another member's wishes.

Etzioni argues that organizations require compliance from their members. This is achieved firstly by the *power* that organizations have over their members, and secondly by the *involvement* of members in the organization, i.e. their attitudes to it. He then distinguishes between three types of power used.

Coercive — the member works because he or she is forced
Remunerative — the member needs or wants a reward, and so has to work
Normative — the member supports the organization because he or she believes in its goals

There are also three types of involvement in the organization.

Alienative — denotes dissociation from the organization (e.g. convicts, slaves)
Calculative — the member is involved in the organization for commercial or other reasons, such as pay
Moral — the member is involved because he supports the aims of the organization (e.g. church and charity workers)

The three types of power and the three types of involvement generate the nine possible types of compliance illustrated in table 4.1. Types 1, 5 and 9 are called 'congruent compliant structures', examples of these are prisons, slavery (1); business enterprises, colleges in which vocational courses are predominant (5); religious sects, voluntary organizations, political parties (9). In these cases, the type of power by those at the top and the involvement of those below 'match' each other, and produce a relatively stable organization.

Other types of structures of compliance ('incongruent compliant structures') are inherently unstable, and such organizations will have a natural tendency to revert to a congruent compliant structure.

Table 4.1 *A typology of compliance*

| | Kinds of involvement | | |
Kinds of power	*Alienative*	*Calculative*	*Moral*
Coercive	1	2	3
Remunerative	4	5	6
Normative	7	8	9

Question

Why are the following not congruent compliance structures?

It is easy to think of many more examples of incongruent structures: the school which makes widespread use of punishments; foreign mercenaries; prisons which aim at rehabilitation (but fail); the idea of the 'short, sharp shock' in institutions for young offenders; firms of professional fund-raisers working for a church, and so on.

Further questions

What is the usefulness of Etzioni's typology of organizations? How far is it applicable to any organization of which you are a member?
Suggestion: Table 4.2 may help to suggest some answers to these questions.

Etzioni's typology applies over a wide range of organizations, showing similarities and differences in a variety of situations. It is useful in alerting us to the sort of false assumptions we may be making about organizations (such as those of management in table 4.2 above), and especially in showing that organizations have a tendency to revert to congruent compliant structures in the long run, in order to function effectively.

It must be stressed that most organizations include elements of all three types, for example a business firm which pays badly but has substantial staff loyalty through their enjoyment of the work. It can sometimes be coercive because jobs are scarce in that field, though normally staff and managers have a good relationship. Particular groups of staff, or individuals at different times, may have alienative, calculative and moral relationships with the company. For example, a secretary made to work late will be alienated; the same person may the next day be happy with a pay rise (calculative); she may move to a new boss for whom she has great respect, and works because she thinks the job very worthwhile (moral).

4   Who Benefits in Organizations?

P. M. Blau and W. R. Scott sought to classify organizations and what they do in a number of ways, for example types of communication and types of managerial control. Perhaps their most useful classification is in answer to the question – who benefits?[8] Table 4.3 is a summary of this.

Table 4.2 *Some examples of compliance in organizations*

Situation	Effect on members of the organization	Comments
• An ailing car manufacturer issues a letter to all its line workers urging them to put in more effort to turn the firm around.	A plant manager, visiting the changing rooms at the end of the day shift, finds the work people have made paper darts out of these notices and are flying them around the room.	This is not a congruent compliant structure according to table 4.1. It looks like category 8. The line workers' involvement is probably calculative; they are interested only in the money, so appeals to loyalty to the firm will have little effect unless bankruptcy is imminent and there are no other jobs, in which case the workers' involvement may still be calculative, but the situation will be coercive (2).
• A leading computer software firm is unable to retain its best young managers, who keep moving on to jobs with brighter promotion prospects. Higher management says 'Stay with the company; it has a great future. Be loyal'.	The young restive managers are thinking of their careers. They have to make it to the top while they are still young.	This is similar to the previous case. Appeals to loyalty may fall on deaf ears. Category 8 describes the current situation, and only a move to category 5 will solve the problem. While the line worker emphasizes pay, the rising manager emphasizes career prospects – both involvements are calculative.
• In Britain the Griffiths Report on the National Health Service recommended that the Health	The medical staff stress professional ethics rather than business efficiency. The two seem odd bedfellows.	Category 9 would seem to be the congruent structure here, but the situation is currently more like 3 or 6. Do you agree?

Situation	Effect on members of the organization	Comments
Authorities should be run by managers brought in mainly from business.		It remains to be seen whether there will be a tendency to revert to category 9 in time.

Source: Nichon Kokusei Zue 1982, p. 326. Reprinted in T. Fukutake, *The Japanese Social Structure*.

Blau and Scott are also interested in efficiency, which they define as the achievement of maximum gain at minimum cost in order to further survival and growth in competition with other organizations. Efficiency is vital in the commercial firm, but in other types of organization, such as the mutual benefit association, efficiency is expected not to interfere with the membership's ability democratically to decide the objectives of the organization. (Efficiency is discussed further in section 10 of this chapter.)

The ideas of Blau and Scott have been criticized.[9] First, they are concerned with efficiency. We should ask 'efficiency for whom?' What is the purpose of efficiency? Secondly, the theory is naïve. In addition to asking who benefits, they should also ask 'Who does not benefit?' and 'Who controls?'. Asking these questions may help to reveal the hidden functions of an organization.

It may be interesting to try answering these questions in relation, say, to a trade union or indeed to any of the examples in table 4.3.

Table 4.3 *Types of organization – who benefits?*

Type of organization	Examples	Prime beneficiaries
Mutual benefit organization	Trade union	Membership
Business organization	Firm	Owners
Service organization	School, hospital	Clients
Commonwealth organization	Prison, police, fire brigade	Public at large

Source: Based on P. M. Blau and W. R. Scott, *Formal Organizations* (Routledge and Kegan Paul, London, 1963).

Another criticism made by Clegg and Dunkerley is that the model of organizations portrayed here is static and cannot explain change, yet there is no reason to believe the beneficiaries would always remain the same. Thus a change in the type of beneficiary may lead to a change in the nature of the organization. An example is the friendly society that becomes a big commercial insurance company.

Finally, it is the controllers of the organizations who really determine the benefit that is to go to an individual or group, and this gives rise to conflict in organizations, particularly over the allocation of resources. Again, this means persisting with the question 'Who really controls the organization?'; often it is *not* the beneficiaries. The following questions may be worth thinking about.

Questions

Why do schools often fail to develop the full potential of their pupils?
Why do claimants fail to get their full welfare entitlement?
Why are many ordinary trade union members dissatisfied with the leadership in their union?
Examine the proposition that some organizations seem to be run for the benefit of the staff. Give examples.

5 Who Makes the Rules in Organizations?

Alvin Gouldner is another leading sociologist interested in organizations. His research could be seen as testing the relevance of some of Weber's ideas about bureaucracy.[10] Weber argued that bureaucracies are governed by the exercise of national rules – but how did these rules come about in the first place? We need to study the *process* of rule-making. To answer these questions Gouldner studied a strike in a gypsum mine in America, describing the effects of introducing a new bureaucratic organization in the face of workforce opposition. Under the previous management, rules were often ignored and the workforce had had a favourable attitude to management. However, a new mine manager arrived, and he tried to enforce the rules fully. The result was a drop in morale and greater conflict between management and the workforce. Eventually this led to what Gouldner called a 'wild-cat strike'.

In analysing this situation Gouldner distinguished between three patterns of bureaucracy: mock bureaucracy, where the rules are imposed by an outside agency; representative bureaucracy, where the rules are made by experts and accepted by all; and punishment-centred bureaucracy, where one side attempts to coerce the other. This is shown in table 4.4.

Table 4.4   *Three patterns of bureaucracy*

Mock bureaucracy	Representative bureaucracy	Punishment-centred bureaucracy
1 Who usually initiates the rules?		
The rules are imposed by an outsider, e.g. the 'No Smoking' rule initiated by an insurance company. Neither management nor workers identify with it.	Both workers and managers identify with the rules, e.g. safety rules.	One party initiates the rule, e.g. time-keeping rules set by management and enforceable ultimately by the threat of dismissal, or 'restrictive practices' rules made by unions.
2 Whose values legitimate the rules?		
Neither party	Both parties	Either party
• Rules are neither enforced by management nor obeyed by workers.	Rules are both enforced by management and obeyed by workers.	Rules are either enforced by workers or management and evaded by the other.
• This usually entails little conflict between the two groups.	This generates a few tensions but little overt conflict.	This entails relatively great tension and conflict.
• Joint violation and evasion of rules is buttressed by the informal sentiments of the participants.	Joint support for rules is buttressed by mutual participation.	Rules are enforced by punishment or threat of industrial unrest.
3 Summary		
Authority is based on expertise.	Authority is based on mutual agreement.	Authority is based on office.

In general, rules may be helpful in that they avoid the need for close supervision (everyone knows the rules), and this in turn avoids conflict.

Gouldner's theory of organization is useful in showing rule-making as a *process*; the reason behind bureaucratization (the making of rational rules to govern situations in organizations) and why attempts to bureaucratize are accepted or rejected. His ideas led to the analysis of the culture (or ideology) of organizations, in which notions of what is proper, fair and legitimate, and how individuals and groups should behave, are enshrined. Thus, in the light of Gouldner's findings, it might be interesting to examine instances of rules being ignored or enforced, and how they are enforced, and then try to answer the question 'what sort of bureaucracy am I looking at?'[11]

Questions

What kind of bureaucracy operates in an institution you know? Whose values legitimate its rules?

6   The Management of Innovation

T. Burns, a sociologist, and C. W. Stalker, a psychologist, wanted to find out why some firms were better at introducing innovation than others, and they studied a number of electronics firms in Scotland. They wanted particularly to answer these questions. 'What were the difficulties of these firms in the face of changing demand and technologies? Why do some firms cope better than others?'[12]

To answer these questions, Burns and Stalker compared these firms against 'ideal types' of organization. At one extreme is the *mechanistic* type of organization, with a clear hierarchy of command and strict demarcation of work and responsibilities. Such an organization could be seen as conforming to Weber's ideal type bureaucracy. At the other extreme is the *organic* (or organismic) type of organization, which has a loose organizational structure and no clear demarcation, in which staff can easily change roles. Here are some of the key differences between mechanistic and organic organizations.

The mechanistic type of organization	*The organic management type of organization*
The mechanistic management system is appropriate to stable conditions.	The organic management system is appropriate to changing conditions which give rise to unforeseen requirements for action which cannot be systematically assigned in the organizational hierarchy.
Characterized by:	Characterized by:
• specialization of tasks	the contributive nature of special knowledge to the common task

• the abstract nature of each task	the realistic nature of each task
• the hierarchical assessment of task performance	the continual redefinition of tasks through interaction
• the precise definition of rights and obligations	imprecise definition of rights and obligations, so it is difficult to shift responsibility
• responsibilities attached to each role	commitment that is wider than the role
• a hierarchical system of communication and control	a network structure of communication and control
• a hierarchy of knowledge	*ad hoc* location of knowledge
• vertical interaction, i.e. management–workers	lateral communication (between workers), consultation rather than command
• instructions	advice
• loyalty and obedience	commitment to the overall task of the organization
• the local organization-based nature of knowledge and prestige	knowledge valid outside the organization

This list may be useful in trying to assess how successful an organization is in adapting to change. Burns and Stalker suggest that any organization could be seen as having three linked social systems. First, there is the *formal organization*, as shown for example by the organization chart which indicates who is responsible for decisions in a particular area. Secondly, there is the *career structure* of an organization. The decisions that members of an organization make may be influenced by their career goals – 'how will this advance my career?' Thirdly there is the *political system* in organizations, in which members compete for power.

Thus while the list above illustrates an organization's adaptability, the three social systems just described may show more clearly why an organization does not adapt.

Question

Can you think of some current examples?

7   The Needs of Members of an Organization[14]

Whereas most of the studies quoted so far may be taken as being sociological in the main, Chris Argyris has used a psychological approach, one that emphasizes the needs of individuals in organizations.[13] (Sociologists do not usually use the concept of 'need'; the nature of needs is discussed more fully in chapter 6.) Briefly, Argyris argues that, as we mature, we pass from a state of dependence to one of independence. Yet many organizations constrain individuals by their organizational structure – the technology and the amount of control by management. The effects of organizational constraints are more strongly felt lower down in the organization than near the top. But more control, and with it more dependence, leads to apathy. Figure 4.1 depicts the vicious circle.

Argyris cites his research at the 'XYZ plant', where manual recruits were carefully examined by the personnel department and potential trouble-makers turned away. Some successful applicants were then assigned to highly skilled work and the remainder to unskilled work. On questioning, it was found that the workers doing the skilled work were interested in the work and its quality and had a high sense of self-worth. However, in the other group, where there was little job satisfaction, workers formed work groups which undermined the authority of supervisors. In response management pressured supervisors to inspect more closely, and this was resented by supervisors, although the workers concerned enjoyed the attention.

Argyris summarizes his own conclusions as follows.

1   There is a lack of *congruence* (coming together) between the needs of individuals and the demands of some formal organizations.
2   This leads to frustration and conflict.
3   This frustration increases:

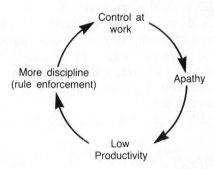

Figure 4.1 *The vicious circle of over-control*

(a) as one goes down the chain of command;
(b) as directive leadership increases;
(c) as management controls are increased;
(d) as jobs become more specialized.
4 The nature of formal organizations gives rise to rivalry.
5 Adaptive behaviour by employees impedes integration with the formal organization. Thus, for example, increased dependency by employees on the organization may lead to adaptation that involves apathy.

Sociologists have been critical of the emphasis on human *needs* which is common among psychologists, because it implies that needs are inherent in the person from birth, rather than culturally acquired and learned from parents, peers and from society generally. One critic, in commenting on the organizational psychology approach, asks:

• How do we validate the existence of needs?
• Are they abstract psychological concepts?
• Do needs really explain behaviour?
• Do needs have to be satisfied by organizations?[14]

He argues that we should not see the employee as an isolated individual with needs, but rather as an individual in interaction with fellows and gaining satisfaction from that. The individual members of the organization are socialized to certain values in the same way that members of a society are socialized to that society's values. The sociologist's role is to try to ascertain what the organization's values are.

8 Why Do Sociologists Study Organizations? Why Do They Theorize about Them?

Much of the literature on organizations comes from sociologists, though psychologists and management theorists make their contribution too. If you understand why sociologists study organizations, you'll be able to see how their studies can help managers and business people in dealing with organizations and their problems. Here then are a few possible 'answers' to the questions that head this section.

1 As mentioned, sociologists are interested in questions of power, authority, values, beliefs, social control and ideologies. Why do people believe in ideologies? Why do they obey rulers or overseers;

how do those in authority maintain control? These concepts and questions, difficult to isolate for sociological analysis in society as a whole, are present with greater clarity within organizations.

2   Organizational problems such as apathy can occur over a wide range of organizations such as the commercial firm, the hospital, the army, trade unions, etc. A sociological analysis of organizations assists our understanding of such problems; for example, apathy has been shown to be frequently linked to over-zealous control.

3   The organizational 'rule books' – the official management instructions – are of great interest for sociological study. Instead of seeing the rules as just rules, the sociologist might ask, 'what do these rules really mean?' What are the underlying assumptions made by managers and managed? Who gains by the rules and do these rules reflect an ideology? Who loses?' This sort of enquiry can sometimes make sociologists unpopular with management, but it is a vital part of the process of understanding what actually goes on.

4   Theories are attempts to get closer to the truth. They are always approximations (sociologists recognize that people have individual characteristics and responses), but they help to illuminate our understanding of situations. Through debate between sociological researchers and others theories are refined or discarded and replaced.

5   The management approach to organizational theory tends to stress how members ought to behave, or could be encouraged to behave, in order, for example, to increase the efficiency of the organization (this is shown particularly in chapter 6). By contrast the sociologist studies people as they actually are in their natural settings, at home with the family, at work with the colleagues, at college with their fellow students and so on. This is one of the ways in which sociologists try to be objective and 'value-free' in their research.

6   So far it has been shown that there is a variety of reasons for the sociologist's interest in organizations, especially the fact that power, authority and ideologies may be more clearly analysed in discrete organizations. But, as just mentioned, organizations are not separate from the rest of society. Organizations could be seen as reproductions of society – reproducing also the social class divisions of society. Thus some have argued that members of the upper social classes can influence the recruitment of members of their own class to high positions in important organizations[15] (and 'self-recruitment' can apply at all levels in the organization). Nowadays the traditional claims of property and inheritance have to be supplemented with relevant education and technical expertise. The success of the higher class in obtaining high positions depends

The value-free approach

Value freedom in sociology means that researchers should not be influenced by the beliefs they are studying. Instead, they should study these beliefs in a 'scientific' and 'objective' way, producing just the facts. They should not make their own judgements about these beliefs, nor advocate particular beliefs, values and ideologies. Many critics of sociology say it cannot be scientific because one cannot measure beliefs and concepts, with which it often deals. It is very hard to attain a value-free sociology because our own values keep intruding. For example, a sociologist researching low-paid workers may sympathize with their feelings, but should not allow this sympathy to influence his findings. Although it is hard, sociologists should either strive to avoid influencing their work with their own values, or make their own values clear in their writing.

partly on wealth, which buys education, for example, and partly on 'correct' social background, and this ensures that high office holders are usually endowed with 'correct' attitudes, values and ideologies.[16] Not only do managers and directors share similar values; they often own a considerable proportion of their firms.

9 A Management Approach to the Theory of Organizations

The theories of organization quoted so far are to a large extent sociological. It would be interesting to examine some management theories on organizations in order to see more clearly any hidden assumptions that are being made. It would be impossible to examine the whole range of management theory;[17] it should also be unnecessary. If readers can sociologically analyse theories for themselves, then there is no need to 'learn' the author's views. Instead it will be useful to tackle what are perhaps the two central problems of most organizations, ones that feature in most management theories of organization, communications and decision-making, and see what the management theorists have to say about them.

Good communications in organizations

Good communication is an essential element in decision-making in an organization. It is also essential for the participation of employees, or at least for genuine consultation. Ideally there should be smooth *two-way* consultation; that is, both up and down the organization hierarchy. What impedes communication downwards? What impedes communication upwards?

One of the impediments to downward communication is the excessive secrecy of leaders and supervisors referred to earlier. British government departments are notorious for excessive secrecy, but many business organizations are guilty of this too. Why is this? One possible explanation, mentioned before, is the link between information and power. It can be argued that control over information is critically important in mobilizing the power needed to put decisions into effect; in one study of a prison where all reports had to pass through a custodial hierarchy, that hierarchy was able to distort the goals of a prisoners' rehabilitation programme being run from outside that prison. A member of an organization who controls the flow of information is known as a gatekeeper. Often gate keepers are in a position of power (such as a head warder in a prison), and often they distort the information they pass on (or do not pass it on at all).[18] It seems from this that handing over information can involve handing over power, keeping knowledge to oneself makes others who rely on the use of the knowledge dependent on oneself; hence secrecy bolsters the position of management. How many times have staff who have been made redundant complained that they were not warned? If they had been warned, they might have come up with an alternative proposal to solve the problem, which management wanted to solve by redundancy. Sometimes there may be a feeling that lower level employees cannot be trusted with information, or that they may misinterpret it. Better not to say anything than to risk causing misunderstandings!

There are other barriers to downward communication, built into the structure of most organizations. One is that communication *takes time*; most managers have large workloads and have not been taught to put communication at the top of their list of priorities (because the effects of communication can rarely be precisely measured in terms of output). Another problem, related to this, is that managers have little training in communication skills.

Turning to impediments to upward communication; often it is lower-level employees who know first that something is amiss. Usually they are not the people who can make a decision about solving the problem. For example, the manual worker on the shop floor may be one of the first to spot faults in the product; the ordinary salesperson may be the one most likely to know why a product is not selling; the private secretary will be aware of the defects of office procedures; the clerk in an outpatients' clinic knows many of the defects in the administration of the system, though they may go unnoticed by the consultant. Why does this information often fail to reach the decision-maker? Managers, administrators and workers may act as gatekeepers for information, for example in preventing undesirable information from reaching the decision-makers. They may not wish to be the harbingers of bad news, especially if it may reflect on their running of their department, or machine.

A further difficulty is that managers and non-managers often have quite different viewpoints. There may be a cultural divide. Communication can be much easier within the workforce itself than between superiors and workers. Often subordinates avoid consulting supervisors for fear of making a mistake.[19] They do not want to be judged. Of course it should be mentioned that there are cliques and conflicts of interest within management itself that also work against horizontal flow of information.

What can management do to improve communications? Management theories argue that as far as possible managers should aim at the free flow of information, up and down, horizontally and diagonally. Having clearly stated goals helps towards clear communication because:

- it lessens misunderstandings;
- it is an aid in discovering where conflict is (which is the first step towards resolving it);
- the setting of goals for the future is an aid in anticipating where the future setbacks might occur.[20]

One way of achieving clear goals in business organization is through 'management by objectives', in which management's aims are translated into particular goals for each person in the organization.[21]

Another method of improving communication might be through setting up joint committees of managers and non-managers in order to decide upon problems of mutual interest. An example of this was the Joint Productivity Councils set up in Britain during the Second World War. It might be objected that such committees blur the fact that decisions have to be taken, and responsibility has to be taken for these decisions. In this respect too many committees could weaken the organization. A committee may be useful as a response to temporary problems such as a move, or a disciplinary matter, or a disagreement on a specific matter, but after the item has been dealt with the committee should perhaps be dissolved. On the other hand, joint committees may be useful for handling long-term issues and planning. It is important to point out that the efficacy of these co-operative committees depends on management's perception of them:

What is the purpose of company meetings? A management view

"In practice, even the most apparently futile of meetings usually serves some wider corporate purpose as well as preserving the mental health of those who attend: it builds and maintains the communication network, it gives a feeling of security, it helps to sort out status and quasi-territory, and it reaffirms identity and the sense of belonging. No corporation could survive or be described as a corporation if every member travelled in from his private house by his private car to his private office, met no one during the day, and travelled back in the evening. Any Corporation Man or Women who found himself or herself in that position for a few weeks would start to wonder how long it would be before he or she got the sack. A certain amount of factory work is in fact very like this, since the noise or the demands of the operation make each person into an island; it is hardly surprising that if the corporation does not bring its members together for regular meetings, they seek assembly and association through the unions. But at the higher and more comfortable levels, most corporations have found ways of channelling this need for association into useful and productive purposes, and in fact the more visibly effective and valuable the meeting the more it fulfils all the social and therapeutic needs as well."[22]

do they regard them as *legitimate* mechanisms in the firm? It also depends on whether the workers respect their 'representatives' and feel that their interests are being properly looked after.

Improving communications may be achieved by improving the communication skills of individuals – especially managers. Examples of this would be training in report-writing, faster reading and 'management', plus advice and counselling, and so on. Against this it might be said that people learn best on the job, and such classes might be resented by older adults (not least by well-educated managers). However, communications skills should certainly be taught to business and management *students*.

A sociological assessment of 'bad communications'

A sociologist might make some objections to the sort of 'solutions' to the problems of communication considered here. It seems a truism that in many organizations people tend to keep to their own groups and not speak to out-groupers. Often there are separate canteens, car parks and toilet facilities for managers and non-managers. Make the test for yourself in your own organization. Thus, if you are a student, look around your college refectory. Do the lecturers have their own separate dining-room? Within the student refectory itself students may look alike and appear to be mixing freely. However, if you look a little closer you will probably see that these students are in their own groups; business studies students talk to business studies students; accountancy students talk to their fellow accountancy students, and so on.

Thus in an organization people are quite likely to keep to their own sub-groups, e.g. an occupational group or, say, their own office or work-group. Secretaries may form one group, computer programmers another. The rule seems to be 'birds of a feather flock together'.

It is not surprising therefore that managers do not mix and communicate much with other organizational members. There is, moreover, a cultural divide that has already been referred to. So too has class difference. As was shown in chapter 3, managers (and professionals) have *careers*; most other employees have *jobs*. Careers confer greater knowledge, information and power on managers, and this is reflected in the organization's communication system. Further a career implies:

- a logical lifelong progression to higher positions through promotion – and competition for these higher positions;
- devotion to the task;
- devotion to the employing organization.

While this may apply also to some other employees, a job normally implies that money is the main consideration. There seems to be a social divide between those who have jobs and those who have careers. Overall the problem with the management theories is that they *ignore* real conflict; they assume that if only management could communicate well to staff, staff would be happy with management's decisions. Yet in reality the involvement of staff is often alienative (see section 3 of this chapter).

Another reason for this lack of contact and communication between managers and others is lack of trust. The two groups sometimes do not trust each other. Some managers may feel that the workforce has to be watched all the time, and only basic information is communicated to them.

Really good communications and good decision-making are vitally linked. You cannot have one without the other. Bad decisions, no matter how 'well' they are communicated, will not lead to harmony or efficiency in the firm.

Decision-making in organizations

Basically the problems an organization faces in its decision-making are: which goals to pursue; what means can be used; what technology is available; what personnel is available. The various strategies are set out below.[23]

		Preferences regarding possible outcomes	
		Certainty	*Uncertainty*
	Certain	Computation	Compromise
Beliefs about cause/ effect relations	Uncertain	Judgement	Inspiration

Good decision-making means trying to reduce the uncertainties involved, making it as routine as possible, as in computation. To achieve this the following suggestions are made.

- Maintain good communications, as discussed in this chapter.
- Do not make false assumptions (easier said than done). Quite often bad decision-making is the result of false assumptions, especially in personnel management and industrial relations. The next section indicates the nature of these false assumptions.
- The theme of this section has been that the better the communication the less the likelihood of false assumptions and therefore bad decision-making. Probably the real barrier is that the different parties tend to have different values and this leads to a biased view of what is really going on (that is to say the parties see only what they want to see). The parties do not see or hear or understand each other because unconsciously they do not wish to – it would be threatening to do so. One example of this is Ian McGregor's book on the miners' strike in 1984/5, when he was Chairman of the National Coal Board. The book's title is *The Enemies Within*.[24] Is this the sort of language that encourages good communication?
- Maybe the emphasis should be less on making right decisions and more on *making decisions come right*. This implies adaptability and listening to others (stop commanding and start co-operating). Section 10 tries to show why this is easier said than done. Perhaps also managers over-emphasize the need for decisions. If there were more genuine consultations and involvement at work – more autonomy and less control – there would be much less need for management decision-making.

Question

What are the obstacles to less control and more autonomy at work?

10 How Rational are Organizations?
A Sociological View

Organizations and the individuals within them are the products of society's institutions and of the prevailing values in society. Just as individuals and societies have beliefs, values and ideologies, so too do organizations. These ideologies cannot be described in purely rational terms; they are based on beliefs, hopes and fears. Nevertheless, they influence organizational decision-making, which is usually intended to be rational. Obviously it is important to understand the nature of these ideologies in order to understand decision-making in organizations. Most ideologies are beliefs that favour the powerful in society – in this case higher management. (See chapter 1 for a definition of ideology.)

Although the values and goals of organizations vary, there are some common organizational ideologies. The management ideology of 'scientific management', discussed in chapter 3, is one – and one that includes several elements. The common elements of organizational ideologies to have been called: structuralism; psychologism; consensualism; welfareism; legalism. These will be considered and explained in turn.[25]

Structuralism

Structuralism assumes that the way the organization is structured is not a matter of choice; that the structure of the organization is neutral in terms of conflict between groups and is based on the application of rational scientific principles. Structuralism stems from the deeper assumption that the principles of management generally are neutral, rational and scientific. This is the basis of a phrase often heard among managers – 'there is no alternative'. The members of the organization are thought to be allocated to their positions in it according to rational criteria. People at the top are there because of their expertise. This 'expertise' tends to become mystified, having its own 'special language' which excludes junior members of the organization.

Structuralism includes an ideology of achievement. Hierarchy and the use of power is seen as inevitable and natural; the opposite is seen as anarchy and chaos. Those in the low-status positions in the organization are there through their own failure or lack of ability. All this is seen as inevitable rather than capable of change.

Psychologism

Progress through the organization is seen in terms of the member's ability and attitude. As with structuralism, the structure of the organization is seen as given; therefore if change is desirable it is the individual who must change, not the organization. Thus, *when things go wrong it is natural for managers to think that the fault lies in the employees* rather than in the structure of the organization or bad decision-making by managers. Personnel are seen as objects and resources amenable to rational measurement, utilization and change. Hence managers and management departments in colleges prefer the term 'behavioural *science*' rather than psychology or sociology, because it implies that behaviour can be measured and modified.

In training, members are encouraged to see themselves as the good 'company' person, to feel more involved in the organization, and to see their future in terms of the company's future. The achievement of this coincidence is the objective of *in-service* training courses, and company conferences.

Consensualism

Consensualism assumes that all members of the organization have the same goal. Where a breakdown occurs in the organization this is due to some fault in the individual or to a failure of communications. To some degree, the members of an organization do have the same basic goals: the survival of the organization; but the stress on consensualism may hide the fact that there is more than one way to achieve a desired end.

Thus consensualism assumes that all members of the organization agree with its goals. In reality the individual member is powerless and cannot influence decisions.

Welfareism

Welfareism is the attempt by management to engage subordinates' commitment through the apparent delegation of authority, through job enrichment and through apparent participation generally. This appears to be reasonable enough except that such actions could be *ploys* to maintain effective managerial control. Even where a democratic leadership style is adopted it is evaluated in terms of, say, productivity rather than the true welfare of the members, and in any case managerial control is ultimately retained.

Legalism

Legalism is based on the idea that there is a free contract between management and the employee, by which the employees contract to sell their labour and commitment to the organization. This also assumes management's right to manage on behalf of the owners, and the employees' obligation to obey instructions.

The objections to these assumptions are firstly that the contract is not free and equal. The employer is more powerful (in terms of rights over employees), and the employee's need of the money is usually strong. Secondly, employees, despite the legal assumptions, do not *freely* agree to obey instructions, but will often combine to try to achieve some control over their pay and working conditions. So when employees strike they may be deemed, by management, to have broken their contract (and this is supported in certain circumstances by the Industrial Relations Act 1983). On the other hand, changes required by management in working practices are assumed to be part of management's right to manage. Resistance to this change in the 'contract' by workers is not seen in the same light as workers' attempts to change things.

Question

Taking as an example an organization with which you are familiar, such as your college, firm, etc., or an organization in the news, give examples of structuralism, psychologism, consensualism, welfareism, and legalism. If you cannot find actual examples of all these, suggest hypothetical ones.

Here are some final general observations. The hierarchical structure of organizations is a reflection of the class-based values of our society. The hierarchical nature of organizations is a result of unquestioned assumptions rather than any necessary relationship.

We must also always question what we mean by efficiency. Efficiency for whom or for what? Thus it may appear efficient to close uneconomic pits in terms of profit for mine owners, but it is not efficient in terms of unemployment, loss of 'social capital', such as derelict houses, schools, roads, etc., and ill health (which imposes costs on the health service). It is efficient for an individual accountant whose firm charges others for her time *not* to keep records of how her time is spent; she can get more 'work' if she spends no time on record-keeping. But for her firm this is very inefficient. Conflicts of this kind arise all the time.

Question

Give examples illustrating the different meanings of efficiency – efficiency for whom?

Suggestion: You could for example examine a firm which is closing down, or laying off some staff, or one that is expanding very rapidly. What does efficiency mean for the firm's directors, for the staff, for the community?

Are centralization and hierarchy really essential; who insists on this? Are alternative arrangements possible? (Some sociologists think organizations can be decentralized.)[26] Many alternative examples exist; the small firm, peasant farms, co-operatives, kibbutzes and so on.

Management objectives (or any other person's or group's objectives) do not exist in a social vacuum. No objective can be studied in isolation from other objectives. Objectives are determined by values and interests. Managers and workers may have quite different interests, and schemes for good communication, increased participation, etc. will not alter this fact. One of the clearest accounts of this state of affairs is given by A. Fox in *Man Mismanagement*, in which he contrasts the management viewpoint which sometimes stresses that we are all part of a team and should pull together, with the viewpoint of the lower members of the organization who are not really consulted on decisions affecting them, and who do not feel part of the organization, and for whom work is a burden. These radically differing views of the organization between management and non-management are discussed in chapter 5, which attempts a sociological analysis of industrial relations.[27]

11 How to Undertake a Sociological Analysis of Business Organizations: Two Examples

How does organization theory, and particularly the sociological view, help us to understand what is going on inside large commercial organizations? Two examples are given here: Marks and Spencer and Imperial Chemical Industries. But first, here are some guidelines on undertaking research into companies.

Some general advice on organizational projects

In examining an organization you could try to do the following:

1 Describe its size in terms of one or more of the following:
- its sales or turnover;
- its premises;
- its brands;
- its share of the market for its product;
- its international standing;
- its value – e.g. on the stock exchange;
- the number of employees.

2 Draw up an organization chart, showing who is responsible for what. Suggest improvements to the organization if you feel this is necessary – for example, would you reduce the hierarchy, cut out some levels of command?
3 Try to show its personnel/industrial relations policy, including one or two of the following items:
- its policy on trade unions;
- its policy on recruitment, training and promotion;
- its policy on the employment of women and racial minorities.

4 Do you feel there are any obvious ideologies in the organization, for example:

• scientific • management	see chapter 3 for definition
• paternalism	defined in this section
• structuralism • psychologism • consensualism	see previous section for description
• welfareism	
• legalism	

5 Is the firm popular with staff and customers? Is it a monopoly?
6 Who owns the firm? Who manages the firm? Are the owners also the managers? Identify where power lies – is it in the boardroom or elsewhere, e.g. a holding company? Who are the board members and what is their social background?
7 Find out what has been the main problem of the firm over the past few years.

You may find the following useful (available in most big libraries):

Annual company reports
Directory of Directors
Extel Cards
Keesing's Record of World Events
Kelly's Business Link
Key British Enterprises
Kompass
Stock Exchange Year Book
Stubb's Directory
The Times One Thousand
UK Trade Names
Who Owns Whom
Who's Who

In addition, many large corporations in Britain and the USA have had at least one history written about them. Bear in mind that the history or description may have been specially commissioned by the company or may be a resumé of the chairman's views, and therefore may be less than impartial. The box on 'the managerial revolution' may also assist you in this project, by indicating what you should look for.

The managerial revolution thesis

Sociologists and others have sought to find out who really owns the bigger companies – thus:

- J. Burnham asked (in 1941) who *controls* large corporations? Is it the owners or the managers?[a]

- Burnham, Berle and Means[b] argued that ownership had become dispersed (among shareholders) and that control of large corporations resided increasingly in the hands of professional managers. This is the crux of the managerial revolution thesis.

- Baran and Sweezy[c] counter-argue that there is no divorce between management and ownership. Managers are still among the biggest owners in their firms.

- Most recently Scott[d] and others have argued that with innovations (especially in informational technology), management is becoming increasingly professionalized, technical and separated from ownership.

- Management is not just technical and neutral – managers are basically interested in profit.

- Increasingly, large financial institutions (bank and insurance companies) are controlling large firms. Your project may help to shed light on who really owns and controls large firms.[3]

[a] J. Burnham, *The Managerial Revolution* (Penguin, Harmondsworth, 1945).
[b] M. Berle and G. Means, *The Modern Corporation and Private Property* (Macmillan, New York, 1947).
[c] P.A. Baran and P.M. Sweezy, *Monopoly Capital* (Penguin, Harmondsworth, 1968).
[d] J. Scott, *Corporations, Classes and Capitalism* (Hutchinson, London, 1985).
[e] E. Herman, *Corporate Control, Corporate Power* (Cambridge University Press, Cambridge, 1981), for USA.

This is a selection of books written about leading companies in Britain and USA, from various standpoints.

A. M. Pettigrew, *The Awakening Giant: Continuity and Change in ICI* (Basil Blackwell, Oxford, 1985)

C. Kennedy, *ICI: The Company That Changed Our Lives* (Hutchinson, London, 1986)

J. P. Wright, *On a Clear Day You Can See General Motors* (Sidgewick and Jackson, London, 1979)

A. P. Sloan, Jnr, *My Years with General Motors* (Anchor Books, New York, 1972)

M. Edwardes, *Back from the Brink* (Rover) (Collins, London, 1983)

I. M. McGregor, *The Enemies Within* (British Coal) (Fontana Collins, London, 1987) (to a large extent an account of the miners' strike 1984–5)

D. A. Simmons, *Schweppes: The First 200 Years* (Springwood Books, London, 1983)

T. Oliver, *The Real Coke: The Real Story* (Elm Tree Books, London, 1986)

A. Sampson, *The Seven Sisters: The Great Oil Companies and the World they have Made* (Hodder and Stoughton, London, 1975) (Although old, this is a good exposé of how some transnational corporations behaved in the past, and probably still do.)

H. Abromeit, *British Steel* (Berg, Leamington Spa, 1986)

B. Phillips, *Conran and the Habitat Story* (Weidenfeld and Nicolson, London, 1984)

P. Kleinman, *The Saatchi and Saatchi Storey* (Weidenfeld and Nicolson, London, 1987)

K.K. Tse, *Marks and Spencer: Anatomy of Britain's Most Efficiently Managed Company* (Pergamon, Oxford, 1985)

G. Wagner, *The Chocolate Conscience* (Cadbury's, Fry's and Rowntree's) (Chatto, London, 1987)

If you need help with understanding the figures you may find the following useful:

C. Hird, *Challenging the Figures: A Guide to Company Finance and Accounts* (Pluto, London, 1983)

Suggestion:

No one book will answer all the questions set in a project, but a picture may emerge of how large companies function. Use all available sources, including newspapers, magazines, company reports, and so on.

Project 1: Marks and Spencer

This is one of the most profitable commercial organizations in Britain. It should be interesting to see how it works, and what lessons can be learned and applied to other organizations.[28] Marks and Spencer will be described and analysed to show what kind of firm it is – its organization, the way it treats its staff and so on. This, and the following project on ICI, show the standard of work expected in such projects.

Marks and Spencer in a nutshell

Size

- M & S is Britain's largest retailer. Over 14 million customers shop at M & S stores every week.
- It has 260 stores in the UK, totalling 600,000 metres squared of selling space.
- It is one of the largest UK companies and has some 250,000 shareholders.

Brand

- M & S stores sell only one brand – St Michael – widely recognized as a symbol of quality and value.
- St Michael merchandise includes: clothing; food and wine; footwear and accessories; home furnishings; household goods; toiletries; books and house plants.
- Over 90 per cent of St Michael merchandise is British-made.

Market share

- M & S has 15 per cent of the national clothing market. It buys approximately one fifth of the clothing production of the UK.
- Of the total UK market M & S accounts for one quarter of the sales of socks and trousers, one third of the sales of underwear, pyjamas, bras and nightdresses, and one half of the sales of ladies' slips.
- St Michael foods is a leading brand in the UK. It represents 37 per cent of the company's total UK sales. It is Britain's largest fishmonger. It also sells one million chickens every week.

Suppliers

- Over 800 companies supply St Michael merchandise to M & S's exclusive specification.
- Nearly 150 suppliers have been manufacturing St Michael goods for over 25 years. Fifty of these companies have been associated with M & S for over 40 years.
- M & S does not have any financial stake in manufacturers.

Employees

- M & S employs over 46,000 staff in the UK. Of these, 20,000 have worked for the company for more than five years, 10,000 for more than ten years. Close to half the total employees own M & S shares.
- Some 200,000 people are engaged in the production, distribution and sale of St Michael goods.

Overseas

- There are seven M & S stores in France, Belgium and the Irish Republic.
- The company also has a controlling interest in over 200 stores in Canada.
- St Michael goods are sold in 30 other countries, including such major customers as Japan and Hong Kong.
- M & S exports more than any other British retailer. It is also the UK's largest exporter of clothing

The Organization of Marks and Spencer

The formal organization structure has been depicted as in figure 4.2.

The staff at Marks & Spencer enjoy a wide range of benefits. The company has been seen by some as 'paternalistic' – that is, giving the staff good benefits will ensure hard work.

Paternalism

Paternalism here refers to the rule of the superior over the subordinate; of the employer over the employee. The subordinates offer loyalty to the employer, who in turn takes a caring (fatherly) interest in the welfare of the staff. In this way paternalism becomes institutionalized, part of the contract of employment, part of the organization of the firm. It may also affect the employee after work, especially, for example, when the employee lives on the employer's premises, such as in a 'tied' cottage, a house which goes with the job.

Paternalism may seem to be beneficial to the staff, for example, providing medical checks, subsidized holidays, etc. But paternalism could also be seen as an ideology justifying the dependency of the employee on the employer and the employer's power over the employee – it depends on the circumstances.

Having read the brief outline of Marks and Spencer above, the reader might like to consider the following questions.

1 How efficient is Marks and Spencer?
2 How does it compare with other companies?
3 How do you measure efficiency?
4 What is meant by paternalism, and does it apply to this company, in your view?
5 How is two-way communication ensured?
6 To what extent do staff really take part in decision-making?
7 How would you assess Marks and Spencer in the light of the organization theories elaborated earlier? What is the managerial ideology (if any); what organizational structure does it generate? What 'rules' operate? Consider other questions based on the theories in making your assessment.

Having seen how questions can be asked once information has been gathered, you might like to try a similar project of your own. Gather the research, information, and apply some or all of these questions. Do not attempt to give too comprehensive an answer. You should try to get into the habit of inquiring into organizations in order to try to answer the question (stated several times in this book): what is really going on here?

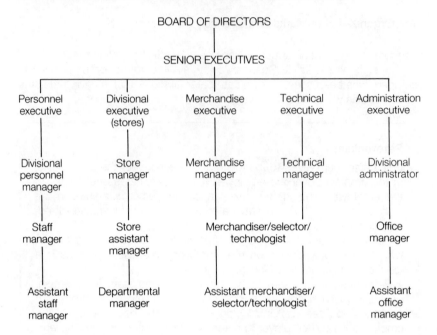

Figure 4.2 *A simplified functional organization structure of Marks and Spencer plc in 1982*

Source: Training Department, Marks and Spencer.

A researcher who has studied the firm, K. K. Tse, does not seem to believe that paternalism applies to Marks and Spencer. Instead she argues that the firm's policy is based on:

- respect for individuals at work;
- attention to all their problems;
- recognition of efforts;
- continuous training and development.

One way in which staff are involved in the company is through the use of 'quality circles'. A quality circle is a group of employees who meet regularly to examine not only the quality of the product but also productivity, working conditions, safety and cost reduction. Quality circles are well established in Japan; in Britain a notable example of their use is at Jaguar cars. Quality circles are seen as a means of two-way communication between management and staff.

Worked Project 2: Imperial Chemical Industries

Growth and change

ICI is one of Britain's most successful manufacturing companies.[29] Table 4.5 gives some indication of its size. Despite its success ICI has one key problem – how to change. It has to adjust to new inventions by others, and new markets; to restructure itself as necessary; to adopt new policies to get the most out of its own inventions; to get the right people at the top.

This section attempts to describe some of the problems of change, and to show how a sociologist might look at some of the problems associated with organizational change.

Imperial Chemical Industries is the second largest industrial organization in Britain. During the 1980s the company has seen a number of changes in organization and manpower in response to the problem of over-capacity. Loss-making plants were closed and the number of employees in the UK reduced from 84,000 in 1979 to 62,000 in 1983.

Reorganization also took place at the top. In the 1970s the main board comprised a chairman, eleven executive directors and six non-executive directors. From figures 4.3 and 4.4 (p. 102–3) it will be seen that there was a focus on product, function (personnel, finance, etc.) and geographical area.

In his book on the company, Andrew Pettigrew charts stability and change in ICI. He mentions some of the forces of conservatism, but also the forces for change such as international competition. Thus his list of characteristics includes:

- the innate conservatism of higher management at ICI;
- the consensus style of decision-making of the main board;

Table 4.5 ICI Group financial highlights

	1986 £m
Turnover (sales to customers outside the Group)	
Chemicals – UK	2,338
– overseas	7,400
Oil	398
Total turnover	10,136
Trading profit	1,049
Profit before taxation	1,016
Net profit attributable to parent company, before extraordinary items	600
(Earnings (before extraordinary items) per £1 Ordinary Stock	92p
(Dividend per £1 Ordinary Stock	36p

Group means ICI and its subsidiaries.
Source: Company Statement 1986.

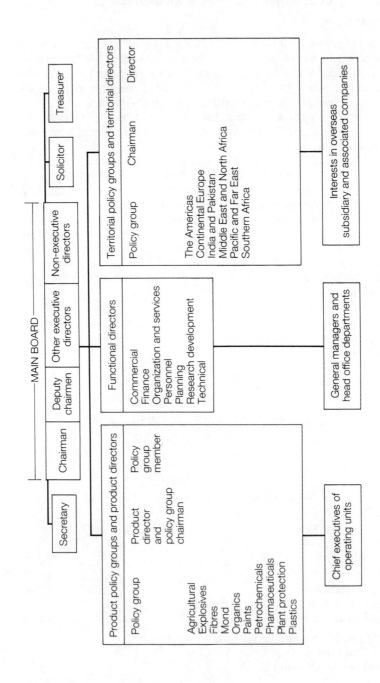

Figure 4.3 The ICI board of directors

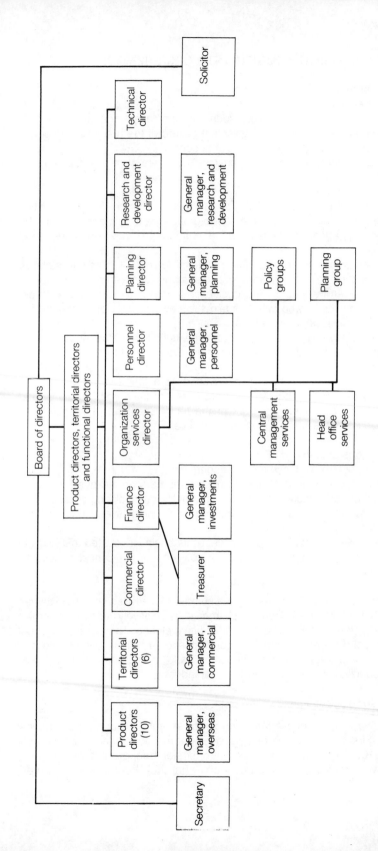

Figure 4.4 *The ICI head office organization*

- the short tenure of non-chief-executive chairmen,
- the power of policy groups;
- the limited time the main board spent on formulating strategy;
- the compartmentalized and intellectual culture of the headquarters;
- an expectation of continual financial success.
- ICI is a multinational company: only 39% of sales were to UK customers in 1981.

Pettigrew argues that a key to successful change is the effective management of links between the senior groups wanting a change, and the operating managers *implementing* the change. In uncertain times good leadership here is vital.

He believes that one of the main problems facing ICI is how to stabilize change, and make sure that rewards, communications and power support 'the newly emerging stage'. The choice of successors in top management should fall on those who will maintain the new situation and later initiate changes themselves as appropriate.

Carol Kennedy, in her book on ICI, comments that the nature of a company is rather like that of a human body; cells die the whole time only to be replaced by new cells. How can a large company selling different products in many markets adjust to conflicting short- and long-term objectives? In short, how can a large bureaucratic organization attain both continuity and growth? Kennedy traced the work of the tenth Chairman of ICI, Sir John Harvey Jones. Here are some of his objectives:[29]

- cutting jobs overall;
- stripping out surplus layers of management;
- setting the divisions of ICI free to operate as hard-edged businesses;
- identifying appropriate new markets and deliberately aiming to meet them by taking bits from all sorts of different technologies and putting them together;
- planning well ahead. (The pharmaceuticals business, started in 1937, did not make money until 1962, but is now one of ICI's most successful businesses.)[30]

Another ICI policy is to maximize the number of markets that can be served by one invention, even if one such market is relatively small in itself. An example of this is ICI's development of polyurethane. There are now about two thousand different kinds of polyurethane, mostly serving quite tiny markets. For example, there is a specific kind for shoe sales. Together, these small specialist markets add up to a big industry.

ICI – a sociological view

As sociologists, we *investigate* control, power, authority and organizational culture. First, then, it is interesting to look at the board of directors. Table 4.6 (p. 106–7) shows the career and social background of the 1987 executive directors, and it is noticeable that their backgrounds are very similar: public schools or grammar schools and 'red brick' universities (only two attended Oxford or Cambridge). Their career profiles are similar. Many are or have been directors of other leading companies, and we might infer that directors of large companies are drawn from a sort of ruling circle or elite, or at the very least a group of people with similar values, many of whom meet frequently at work and leisure. (See the discussion in chapter 3 of top people's backgrounds.) It will be seen from Chapter 3 that the chairmen of boards and insurance companies seem to have higher social status than the directors of large industrial companies in Britain such as ICI.

Question

Do you agree? If so, what are the implications? (See p. 43.)

On the question of who controls ICI, it should be noted that the founder of ICI, Sir Alfred Mond, was one of the first industrialists to advance the idea of workers becoming shareholders in their own companies. However, unlike co-operative workers, shareholding leaves control undisturbed and has been advocated as the answer to socialism in making workers into capitalists. Mond's ideas have now become the foundation of the British government's privatization policy.[31]

The sociologist should enquire further into the question of control. Is the ideology of 'scientific management' being applied here? Further research would be needed to establish the position.

On the question of organizational ideology, it seems that a keynote is the emphasis on change despite some conservative tendencies. Change is necessary in the highly competitive world inhabited by ICI – but it could be exaggerated. Does the emphasis on change indicate or dictate policy? Is belief in change itself an ideology? Does the young ambitious executive have to prove his or her commitment to change? This is an extract from the Chairman's Report of 1986.

Convinced that we must not allow the momentum of constructive change to slacken, we took five main actions in 1986 to accelerate progress. First, we acquired Glidden, a leading paint manufacturer in the United States, making ICI the largest paint supplier in the world. In a full year Glidden should add around £500m to Consumer and Speciality Products sales. Second, we announced the formation of the ICI Chemicals and Polymers Group, a fundamental reorganisation of our West European industrial chemicals businesses, which is aimed at making them the most efficient low cost suppliers of bulk chemicals in Europe. This clearly signals our determination to continue profitably in these businesses. Third, we have merged our Oil and Gas interests with Enterprise Oil, one of the larger independent oil companies operating in the North Sea. We consider that the enlarged company has the strength to protect ICI's position in this important area. Fourth, the joint venture with EniChem SpA which I told you about last year has now come into being in the form of the European Vinyls Corporation. This major initiative to improve the prospects of the vinyl chloride monomer and polyvinyl chloride businesses of the two companies

Table 4.6 *The background and careers of ICI directors, 1987*

Executive director	Career	Social status (as indicated by education)
Denys Henderson	A Director since 1980 and Chairman since April 1987. He has particular responsibility for group planning and group public affairs. He also has overview responsibility for group identity and marketing. Also a non-executive director of Barclays Bank PLC.	Aberdeen Grammar School and Aberdeen University.
David Barnes	A Director since August 1986. Currently Business Director for the agrochemicals, seeds and plant-breeding, colours and pharmaceuticals businesses. Also a non-executive director of Thorn-EMI PLC.	
Alan Clements	A Director since 1979. Currently Finance Director, a Director of ICI Chemicals and Polymers Group and Territorial Director for Africa, the Middle East and Pakistan. Also a non-executive director of Cable and Wireless PLC and of Trafalgar House PLC, and a lay member of the Stock Exchange Council.	Culford School and Oxford University.
Ronnie Hampel	A Director since 1985. Currently Business Director for the advanced materials, paints, polyurethanes and speciality chemicals businesses and	

Territorial Director for the Americas. Also a non-executive director of the Commercial Union Assurance Co. PLC and of Powell Duffryn PLC.

Tom Hutchison	A Director since 1985. Currently Business Director for the electronics, explosives and films businesses and Territorial Director for Continental Europe and for the Pacific and Far East. Also a non-executive director of Cadbury Schweppes plc, of the Bank of Scotland and of Enterprise Oil plc.	Hawick High School and St Andrews University.
Sir Robin Ibbs	A Director since 1976, apart from two years' secondment to the Cabinet Office. He assists the Chairman on planning and public affairs and is a Director of ICI Chemicals and Polymers Group. He holds the part-time appointment of Prime Minister's Adviser for Efficiency and Effectiveness in Government, and is also a non-executive director of Lloyds Bank plc.	Universities of Toronto and Cambridge.
Charles Reece	A Director since 1979. Currently Technology Director and Management Services Director, and Territorial Director for India. He is also a non-executive Director of APV Holdings plc.	Pocklington School and Leeds University.
Frank Whiteley	A Director since 1979. Currently Personnel Director, and Chairman of ICI Chemicals and Polymers Group.	

Source: Company Reports, 1986 and 1987, and *Who's Who*, 1987.

has made a good start. Finally, we have increased our borrowing limits enabling us to supplement organic growth by further acquisitions should opportunities arise.

Now try your hand at analysing other large organizations.

12   Conclusion

The following summary is intended to expose the taken-for-granted world in organizations, and provide fresh insights for the manager.

Layperson's views of organizations	*Some sociological reflections*
The goals of organizations seem obvious. Commercial firms seek to make a profit; trade unions to protect their members' interests; schools educate their pupils; hospitals try to cure their patients, and so on.	Sometimes the organization's goals get distorted; for example there may be a tendency for trade union officials to lose touch with the ordinary members. Schools may have *latent* functions, such as keeping young people out of the labour market; socializing their pupils for their place in society (high in the case of independent schools, low in the case of 'slum' comprehensives; socializing working-class children to a lifetime of manual labour). Even where the goal is obvious – such as most commercial firms' goal being to make a profit – this may get distorted, for example, in order to show the firm in a good light by emphasizing non-profit-making aims (consider drug companies, some multinational enterprises: see chapter 2).
Even if the aims of organizations get distorted, the means of achieving these aims is clear and rational. Thus, for example, most firms have an organization chart showing who	The criticisms of Weber's bureaucracy in this chapter show that seemingly rational organizations have many dysfunctions (goal displacement, internal competition, cliques

is responsible for what, and this structure comes about as a rational way of achieving the ends.

and so on). There is a limit to what the official organization chart and the official rule book can tell you; for example, they say little about the quality of leadership, morale, or how informal work groups operate (and sometimes thwart management's aims).

Even if the aims and the means of achieving them get distorted, the members of the organization behave rationally in dealing with the work tasks and with each other.

The discussion here has shown that organizations are prone to ideologies which distort what is going on. These ideologies are adopted by the members unconsciously; they become part of their everyday world; they are not even noticed, let alone criticized. Structuralism, psychologism, consensualism, welfareism, and legalism have been cited here, but the list can be extended.

Even if there are organizational ideologies which distort reality in organizations, better communications will help to overcome this by showing clearly what is really happening.

Good communication is more than consulting people or telling them what is happening. Good communication really comes from sharing similar goals and values. Where this does not happen then no amount of 'communicating' will really get different groups or members of the organization seeing fully eye to eye.

Improving the quality of decision-making by management will help to overcome most of the problems mentioned here. Surely it is part of the manager's job to overcome these difficulties.

Perhaps the real problem in organizations is too much control by management, leading to alienated involvement by members. Probably the sociologically informed manager will have a clearer view of what is really going on in the organization and this will result in better decision-making.

Exercises

Essay or discussion questions

1 Give examples of the following in organizations (preferably from your own experience):

- power
- authority
- leadership
- compliance
- good and/or bad communications
- structuralism
- psychologism
- consensualism
- welfareism
- mock bureaucracy
- representative bureaucracy
- punishment-centred bureaucracy
- mechanistic organization
- organic organization
- needs
- paternalism
- legalism

2 A sociological approach to organisations must not, if it is to be useful or perceptive, accept available common sense conceptions of the problems of organisations. (from G. Salaman, *Work Organisations*)

Discuss.

3 In what ways can a sociology of organizations help us to understand the exercise of power in organizations?

4 Control has been singled out as a major practical problem by managers themselves and also as the greatest problem about management practice by critics of the system. In fact many writers regard the main contribution of organisational design to be the means it provides for controlling the behaviour of employees. (from J. Child, *Organisation: A Guide to Problems and Practice*) (Harper and Row, London, 1977, p. 117)

Why do some managers and others adopt this view?

5 *'Taken for granted' thinking in an organization: a simple exchange*

Sociology student: I would like to ask you about this organisation's corporate culture.

General manager: We don't waste our time on airy-fairy twaddle like that. We're here to make fork-lift trucks.

Sociology student: Thank you for straightening me out right at the start. Don't you mean make and *sell* fork-lift trucks?

General manager: Sorry, when you make them as well as we do, they sell themselves.

Sociology student: Is that what your salesmen think?

General manager: They're not paid to think, they're too busy seeing our customers, finding out how many more they want.

Sociology student: So this is a production led company, right?

General manager: Design and production. Got to design them right as well as make them good.

Sociology student: I suppose that means you take on lots of young science graduates with plenty of good design ideas?

General manager: . . . You what! Practical design is what we're good at. You want to be design director here, you start as a tool room apprentice.

Sociology student: Does your managing director approve of this view?

General manager: Approve of it! He is it! Started on the shop floor at fifteen. Most of the board are ex-apprentices. No college boys here, we're all grafters.

Sociology student: What's company policy on co-determination? Do you have a works committee?

General manager: None of that. When we've got something to tell them, the Old Man lays it on the line for them. When they've got something to tell us, well, we usually pick it up Friday night at ten pin bowling.

Sociology student: It doesn't sound as if you stand on ceremony here.

General manager: You kidding. Know where the directors went for their Christmas lunch last year? Joe's Hamburger Saloon. Old Man's always liked a good hamburger since that sales trip to Minneapolis years back.

Sociology student: Well I mustn't take up too much of your time.

General manager: Don't worry. It is just that I don't know anything about whatever you said at the beginning. (from R. Lee and P. Lawrence, *Organisational Behaviour* (Hutchinson, London, 1985), p. 106)

What is being taken for granted here?

Try to answer this question first before reading the suggestions. Then compare the ideas raised by the suggestions with your own. Did you miss any ideological elements because you, too, took them for granted?

Suggestions: It may be interesting to enlarge on the following (the possible ideologies are in brackets.)

- The hierarchy of the corporation is taken for granted (structuralism).
- People do as they are told (Taylorism).
- The goals are obvious (consensualism).
- Management has the right to manage (Taylorism)
- There appears to be extreme emphasis on practicality – so much so that it could be described as an ideology and be called 'practical*ism*' – do you agree?

Try out this type of analysis in your workplace, college and family. Look for what is taken for granted; look for hidden ideologies. Note how successfully the discreet prodding of the (very astute) sociology student actually brought out the information the first (overly formal) question sought.

Case study 1

Read the following passage and then answer the questions below.

> For centuries managers have attempted communication 'downwards'. This cannot work, no matter how hard and how intelligently they try. It cannot work, first, because it focuses on what the manager wants to say. It assumes, in other words, that the utterer 'communicates' – when in fact communication is the act of the recipient. The emphasis has been put on the emitter, the manager, the administrator or the commander, to make him capable of being a 'better communicator'. But all that can be communicated downward are commands, that is, prearranged signals. Nothing connected with understanding, let alone with motivation, can be communicated downward. They require communication upward, from those who perceive to those who want to reach their perception. (From P. Drucker, *Drucker on Management* (Management Publications Ltd London 1970) p. 121)

1   What is Drucker trying to achieve?
2   What are the obstacles to achieving his goal?
3   Take an organizaton with which you are familiar and analyse the obstacles to good communications.

Case study 2/Project

> Jack Roth looked out from his window over the roof tops of the office and workshop blocks of his firm. His firm was now one of the leading manufacturers and distributors of office equipment, with a staff of 600, in this country. But it had not always been like this. His mind went back many years to the days when he was an out-of-work furrier in London's East End. His first semi-permanent job was selling typewriter ribbons and carbon papers on commission, trudging from office to office, being kept waiting, and enduring minor insults. He had worked hard though – hard enough to set up a retail shop employing salespeople. As this expanded he brought in his brother-in-law, Luke, to be a partner in the growing enterprise. Jack was always optimistic and expansion-minded. He saw difficulties as challenges to be overcome. He knew how to get things done and inspire others. He persuaded Luke, a cabinet-maker by trade, to set up a workshop to make office furniture to customers' orders. Luke selected cabinet-makers from friends in the trade whom he had known for years.
>
> With further expansion it was decided to make office furniture for the mass market, to employ more salespeople, to use marketing and advertising consultants to advise on which lines should be developed and which should be dropped. Jack was the inspiration behind this expansion even though times were bad. He would have liked to set up branch factories and retail outlets and

had hoped his son, Ben, would take this on, but Ben seemed set on an academic career. Luke, on the other hand, was always keen to help. In particular, he looked after his staff, many of whom were friends anyway. Jack's wife, Rosie, was also a great help in the firm, especially on the secretarial and personnel side.

All these thoughts were going through Jack's mind. He was getting on now and it was a disappointment to him that his son did not seem to be interested in the business, and Luke was getting too old to want the worry of running a large business.

As a business consultant, write a report to Jack on what should be done. In particular, your report should include the following.

- A full introduction specifying the problem and how you propose tackling it in the report.
- A full conclusion summarizing the main points and setting out recommendations.
- An organization tree showing how the business could be split into departments.
- Comment on what an organizational tree can show and what it cannot show (for example, on the nature of leadership, authority and communication).

Then answer the following questions.

1 What is meant by 'charismatic authority' – to what extent does Jack have charisma?
2 What is meant by 'paternalism' – to what extent does this apply to this firm?
3 How should the staff be kept informed as to what is going on?
4 What examples can you quote of the sale (or 'going public') of a large family firm? Comment on what happened in these cases.

Case study 3: where organizations go wrong

The following article was prompted by a scandal surrounding the Nye Bevan Lodge for old people in South London in 1987.

Another scandal breaks into the public consciousness alleging cruelty and abuse to old people and everyone takes a sharp intake of breath. Isn't it awful? How could it happen? But in a few months' time it will be a children's home that hits the headlines, then the elderly again.

It isn't that every children's home is run by a paedophile or every home for the elderly is run by a geriatric-hater, but each dreadful incident exposes an element of institutional life which should be investigated as thoroughly as each case of brutality or neglect.

I have worked in children's homes, in homes for the elderly and in various educational establishments. The fundamental attitude which I have found common to people working in institutions (or organisations) such as these, is irritation that the 'customers' – clients, inmates, residents – create a major obstacle to the smooth, efficient, orderly running of the place, and that they also pose a potential threat to the freedoms and comforts that the employees enjoy, always informally and occasionally illegally.

Every member of staff concentrates on their own job as an end in itself, removed and seemingly unconnected to the overall *raison d'être* of the establishment. Thus, the cleaners are repairing the violations committed daily in their domain, not making life more pleasant for the old folk corralled into the TV room, forbidden to go to their rooms while hoovering is in progress. The cook is planning menus on the basis of thrift and economy for minimum nourishment, maximum predictability and least effort.

The 'care-staff' are often kind, concerned and well-intentioned people, but powerless, status-less, poorly paid and usually part-time; they are sandwiched so tightly between the unyielding crusts of maintain-the-status-quo full-time staff that their voices and potential influence go unheeded.

Senior residential staff or the management team spend their time submerged in reports, rotas, orders and invoices, pension books, and pay claims, and, of course, the three or four times daily sortie to the drugs cupboard in order to maintain the residents at the lowest possible level of likely disturbance. The most welcome time of day for these workers is when the old people, the pale and silent handicapped have vanished away into their rooms, into the fabric of the building, and the miles of contract carpet are no longer dotted with human obstacles who might suddenly shout or weep, fall or wet the floor. (from N. Foster, *Guardian*, 19 August 1987)

1 What is wrong with these organizations?
2 What suggestions would you make for putting them right?

Suggestions:

- Draw on the organizational theory set out in this chapter. Demonstrate that you have analytical skills and that you are able to pursue your analysis beyond that of the average lay person.
- Concentrate on ideologies. Consider the ideology of ageism (you concentrate on the old person's *age* rather than seeing them as a whole person).
- Consider the dysfunctions of organizations – obsessive cleaning, cooking and the drugs cupboard. For whose benefit is the organization run – the clients or the staff? Do the means become more important than the ends in these organizations?
- You could, as an exercise, write this up in the form of a report from a local authority Chief Welfare Officer to the Chairperson of the Welfare Committee.
- You may find the following useful (use the Further Reading list at the end of the chapter too): E. McNally, 'In Place of Fear', *New Society*, 31 July 1987; C. Cousins, *Controlling Social Welfare: A Sociology of State Welfare, Work and Organisation* (Wheatsheaf, Brighton, 1987).

Further Reading

M. Albrow, *Bureaucracy* (Macmillan, London, 1970)
S. Clegg and D. Dunkerley, *Organisations, Class and Control* (Routledge and Kegan Paul, London, 1980)

L. Donaldson, *In Defence of Organisation Theory* (Cambridge University Press, Cambridge, 1985)

A. Etzioni, *Modern Organisations* (Prentice Hall, Englewood Cliffs, NJ, 1964)

A. Etzioni, *A Comparative Analysis of Complex Organisations* (Collier Macmillan, London, 1975)

A. Fox, *Man Mismanagement* (Hutchinson, London, 1985)

H. H. Gerth and C. W. Mills, *From Max Weber* (Routledge and Kegan Paul, London, 1948)

C. B. Handy, *Understanding Organisations* (Penguin, Harmondsworth, 1985)

D. S. Pugh et al., *Writers on Organisations* (Penguin, Harmondsworth, 1983)

D. S. Pugh (ed.), *Organisational Theory* (Penguin, Harmondsworth, 1984)

M. Rose, *Industrial Behaviour* (Penguin, Harmondsworth, 1985)

G. Salaman, *Work Organisations: Resistance and Control* (Longman, London, 1979)

G. Salaman, *Class and the Corporation* (Fontana, London, 1981)

G. Salaman and K. Thompson (eds), *Control and Ideology in Organisations* (Open University Press, Milton Keynes, 1980)

D. Silverman, *The Theory of Organisations* (Heinemann, London, 1970)

T. J. Watson, *Management Organisation and Employee Strategy* (Routledge and Kegan Paul, London, 1986)

Notes

1. A. Etzioni, *Modern Organisations* (Prentice Hall, Englewood Cliffs, NJ, 1964), p. 1.
2. H. Becker et al., *Boys in White* (University of Chicago Press, Chicago, 1963).
3. H. H. Gerth and C. W. Mills, *From Max Weber* (Routledge and Kegan Paul, London, 1948), p. 296.
4. Ibid., p. 295.
5. Ibid., p. 59.
6. M. Albrow, *Bureaucracy* (Macmillan, London, 1970), p. 45.
7. A. Etzioni, *A Comparative Analysis of Complex Organisations* (Collier, Macmillan, London, 1975).
8. P. M. Blau and W. R. Scott, *Formal Organisations* (Routledge and Kegan Paul, London, 1963).
9. S. Clegg and D. Dunkerley, *Organisations, Class and Control* (Routledge and Kegan Paul, London, 1980), pp. 142–3.
10. A. W. Gouldner, *Patterns of Industrial Bureaucracy* (Collier Macmillan, London, 1954); Clegg and Dunkerley, *Organizations*, pp. 158–61.
11. G. Salaman and K. Thompson (eds), *Control and Ideology in Organisations* (Open University Press, Milton Keynes, 1980).
12. T. Burns and G. W. Stalker, *The Management of Innovation* (Tavistock, London, 1966).
13. C. Argyris, *Integrating the Individual and the Organisations* (Wiley, London, 1964).
14. D. Silverman, *The Theory of Organisations* (Heinemann, London, 1970), p. 102.

15. J. Scott, *Corporations, Classes and Capitalism* (Hutchinson, London, 1985), pp. 266–8.
16. G. Salaman, *Class and the Corporation* (Fontana, London, 1981).
17. For an overview of other organizational theories, see D. S. Pugh et al. (eds), *Writers on Organizations* (Penguin, Harmondsworth, 1983).
18. A. M. Pettigrew, *The Politics of Organisational Decision-Making* (Tavistock, London, 1973), p. 28.
19. P. M. Blau, *The Dynamics of Bureaucracy* (University of Chicago Press, Chicago, 1963), pp. 126–7.
20. J. O'Shaughnessy, *Patterns of Business* (Allen and Unwin, London, 1966).
21. J. W. Humble, *Improving Business Results* (McGraw Hill, Maidenhead, 1966).
22. A. Jay, *The Corporation Man* (Jonathan Cape, London, 1972), pp. 201–2).
23. Adapted from J. D. Thompson, *Organization in Action* (McGraw-Hill, London, 1967), p. 134.
24. I. McGregor with R. Tyler, *The Enemies Within* (London, Fontana/Collins, 1986).
25. Most of this section is based on G. Salaman, *Work Organisations: Resistance and Control* (Longman, London, 1979).
26. Burns and Stalker, *Management of Innovation*.
27. A. Fox, *Man Mismanagement* (Hutchinson, London, 1985), p. 32.
28. K. K. Tse, *Marks and Spencer: Anatomy of Britain's most efficiently managed company* (Pergamon, Oxford, 1985).
29. A. M. Pettigrew, *The Awakening Giant: Continuity and Change in ICI* (Basil Blackwell, Oxford, 1985).
30. C. Kennedy, *ICI: The Company That Changed Our Lives* (Hutchinson, London, 1986).
31. W. Jones (ed.), *Political Issues in Britain Today* (Manchester University Press, Manchester, 1987), p. 104.

5 Industrial Relations: A Comparison of Viewpoints

1 Introduction

Industrial relations refers to the relationship between employer and employee, and of course it centres on pay and conditions at work. This chapter presents briefly the conventional view of the employer/ employee relationship and then compares this description with a sociological viewpoint, showing the contrast in beliefs about what is really going on, especially in disputes. The sociological view concentrates on the ways in which power is wielded in organizations, particularly management's *control* of work and how it is to be done. The sociological approach highlights the importance of class at work, and shows unions and shop stewards weaker, and management stronger, than is commonly supposed. As is the case throughout this book, an underlying question here is 'How can a knowledge of sociology improve decision-making by management?' – *without the discipline losing its integrity as an unbiased investigatory discipline*. Better decision-making can only come from utilizing the conditions of independent analysis – the sort of analysis that sociologists attempt to make.

2 A Management Approach to Industrial Relations

Industrial relations (also known as labour relations) include the formal work relations between employees and management. The subject deals with questions such as 'How do people get better pay and conditions at work?' 'How can productivity be raised?' 'How should redundancy be dealt with?', and so on. Usually the term 'industrial relations' is seen as applying to large organizations rather than small private firms, but really it could apply to most types of organizations, including hospitals, shops, schools, the civil service and local government.

Many writers have tried to analyse industrial relations. Some believe that *fairness* is the key concept from the workers' point of view, indicated by such items as:

- fair wages;
- fair income;
- fair effort;
- a fair day's pay for a fair day's work;
- unfair dismissal.[1]

The trouble is that there are differing views as to what is fair or unfair. Really fairness is not a question of fact, but rather a subjective judgement – such as what workpeople feel when comparing themselves with others who have similar jobs.

Again, although a group of workpeople may have a strong and shared view as to what is a fair wage, this can be completely contradicted by the operation of market forces. If there is no market demand for their product, or their particular skill is now obsolete, then they would have to accept a wage below what they consider fair (or they may be prepared to be unemployed rather than accept an unfair wage).

Question

Can you think of any recent examples?

In the long run, the feeling of fairness is important, even though it may have to be constantly fought for.

If fairness is the *aim* of unions, what are the means of achieving it? Here are three possible ways.

1 *Voluntarism* – complete autonomy for the wage bargainers on both sides, without for example the use of the law to enforce conditions. Voluntarists believe that the state should not interfere in the process of collective bargaining. Thus trade unions oppose, say, bringing in the law to stipulate how many pickets should stand outside a factory during a strike.

2 *Collective bargaining*, where both sides fully represent their members and meet as equals to come to an agreement on wages and conditions acceptable to all. Collective bargaining helps to

regulate conflict at work and gives the individual employees some power and some say on pay and conditions at work.

3 On the trade union side *solidarity* is often stressed. The workforce should be fully behind their union. An individual worker may be in a weak position against a strong employer, but if he or she joins with others their strength will increase. Hence trade unionists often say that unity is strength, and 'one out – all out' is a rule in the event of a strike.

In spite of the quest for fairness it is clear that employer and employee may have different objectives in industrial relations (and different ideas of fairness), as the following list indicates.

Employer's objectives	*Employee's objectives*
To contain overall labour costs (the need to recruit the necessary amount of labour of the appropriate quality at the least cost).	To maximize pay for a given level of effort.
To pay no more than a 'fair' wage.	To achieve a fair wage.
'Fairness' from an employer's viewpoint may be based on what other employers pay for similar work.	'Fairness' may be based on: (a) the individual's need for a living wage; (b) what is felt to be fair in relation to similar occupations; (c) a collective feeling as to what is fair (rather than a personal view of what is fair).
Wages are based on the need to recruit and maintain the type of employee wanted.	Wages are related to what those in similar types of work get, i.e. there is a need to maintain appropriate differentials between different types of work – there should be an appropriate increase for skill, etc.
The employer seeks to control the work situation. The premises, the production and everything associated with production is controlled by (and often belongs to) management.	Work people in factory or office seek some control over the workplace situation – which after all is an important part of their everyday life.

Usually a reasonable employer wishes to make the work more interesting (provided this does not reduce productivity).	Often employees do not seek more fulfilling work. Their main wish may be for more pay (fair pay) and acceptable working conditions.[2]

3   A Sociological View of Industrial Relations

As will be seen, the above approach to industrial relations would, among other things, stress agreement about pay and conditions at work, job regulation, fairness, and the reconciling of the different objectives of management and employees.

A sociological viewpoint may see the term 'industrial relations' as a euphemism for the apparent constant state of war between management and labour. Probably the key concept to many sociologists would be *control*. Management seeks to control the whole work situation: working conditions, pay, hours and the speed of work. Accordingly sociologists are not so interested in the study of job regulation as such, or in the quest for fairness, but rather in *power*.

Power is usually thought of as the rule of the few over the many. This rule is justified by ideologies – in this case managerial ideologies. The most important such ideology is that of scientific management, discussed in chapter 3. Briefly, this sees management as entitled to control not only what is to be done but how it is to be done; it stresses the managerial prerogative, management's right to manage. Management and to some extent employees and unions accept the ideology of scientific management, and this is supported by other ideologies. One ideology not mentioned before is the 'pluralist' idea of the firm. (This is rather similar to the view of management as balancing interests discussed in chapter 3, section 3.)

In the pluralistic view of the firm, power appears to be diffused, and management and workforce appear to have common goals including the continuing prosperity of the firm, rising output, improved quality and so on. Management manages in the interests of all concerned: employees, customers and shareholders.

In contrast, a 'radical perspective' has been offered by sociologists who concentrate on the differences in power between the various groupings.[3] This approach shows that management's power is greater than it appears. Employees in the more lowly positions of the organization are totally dependent on it. They have little power or influence. They only really gain power by combining in trade unions. Even then, they are little threat to management's power, since in the main what the unions usually seek is more pay, or better working conditions, rather than, say, taking over the firm or demanding seats on the board.

Management's power derives from the acceptance of managerial ideologies, not just within the firm, but within society. When there are strikes, public opinion and government policy often tend to support employers; in addition many workers themselves do not support their unions (hence management sometimes prefers to talk to its workers direct, rather than negotiate with their unions). Management, of course, also owns and controls the property, the technology and the investment. Two instances may help to illustrate the climate in which unions operate in the West. Firstly, the media support the *right* to strike, but very seldom a real strike. Secondly, the media support trade unionism in Poland while lambasting unionists at home.

Question

How true is the preceding paragraph? Test it with reference to current or recent disputes.

But why should there be conflict between management and workforce anyway? Do they not really share the same interests in the end; the prosperity of the firm, higher wages, higher profits, higher productivity? Really this assumption lies at the root of much bad decision-making by management. From the viewpoint of, say, an unskilled manual worker, or a clerk doing routine work in front of a VDU all day, there may be little interest in the work. In addition to the fact that much of the work is routine and monotonous, there are often no career prospects, the people feel of low status, and they have little say in the decisions that affect their everyday working lives. They can see for themselves no benefit in working harder. It is little wonder that such people appear to be unreasonable in disputes. Their main interest in the work is the pay packet. Understandably management's appeal for reason, for loyalty to the firm, for all to pull together, falls on deaf ears. These pleas may influence managers and those with career prospects, but then managers should not assume that others have the same outlook.

Question

Is it not ultimately in workers' interests that the organization for which they work should prosper?
Suggestion: It is difficult to see how, given the current capitalist world order, it is not normally in their interests. What exceptions are there to this idea? Consider the person who is working out their notice, or who is grossly

overworked or underpaid. Look at examples of non-cooperation, such as the Case Study/Role Play on Ford at the end of this chapter. Why did co-operation break down? Use the concepts explained here, including those of scientific management and alienative and calculative involvement, in order to account for this. You may like to return to this question when you have got further through the book. It is fundamentally important.

4 Are Class Differences the Cause of Bad Industrial Relations

A Marxist view of industrial relations argues that industrial relations are really based on class relationships and that labour is bought and sold on the market just like any other commodity, with the employer trying to get it at the minimum price.[4] (What evidence is there for these views?)

It is clear that there are enormous pay and wealth differences between the top and bottom classes, with the top 20 per cent of the population having about half the income (see table 5.1). Pay differentials at work are closely based on the class-based wealth and pay differentials throughout society generally. The highest paid normally have pleasant working conditions, generous sickness and pension schemes as well as good career prospects, while the lower paid have poor working conditions, job insecurity, are often exposed to accidents and disease (see table 5.2), have to 'clock in', work shifts, and suffer inferior status generally. Again, the lowest-paid, lowest-class occupation has least autonomy at work. As table 5.3 shows, they also work longer hours.

Because of competition, the pressure on the commercial firm to remain profitable, especially in a time of recession, is strong and constant. This forces firms to reduce wages or keep them as low as

Table 5.1 *The distribution of income between households in the UK, 1976 and 1986 (percentages)*

| | Percentage of total household income received by | | | | | |
	Bottom Fifth[a]	Next Fifth[a]	Middle Fifth[a]	Next Fifth[a]	Top Fifth[a]	Total
1976	0.8	9.4	18.8	26.6	44.4	100
1986	0.3	6.1	17.5	27.5	48.6	100

[a] of households by income.
Source: Adapted from *Social Trends*, 1989.

Table 5.2   *Standard mortality ratios for different classes in the UK*

	Social Classes I and II	Social Classes IV and V
Men	74	129
Women	76	116

Standard Mortality Ratios (SMRs) are measures of averge death-rates, commonly used in comparisons of health and ill-health. The average for the UK population is taken to be 100. Social classes are taken to be based on occupation. Social classes I and II are professional and managerial people; social classes IV and V are semi-skilled and unskilled people. In all common diseases, including heart disease, the SMR in social class V is considerably higher than that of social class I. There may be a variety of reasons for this, including harsher conditions at work.
Source: R. M. Whitehead, *The Health Divide* (Health Education Council, London, 1987), table 4.

Table 5.3   *Average weekly hours of full-time male employees in Great Britain*

	Male manual worker (%)	Male non-manual worker (%)
Under 40 hours	51	82
Over 40 hours	49	18

Source: Adapted from *Social Trends*, 1985.

possible. The lowest-paid suffer most, as they are least powerful. So the enterprise constitutes a major arena in which class relations take place.[5] It could be argued therefore that class differences, because they go along with ideological differences (and power), necessarily underline bad industrial relations. Thus antagonistic class relations in society are reflected in poor industrial relations.

Suggestion:

Working through the projects at the end of this chapter may help you in dealing with the question at the head of this section. The relationship between class and occupation and ideology is not a simple one (see chapter 3).

5   How Powerful is Management?

It has been suggested that management's right to manage appears to be supported by a number of managerial ideologies, most notably by the concept of scientific management or 'Taylorism', which argues that management must control not only what must be done but also how it should be done. But how far do management and workforce *really* believe managerial ideologies? Here is a brief list of some specific ways in which management's control is legitimized (made to seem 'right'). (Think too of the elements of managerial ideologies discussed in chapter 4.)

- There are some legal rights and duties conferred on management by law – management *must* do this (for instance, safety regulations).
- A free contract is said to exist between the employer and employee (see the ideology of legalism discussed in chapter 4). ('If you don't like working here, you are free to go', says the employer to the complaining employee.)
- Managers appear to be exercising managerial rights within their own domain, for example, a manager may refer to 'my department'.
- Managers talking to staff sometimes invoke a higher level of authority (e.g. in suggesting that top management would be annoyed if they knew what was going on).
- Managers rely on greater expertise than that of workers, especially in the production process, where a manager may also be a professional engineer. Only the manager can decide what is acceptable or right.
- Managers may stress their responsibility. They take the blame for mistakes, they argue, so they have the right to make the decision.[6]

Here the reader might like to consider how the list might be extended. Look for common phrases you may have heard of or seen mentioned (like 'you could always try your luck elsewhere').

Question

How far do you accept the above arguments? What answers could you give to them?

Sometimes management appears to be in a weak position, for example during a strike when unions are pressing what seems to be an unreasonable wage claim, or where a union is refusing to reduce manning levels, or refusing to agree to the introduction of new technology. As discussed above, frequently the media portray strikers as unreasonable. Surely management ought to manage and be allowed to do so? Strikes, militant unions and shop stewards, government intervention, all appear to be infringements of management's right to manage.

Unions are in fact weaker than they appear; they are essentially *reactive*. They have to react to management's policies rather than initiate their own. This limits their role.

6 The Nature of Trade Unions

Trade unions exist to improve the pay and conditions of their members. They are mutual support societies; their prime aim is to help their members. It is important to realize that it is not the function of a trade union to bale out the employer during difficult times, or to keep their members' wages down in order to help a government's policy, unless it is in the interests of its members to take these actions.

Two concepts may help to convey the nature of trade unions – *density* and *unionateness*. *Density* or completeness is a measure of actual union membership in an employment group divided by the total members of that group, i.e. how 'unionized' a group of workers is. It is expressed as a percentage. How is this concept useful? Because density affects the power of the union in a particular industry. Tables 5.4 and 5.5 show how union membership has declined in recent

Table 5.4   *Trade union membership in the UK, 1975–84*

	Number of unions	Total membership (thousands)
1975	470	12,026
1979	453	13,289
1984	371	11,086

Source: *Social Trends*, 1987.

Table 5.5   *Membership of selected UK trade unions, 1979–1985*

Union	1979 (thousands)	1985 (thousands)	% change
Transport and General Workers' Union	2,086	1,434	−31.2
National and Local Government Officers' Association	753	752	−0.1
Iron and Steel Trades' Confederation	110	45	−56.4
Confederation of Health Service Employees	213	213	0.0

Source: *Social Trends*, 1987.

years, along with the number of unions, and the number of traditional working-class jobs.

Question

What employment pattern does table 5.5 indicate?

Unionateness is a different kind of measure.[7] It shows how far any individual union is committed to the general principles of trade unionism, as shown by its answers to the following questions.

- Does it call itself a trade union?
- Is it registered as a trade union?
- Is it affiliated to the TUC?
- Is it affiliated to the Labour party?
- Is it independent of employers in negotiations?
- Is collective bargaining with employers a major function?
- Is it prepared to be militant?

A few cases may help to explain this. For example, in banking or insurance some unions are really 'company unions' or staff associations. They may be run by the employers. Some may call themselves unions but lack some of the other attributes mentioned above. Is the Royal College of Nursing a trade union or a professional body? It says its members will never strike, as this would hurt patients. (Incidentally, should a nurse join the Royal College of Nursing or the Confederation of Health Service Employees (COHSE), which satisfies all the items of unionateness?) What about the National Union of Teachers? This satisfies nearly all the items, yet teachers firmly consider themselves to be professionals. Further, how would you classify the National Union of Students, the Union of Democratic Mineworkers, the Professional Association of Teachers and the British Medical Association?

Union membership

A craft union limits its membership to those who are members of the craft, for example the National Graphical Association.

An industrial union seeks to recruit all those within a particular industry, for example the National Union of Railwaymen.

A 'white-collar' union represents white-collar workers in a variety of organizations.

Some trade unions are very large organizations. At the lowest level of the union are the branches, often based on the place of work, the office, the mine or the factory. For miners, the branches are called lodges, and for print workers, chapels. The organization of some trade unions can be seen as a pyramid of power, as depicted in figure 5.1.

7 Changes in Trade Unionism and Managerial Practices

Over the last ten years there has been a considerable change in the position of trade unions. The main change seems to derive from unemployment, the decline of traditional industries, and legislation which has weakened the legal position of trade unions in Britain.

Sociologists have examined the belief that mass unemployment encourages management to be more aggressive towards trade unions. They found that to attack those institutions which employees have

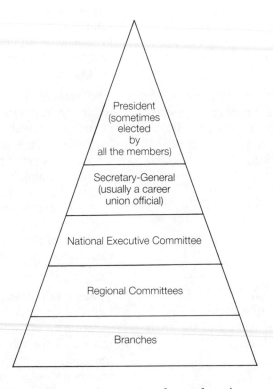

Figure 5.1 *The organizational structure of a trade union*

built up over many years is to invite employees' distrust and make them inflexible when management want to change working practices in order to achieve higher productivity. It seems that it is in managers' interest to maintain their relationship with the unions, so that they can persuade them to accept flexibility. One writer, quoting the Vice President of the Institute of Personnel Management, says the trend towards more employee-oriented management and the reluctance to attack organized labour in most cases is a management strategy for coping with change by achieving *flexibility* in labour.[8] The unions have responded with more flexibility. Some of the more important changes in the position of trade unions are summarized as follows.

From	*To*
• Strong solidarity among the members, especially during strikes.	A loss of solidarity in some cases, for example, Nottinghamshire miners worked during the pit strike; members of the Electrical, Electronics, Telecommunications and Plumbing Union worked the presses at Wapping during the strike of their Fleet Street colleagues.
• Strong collective bargaining, i.e. the members supported leaders in their negotiations for more pay and better conditions.	The weakening of trade union solidarity (referred to above) has in turn weakened collective bargaining, since employers suspect a union cannot maintain a strike. Examples are the failure of the civil servants and teachers' strikes in 1987 (including the government's abolition of the Burnham Committee which settled teachers' pay).
• Traditionally there has been a strong link between the Labour party and the trade union movement.	Though still strong, this link has weakened. A Labour government is unlikely to restore all the immunities for the effects of strike action that unions previously enjoyed.

- A high proportion of trade unionists came from the older traditional industries: mining, steel, railways, etc.

  Increasingly unions are recruited in the service and white-collar sectors.

- Shop stewards, the informal union representatives, played a prominent role in industrial relations.

  Shop stewards seem to be weaker now, owing to the general weakness of trade unions.

Question

The list above is mainly descriptive. What do you consider to be the underlying causes of the trends depicted? Could these trends be reversed (e.g. in times of full employment)?

Suggestions:

- It could be suggested that unemployment and strong government are the underlying causes (in the USA as well as in Britain).
- Use the *Employment Gazette, Social Trends*, etc. to show these and other relationships of trade union membership to unemployment.

It is clear that there has been a decline in the power and influence of trade unions. How have unions and management responded?

First, a few unions, especially the electricians, have tried to co-operate with their employers; for example, the Electrical, Electronic, Telecommunications and Plumbing Union (EETPU). This union has offered 'no strike' deals, equality of status for all workers, flexibility of labour, joint consultations, and so on.[9] The difficulty is that genuine industrial relations tend to be adversarial (because the interests of the two sides *are different*), a contest between employers and employees. In these circumstances, can a union offering 'no strike' deals (the strike is the ultimate sanction) be a real union? (See the tests of 'unionateness' above.)

Other unions have tried to adjust to the new situation by, for example, recruiting workers from the expanding service sector, where membership has been low in the past. Thus the General, Municipal and Boilermakers Union (GBMU) has been making a broad appeal to what it calls the new 'servant class', likely to be around six million in the 1990s, and larger than the manufacturing sector.[10] This includes those in contract cleaning, hotel and catering, shops and laundries.

Table 5.6   *Part-time employment in the UK,*
1971–1984 (thousands)

	1971	1981	1984
Males	584	718	—
Females	2,757	3,781	4,172

Source: Adapted from *Social Trends*, 1987.

These trades currently are low-paid; the workers have no fringe benefits; no welfare; no security of employment; no union representation. The position of these people has recently been worsening – for example, wage councils which set minimum wages for a trade have had their jurisdiction for those under 21 removed, leaving employers free to pay very low wages to this group.

8   What Does the Future Hold for Industrial Relations?

Industrial relations have been, and will be, further affected by high unemployment, new technology and the need for flexibility in the face of world competition and uncertainty. Unions, management and individuals are all involved in the following developments.

- A reduction in full-time jobs and an increase in part-time ones. In 1980 one in five employees worked part-time. In the 1990s there may be one in four.[11]
- There has been a large increase in self-employment in recent years. Between 1979 and 1985 the number of self-employed increased by a third to 2.6 million.[12]
- There has been a big increase in temporary jobs and the numbers of temporary agencies. It is estimated that 1.6 million workers were temporaries in 1985.

Note that many of these changes strongly affect women; for example, their part-time employment has shot up. (See chapter 7 for further discussion.)

• In July 1985, Borg-Warner, an American-owned automatic transmission company, clinched an agreement with the unions at its plant
in West Glamorgan which swept away demarcation lines, enabling
workers to operate, maintain and even clean their own machines.
As icing on the cake, it signed a pay agreement for the next SIX
years.

Findus operates its factory at Long Benton, in the north-east,
with two categories of manual workers. The first, some 30 per cent
of the workforce, have a special clause added to their contracts
saying that their employment could be ended without their unions
having any comeback. The second is without this insecurity clause.
A worker can move from the first to the second group only when
someone leaves the latter.

Control Data, manufacturer of computer tapes and discs at
Brynmawr in South Wales, ensures that 15 per cent of its workforce
are 'supplementals'. Supplementals are on ten-month contracts, work
no more than 30 hours a week and are told that there could be
periods when no work is available.

British Caledonian (now part of British Airways) signed an
agreement with its unions which relaxed demarcation lines, ended
paid overtime working and moved its manual workers onto a $37\frac{1}{2}$
hour week with salaried status.[13]

In trying to explain the significance of these changes it may be helpful
to divide workers in firms into two segments, the *core* and the
periphery. Employees in the core receive good wages and conditions
and are flexible, while workers in the periphery are taken on to do
specific jobs and dispensed with when they are not needed.[14] The
foregoing quotation illustrates some of the core–periphery differences
by actual examples.

Question

Is the 'core' and 'periphery' distinction replacing the blue-collar and white-
collar distinction?

• There is an increase in smaller units of production, partly as a
result of the government's promotion of small businesses. There is
also some change in class attitudes, with a new and growing section
of the working class which refuses to think of itself in traditional
terms, a trade union movement in which the majority of members
now work in the public sector, and a lack of trade union solidarity
in many disputes. Some have argued that the trade union movement
must adjust to the changing employment market. Perhaps unions

should offer to train their members (like the EETPU) and be less defensive generally.[15]

• Another development in industrial relations is the increased emphasis on 'human resource management' (making the best use of personnel), especially in the USA. Flexibility is increasingly being sought *outside* collective bargaining, through human resource management (HRM). The important questions are:

(a) *Commitment* – to what extent do HRM policies enhance commitment to the organization?

(b) *Competence* – to what extent do HRM policies develop people with skills and knowledge needed by the organization?

(c) *Cost-effectiveness* – what is the cost-effectiveness of a policy in terms of wages, labour turnover, absenteeism and strikes?

(d) *Congruence* – HRM policies should be congruent as between management and workforce. Lack of congruence (one 'law' for management and another for employee) results in loss of trust.[16]

• Suggestions on techniques include 'open door' policies – the manager always being available. This of course helps to improve communications by keeping managers in touch with employee attitudes. In criticism of HRM, it was shown in the last chapter that there are general difficulties in communication in organizations, arising from the fact that the two sides seem to speak 'different languages'; have conflicting interests.

9 A Sociological View of Trade Unions

A sociological view of trade unions might emphasize the control of the union, and the institutionalization of conflict in industrial relations; that is to say it might examine how the parties (employers and trade unions) agree on pay and conditions without resorting to violence. ('Union-busting' activity in the USA before the Second World War could be very violent.)

Question

Briefly how would you account for the clashes on the miners' and print workers' picket lines in recent years, during the 1984/5 coal strike and the 1986 dispute between SOGAT 82 and Rupert Murdoch over Wapping.
Suggestions:

• Consult *'Keesing's Record of World Events* or other library reference material, including weeklies like *New Society*, *New Statesman* and *The Economist* (see also the list of Further Reading at the end of this chapter).

• Avoid being too descriptive or historical. Be analytical.

• Analyse the reasons for the comparative weakness of the unions and the corresponding strength of the government.

Given the changes in industrial relations outlined above, it is appropriate to ask: 'How powerful are the unions now?' This question will be dealt with by asking three basic questions: (1) Are trade unions too powerful?; (2) Are shop stewards too powerful?; and (3) Are trade unions a political threat to society in the West? These questions will now be dealt with in turn.

Are trade unions too powerful?

Despite recent losses, unions are still powerful. In Britain they have over nine million members. Because Western economies are complex, union constraints can hurt; thus a strike in the motor industry has a knock-on effect for hundreds of suppliers. Again, the international economy is increasingly competitive. Employers lose markets to competitors if there are strikes. But how powerful are the unions really? Are they too powerful? The public may see the unions as being threatening and unreasonable, calling a strike which inconveniences people, challenging the police and the government as well as the employers and the customers. The unions have often been blamed for Britain's industrial decline. Thus when unions are in the news it is usually because the news is bad – a strike, say – but when all is well they disappear from view.[17]

The following quotation comes from the Glasgow Media Group and is the result of a careful examination of media reporting of trade union activities.

> The almost universal complaint from the trade unionists interviewed was that both television and press coverage focused upon unions exclusively as 'dispute' organisations. They argued that this obsession with strikes and 'disruption' on the part of the media led to an almost total neglect of the wider role which trade unions play in the general organisation and administration of the economy. In addition, it was often commented that an advanced industrial economy could simply not survive without this constructive co-operation on the part of trade unions.
>
> A second complaint, frequently made, was that not only did media coverage focus mainly upon strikes but when it did so it concentrated upon the most trivial and sensational aspects of them.[18]

Unions are often weaker than they appear. Their only strength is in their solidarity; the fact that managers need men to run firms. Their actions are curtailed by law. For example, not more than six pickets are allowed at a works entrance. Most importantly, unions are reactive bodies. They rarely take the initiative, and they are not revolutionary – they don't want to change the system by taking over control from the managers, for example.

There is another reason why unions are weaker than they appear. There may be dissensions within the unions, between the leaders and the ordinary members. It has been argued that because of the kind of work they did, such as negotiations with employers and managing strikes, trade unions became bureaucratic and oligarchic (ruled by a remote few at the top). The leaders sometimes lost touch with the members.

It could be said that conflict is natural in an open society and that trade unions help to direct that conflict through legitimate channels. Strikes are often for more pay and such strikes do not really threaten society; sometimes they help to formulate the issues in such a way that they can be settled. In short, strikes are not a menace to society but show that there are many competing interests. We should not feel threatened by allowing these interests freedom of expression. Countries with very successful economies, such as Australia and the USA, have far higher strike figures than does Britain. People feel threatened by strikes because they depend on services or goods – but is this fear well founded? How often have you been seriously affected by a strike? The number of days lost each year through strikes is minute compared with those lost through illness.

Are shop stewards too powerful?

Shop stewards are the local officials of trade unions. They are elected by the members, and they are unpaid. They usually work alongside their fellow trade unionists and because of this closeness they are often more in tune with what the members really want than perhaps the more remote paid union official in the union's head office. In fact, the power and influence of shop stewards depend on the trust and support members place in them. It is important to mention this because shop stewards have sometimes been portrayed as trouble-makers. But they can be useful to management *because* they are closely in touch with members' complaints: they can be an important link in the chain of communication. Shop stewards are weakened by the fact that their role is ambiguous (whose side are they on – that of the members, the union, the management or themselves?).

Are trade unions a political threat in the West?

So far it has been suggested that trade unions are not a threat to society. It may be interesting to examine what some political writers have to say on the political power of the trade unions.

Early Marxist writers, including Marx himself, saw the trade unions as a means of preparing the working class for the great struggle that cannot be avoided, the overthrow of the bourgeois society. Strikes were seen as increasing solidarity and as the military school of the workers. The nature of capitalist society assisted this by concentrating together in the factories a crowd of strangers who, by association and combination, would acquire *class consciousness*, a realization of their true class position – property-less and exploited.

In fact, in the course of the nineteenth century in Britain events took a different turn, with the collapse of the Chartist Movement which sought full political rights for all, and the rise of craft unions concerned solely with the workplace interests of their members rather than political activity.

Can trade union activity ever really be a threat to 'capitalist society'? Leon Trotsky argued that in economic depression trade unions are dangerous to capitalism because members' aspirations (higher living standards, etc.) cannot be satisfied.[19] These aspirations could only be achieved by a fundamental reorganization of society. On the other hand, the trade union leadership does not want this sort of fundamental change. Union leaders are often very conservative in their ideology (certainly this has been true in Britain, from Bevin and Deakin in the post-war period to Brown, Gunter, Gormley, and Weighill in the sixties and seventies, and to Willis (but not Scargill) today). To counter tendencies to bureaucratic control in unions Trotsky, and writers and activists since, have stressed the need for 'rank and file' control in trade unions. (Indeed this can be seen as one of the main differences between the Communist party in Britain, which seeks to capture top posts in trade unions, and the Trotskyist Socialist Workers' Party, with its drive for rank and file control through the union shop steward movement. In neither ventures have Marxists been particularly successful.) Thus in good times unions simply press for higher wages. This has been called *economism* (signifying that workers want better pay and conditions within capitalism rather than the overthrow of capitalism). In economic depression, unions are weak through loss of members and members' fear of unemployment. Despite the optimism of Marx and Engels, trade unions, for the reasons given by later Marxists themselves, pose little threat to society (either in the recession of the 1930s or that of the 1980s).

In fact it has been argued that there is little class consciousness among workers in the West. They do not realize their exploitation fully, and try to compensate for alienation at work by non-work activities. Basically, work people seek more money (economism), and some degree of job control at shop-floor level. Neither of these endeavours challenges the overall class structure. The institutionalization of industrial relations through the establishment of trade unions narrows conflict down to these two items. One sociologist concludes that workers have a feeling of interdependence with their employers, that despite some apparent surges of class consciousness capitalism survives through economism, and that even when the economy is stagnant capitalism is not threatened. Instead of seeing capitalism itself as the cause of their problems, workers sometimes seek scapegoats, for example immigrants.[20]

10   Possible Reasons for Poor Productivity

Perhaps the first reason to spring to mind here is strikes. Yet are these really the main cause of loss of output? For example, there is evidence to show that in most years Britain loses more working days through industrial accidents than through strikes; between 10 and 20 times more days are lost through sickness; and 20 to 40 times more days are lost through absenteeism.[21]

If strikes are not the main problem in industrial relations, then what is? One possible answer is alienation. People are not motivated. Management ideologies leave little room for their real participation at work, so they react in a number of ways – not necessarily by strikes or seeking more pay. Basically they will seek control of their own work situation by a variety of strategies or reactions, or they will avoid work as far as they can.

First, workers may try to thwart management's wishes if they feel that management is too controlling and oppressive. They may try to establish their own output norms in opposition to those laid down by management; they may try to do the job in their own way in opposition to that laid down by management. As discussed in chapter 6, the work groups sometimes establish their own output norms. In one case those who exceeded these norms were known as 'rate busters' and those who did not work hard enough were known as 'chisellers'.[22] In this way a work group might try to maintain solidarity against an oppressive management.

Secondly, the work group may give strong support to their shop steward in order to gain a voice in management's decisions that affect their everyday life at work.

Thirdly, workers may react in a less planned and concerted way. This may include high labour turnover, high absenteeism, high sickness rates, high accident rates, stress and fatigue.

Fourthly, the workforce may react more aggressively, through pilfering and sabotage. Pilfering could often be seen as a reaction to low pay; an attempt to redress the balance. It is quite common in the hotel and catering industry, which is notorious for low pay. There is little evidence of widespread sabotage; more important is working without enthusiasm, a common reaction to 'scientific management'.

In some of these examples there does not *appear* to be a direct relation between the employer's action (say, tight control) and the employees' response. One can see that where employees feel pushed around at work, absenteeism may be an understandable response. In other cases the relationship is less clear. What, for instance, is the relationship between control at work and accidents? A survey of the literature on industrial injury shows a wide variety of apparent causes, but behind many of them is the pressure to maintain or increase production, leading to cutting corners where safety is concerned.[23] The situation is aptly summed up by a comment a worker made about the role played by a factory foreman: 'If he hears them rollers stop he's out of that office like a shot.'[24]

The title of the article from which this quotation comes is interesting and self-explanatory, 'The Sociology of Accidents and the Social Production of Industrial Injury'. In other words, accidents are not just a question of bad luck, or just the fault of an individual; they reflect the sort of society we are. Thus accidents are often the result of commercial pressures, speeding the production line, cutting corners, subcontracting and so on. There is a widespread belief that uninterrupted production is the chief goal, and this naturally sometimes conflicts with safety. On a practical level, there is role conflict. The production officer or supervisor should not also be in charge of safety at work.

The article ends:

> To sum up: each of these accidents occurred in the context of a process failure and whilst the men concerned were trying to maintain or restore production. In every case the company's safety rules were broken. The process failures involved were not isolated events. Nor were dangerous means used to deal with them. The men acted as they did in order to cope with the pressure from foremen and management to keep up production – the foremen themselves going out of their way formally to acquaint themselves with how the men were coping. For them – the foremen, that is – it was safer that way. This pressure was continual, process failures were fairly frequent and so the short-cutting methods used to deal with them were repeatedly employed. They didn't drift into danger, they were pushed into it via a choice between working harder or taking risks. In each case it was only a matter of time before somebody's number came up.[25]

11   Is Industrial Democracy Possible?

Industrial democracy implies that workers will at least take part in decisions that affect them at work. In Britain the Bullock Committee (majority report) 1977 recommended that firms employing more than 2,000 people should have a single board comprising management, employees and neutral representatives. The report was opposed by both employers and trade unions – why?

It is easy to understand the employers' objections. They put up the capital and take the risks. They have the power and authority now – why should they give it up?

The trade union objection also derives from the loss of power such a change would involve. Trade-union power comes from their facing the employer as a collectivity, as representative of the workforce. If workers are in effect part of management, the basis of this power evaporates. This is not a purely selfish objection. Trade unions are workers' institutions built up over many years. They are seen by some unionists as virtually the only institutions employees have to protect them in a competitive society.

A second trade-union objection to industrial democracy is that workers do not want it. Is work a central life-interest, especially if the work offers no career prospects and is generally soul-destroying? This chapter has indicated that work is often *not* a central life-interest – indeed the major interest in it for many people is the money.

There are circumstances in which workplace democracy is possible, for example, in small co-operatives where participants own a share in the equity of the concern. But there are many major problems with it in large industrial firms. This does not mean to say the goal of industrial democracy should not be pursued, but it does show that sociological analysis can spot some of the difficulties. Incidentally, the degree of industrial democracy in Britian is quite low compared with that in other European countries.

Some have argued that industrial democracy and employee participation is overdue in Britain. They advocate the following steps:

● Legislation setting out rights and duties of employers and employees.
● An emphasis on democratic leadership styles (see chapter 6 for a definition of democratic leadership style). (Also more women should be encouraged to become managers.)
● Employees should have an effective power base, for example, a trade union.[26]

Industrial democracy has often been proposed as an alternative to voluntary collective bargaining. But this is difficult during a recession in which competing groups of labour clash. Worker directors with responsibility for decisions are not likely to be an acceptable way forward for labour. Nor is employee participation in management, which might include profit sharing, likely to be successful, for two reasons. First it is likely to be seen as a control over wage bargaining where profits are low. Second, it emphasizes economic incentives and ignores the basis of labour's claim to a share in management.

Other forms of industrial democracy include co-operatives and autonomous work groups, but these have seldom been really popular in Britain (although there have been some successes on the Continent, most notably the Mondragon Co-operative in Spain; see next chapter). Autonomous work groups have been successful, though, when their role is akin to that of a subcontractor (for example on a building site where the 'lump' operates – where the worker is a subcontractor, self-employed, and the employer does not have to pay national insurance, etc.).

12   Conclusion

The aim of this chapter has been to present a sociological view of industrial relations by looking at the situation from the viewpoints of all concerned and showing that strikes are not the main problem in industrial relations. The following is an attempt to summarize the sociological approach. Some items mentioned in this chapter are discussed further in other chapters, so:

- for the labour process see chapter 3;
- for managerial ideologies see chapters 3 and 4;
- for alienation at work see chapter 6;
- for the changing occupational structure see chapter 8.

A common view	*A sociological view*
The various members of an organization, manual workers, clerical workers, professionals, and managers should all pull together. Management manages in the interests of all concerned.	'Lacking property or command over resources the employee is totally dependent on employment by the owners or controllers – and a dependence relationship is a power relationship.'[27] Employees may seek higher pay or better conditions, but these claims are no threat to management.
Class differences at work are much less important now.	Many large organizations still have separate dining rooms, car parks, and toilets, for managerial/professional staff.

Class divisions at work are still strong and this probably affects productivity.

The class gap at work may still exist but it is much less now. Well-paid (affluent) manual workers are becoming more middle-class. Sociologists seem to exaggerate the importance of social class.

Affluent worker studies show that such workers have an instrumental (or calculative) approach to their work, to trade union membership, to politics and to education.[28] These workers do not aspire to become middle class, nor perhaps do middle-class (white-collar) workers seek their company.

Class is still important. It seems to determine where you live, how you live and when you die – the lower your class the less your income and the shorter your life expectancy.

Management is more enlightened these days; it does not order people arround. Taylor's book on 'scientific management' (which stressed the right of management to manage) was written at the turn of the century and is out of date now.

Management can be very harsh and petty sometimes (and enlightened at others). Managerial ideologies still abound and 'Taylorism' is rife. Strict managerial control is legitimated by a variety of ideologies, as shown throughout the text. Against a background of high unemployment in the eighties some managements seem to be exercising even stricter control. This appears to be succeeding (but perhaps employees may regard a return to full employment as a time for settling old scores).

Although trade unions are weaker now through unemployment, a decline in membership, and legislation

Trade unions are less powerful than they appear. Basically they seek more money for their members and regulating their activity, they are still too powerful. They can still call strikes and intimidate employers. Strikes and other union activity seem to have weakened Britain and seem to be the cause of the country's decline.

better conditions at work. They do not really challenge the 'system'. They are not revolutionary and do not want to take over management. Britain is not particularly strike-prone. It is too simplistic to say that trade unions have weakened the British economy; strikes are far fewer in Britain than in the USA or Australia, two countries consistently successful economically. The roots of Britain's industrial decline lie deeper (as chapter 2 indicates). It is lazy thinking just to blame the unions.

There is little that could be said for strikes; they are a throwback to an earlier age. Industrial relations should be more civilized now and made dependent on reconciliation and mutual respect.

Conflict is a fact of life and indeed may be a healthy sign, helping to bring matters out into the open, thus clarifying the issues. Some strikes may appear to be 'senseless' but it is the task of the sociologist to find the causes.

Exercises

Self-examination questions

1 Define briefly:
- trade union
- shop steward
- industrial relations
- industrial democracy
- fairness
- voluntarism
- collective bargaining
- solidarity
- density
- unionateness
- core
- periphery.

2 What is meant by:
- instrumentalism
- institutionalization of conflict
- work norms
- pluralist perspective
- radical perspective
- control
- economism?

Essay or discussion questions

1 In your opinion, do workers still need trade unions? If so, why?
Suggestions: Consider the weak position of the individual worker. Analyse the changing scene in industrial relations and show how unions can adapt to this while at the same time protecting their members.
2 Examine the view that trade unions should keep out of politics.
Suggestions: Consider how political trade unions are. They do give financial support to the Labour Party. Is this acceptable?
3 What are the causes of the present apparent weakness of shop stewards?
Suggestions: Show this is part of the picture of current trade union decline, e.g. loss of members, lower density, high unemployment. You could consider whether shop stewards were not as strong as they were made out to be in the past.

Case study 1/project

Take any important strike or dispute that is happening now or has occurred in the recent past, and try to analyse what is *really* happening. You could work through the following stages:

1   give a very brief history of the dispute;
2   summarize the accounts of this dispute as given by the press and broadcasting media;
3   give an account of the dispute from the viewpoints of management, trade unions and the workforce generally.
4   Who has power in this dispute and how is the power wielded?
5   How would a sociological account of what is happening differ from other accounts?

Case study 2

A Parliamentary Select Committee is seeking the views of experts on the causes, consequences and conduct of the miners' strike, 1984/5. As a sociologist with a good record for research in industrial relations your views have been sought on these questions. Read the passage and then make your report to the Committee, including, among other matters, the issues raised in the questions that follow the passage.

The Miners
In one obvious sense, a coal dispute in 1926 was a more significant event. There were over a million miners then compared with approximately 180,000 in 1984. South Wales, the radical vanguard of the Miners' Federation, had about 200,000 miners in 1926; still demonstrating its traditional solidarity today, the number is little over ten per cent of the old figure. Besides this diminishing industrial significance, the old stereotypes of the mining community, industrial

homogeneity and solidarity are of diminishing relevance. Massive closure programmes have often ruptured the umbilical cord between the pit and the community. The solidarity of miners – 1984 style – is not a timeless quality inherited readily from past battles. It has had to be constructed, often in the face of forbidding difficulties.

But a significant parallel does stand out against this kaleidoscope of changes. The issues at stake in both disputes involved much more than the future of the coal industry. The complex Glaswegian politician John Wheatley expressed this judgement forcibly in 1926, as he condemned the weakness of many of Labour's most prominent figures: 'The miners are fighting alone but they are fighting the battle of the whole nation. If they lose, we all lose.' Then, the miners stood out against the doctrine that the export trade demand required wage reductions. Moreover '1926' marked the last battle in a series of confrontations that had dominated industrial relations since 1910. In 1984, the battle raised issues fundamental to Thatcher's Britain – employment, the 'rights' of management, and above all responses to that harsh process that is turning large tracts of Britain into a separate country where the age of retirement is often sixteen. And again, there is the longer perspective: for the Government, 1984 could count as a second leg to 1972 and 1974. This time, as in 1926, the Government played on its own ground.

One reason for the unfavourable terrain in 1984 has been the issue. The solidarity achieved in 1972 and 1974 over a national wage demand has been eroded, firstly through the introduction of area productivity schemes, and then by the nature of the closure issue. Among the many propagated in recent months, there exist few more misleading stereotypes than the claim that miners' disputes have always been notable for their solidarity, and that the recent actions of some NUM officials have damaged this resource. But '1972' and '1974' were, arguably, exceptional. In 1926, the issue was again potentially divisive. The threatened shift to District Agreements indicated draconian reductions in exporting coalfields such as Durham and South Wales, but in Derbyshire, Nottinghamshire and other Midlands Districts, the likely wage cuts often seemed small. In both disputes, it was in the latter coalfields that the union's strategy had its weakest point. It was there in 1926 that the return to work began in the late summer. The problem of solidarity was reflected in the loose structure of the Miners' Federation; it still leaves its mark on the organization and actions of the NUM. Solidarity within a mining community has been achieved frequently; solidarity between coalfields has often been far more problematic. 1926 and 1984 stand as sombre monuments to this.

The problem of mobilizing the NUM membership over the issue of pit closures was highlighted in the argument over the absence of a national ballot. It was an issue in which Labour parliamentarians largely accepted the orthodoxy that such an individual ballot counted as the ultimate in democratic procedures. Accordingly they not only marginalised other participatory forms of decision-making but also failed to focus on a fundamental problem of democratic theory. Whilst it may be argued that a national ballot would be appropriate on an issue that affected all participants equally – a national wage demand, for example – it is less obviously appropriate for dealing with so divisive an issue as pit closures. In such cases the impact may be seen not simply as uneven, but as bleak for some while advantageous for others. The basic argument has been heard before. In June 1926, a Derbyshire coalmine-owner wrote to *The Times*: 'If the ballot were secret, taken in a constitutional manner, the men would go back to work immediately . . . Neither Mr Smith nor Mr Cook dares face a secret ballot.' On both occasions, a union forced to fight on an issue that worked against the maximisation of solidarity had to develop methods of achieving and maintaining unity. In 1926, the initial stoppage was more complete, but significantly less than unanimous; divisive tendencies were present then as in 1984. (from David Howell, 'Where's Ramsay MacKinnock?: Labour Leadership and the Miners', in H. Beynon (ed.), *Digging Deeper* (Verso, London, 1985), pp. 182–3).

1   Why could the coal strike of 1926 be considered a more significant event than that of 1984/5? What is the significance of each strike?
2   What would you say is the basis of the strength of community felt by many miners?
3   How has the miners' solidarity been eroded in recent years?
4   What were the arguments for and against holding a pithead ballot in 1984?
5   Briefly outline the argument for and against keeping open 'uneconomic' pits. How might a sociologist approach this issue?

Do not spend too much time on the history of the dispute or a description of events. You should concentrate on sociological analysis and especially expose hidden assumptions or misconceptions by all concerned.

Case study 3: role play

The following passage describes a strike at Ford. It can be used either as a role play or as a case study or both. If used as a role play it is important that the players stay in role throughout the exercise. The cast could be increased or reduced as required. It is suggested that the play be enacted in two scenes.

The anatomy of a strike: a role play for seven people

Characters

John Dillon	Ford Shop Steward
Ken Brown	Second Shop Steward
Reg Jones	Foreman
Bill Finch	Plant Manager
Sally Grant	Reporter
Bob Ramsey	Ford Labour Relations Director
Brian Smith	Chief Union Negotiator

Scene one: the shop floor
Each character should speak their part with a view to clearly establishing what actually happened – what sparked off the conflict?

Scene two: a seminar to analyse what really happened
At first the parts should be played as described in the text but then all actors should be feeling for a solution. In this seminar an additional character could be introduced – that of a sociologist, to discuss the findings.

A case study

As an industrial relations consultant you have been asked by the management to write a report analysing the dispute at the plant and make recommendations for improvements. Your report should comment upon the items mentioned in Cas Study 2. You should also devote a major section of your report to giving sociological insights into what is really going on at this plant. You should include examples, from the text, of 'Taylorism', alienation, union power, shop steward power, solidarity, an unofficial strike.

The issue

On Monday 14 June a shop steward, John Dillon, was summarily dismissed by Ford management; the reason given was that he had held an unofficial meeting during working hours and had taken a leading part in an 'unruly demonstration' on company premises. Since Ford's account of this episode was challenged by union representatives, it may be useful to cite the account given in the *Sunday Times* of 20 June.

'Under Ford procedure agreements, embodied in a Blue Book, shop stewards may not hold meetings on company premises or during working hours; they may not leave their ordinary jobs to act as shop stewards in a dispute between workers and foreman unless the foreman has first had two shifts to sort it out; and they must accept a foreman's instructions, unless these are over-ruled at a higher level.

'Mr Dillon has been suspended twice, and was ultimately dismissed for breaching these and other rules. According to union sources, the first suspension was for leaving his job in the paint shop when a group of men got him to represent them in an argument with a foreman, in spite of the fact that the foreman had told them that a shop steward should not be brought in at that stage.

'The second suspension, again according to a union account, was for 'advising' a group of men to continue doing a job a particular way, although the foreman had said it should be done differently. Three men had been taking turns at using either hand or power-driven sanding equipment, but the foreman had said that each man should stick to the same piece of equipment. Dillon argued that it didn't seem to him to matter either way. The plant manager's letter said that the second suspension was for 'telling employees to disobey their supervisor who had instructed them in the way in which the job should be done, then telling them not to listen to the supervisor's advice'.

'The third and final incident arose last Wednesday week (i.e. 9 June) over a manning dispute. One man, union sources say, was taken off a job usually done by five men (it involved manhandling car bodies from overhead to lower-level conveyor belts). The men objected, but Mr Dillon advised them to try it, which they did for two days and nights. The foreman complained about the way the job was being done and warned them that if it wasn't done properly, they would be dismissed. Rather than risk being dismissed for failure, the four men stopped work altogether. The foreman promptly suspended them.

'About thirty other men also stopped work (union sources say they were laid off; the company says they struck). A shop steward takes up the story: "On the way out, some of them got hold of Dillon and asked him what the hell was going on. He said: 'Let's go outside and talk about it with the others.' They said: 'Come on, John. Tell us what it's all about.' So he told them about the manning dispute.

"'Some of the men said: 'Let's go and get hold of the manager.' Dillon said: 'You can't do that.' So he went to the shop manager's office instead and asked him if he would come out and talk to the men. Dillon came out of the office and said the manager wouldn't talk to them. But the men pushed him back and went into the shop manager's office. He followed them in to see what was going on. There was a bit of shouting, but not by Dillon. Eventually he persuaded them to go outside."

'For the next two days, the management carried out its own investigation into what happened. Last Sunday two senior Ford labour relations officials travelled to Liverpool and in the Adelphi Hotel heard the results of the investigation. District officials of Mr Dillon's union, the Transport and General Workers, were informed on Monday that he would be dismissed, and dismissed he was.'

The background

There had been a long pay strike earlier in the year which had been costly to the company and the unions. After the strike management's attitude had hardened. *The Times* of 17 June argued that 'behind the apparently simple issue of the dismissal of one shop steward for what the company calls "continual breaches of Company agreements" has been a much more deep-rooted problem of a power struggle between the Halewood management and the shop steward organization at the plant.

The stoppage

John Dillon was dismissed by the company on the morning of Monday 14 June. Men at the assembly plant (Dillon's factory, one of three in the Ford Halewood complex) held a lunchtime meeting and voted to strike. By Wednesday, workers at the adjacent body and transmission plants had joined the stoppage, involving over 10,000 employees and bringing production at Halewood to a standstill.

On the Tuesday and Wednesday, meetings were held at national level between Bob Ramsey, Ford Labour Relations Director, and Brian Smith, Chief Union Negotiator. The union insisted that Dillon must be reinstated, but suggested that he could return to work as an ordinary employee pending a joint investigation of his activities as a shop steward. The company rejected this, refusing even to discuss Dillon's case until after the strikers returned to work. The talks thus ended in deadlock, with no fixed date for any further discussions. This led senior shop stewards from nineteen Ford factories to meet in London on Friday, and the outcome was a call for the unions to declare a national strike of all Ford workers. (adapted from R. Hyman, *Strikers* (Fontana, London, 1984), pp. 11–19)

Project 1

A London evening newspaper has just published the result of a survey on the general public's attitude to the trade unions, and it makes dismal reading for a number of union leaders who are now in town to discuss the formulation of a joint policy towards new legislation in connection with industrial relations which has been proposed. An extract from the survey is given below.

The union leaders see the connection between the problem they are dealing with and the findings in the survey. As a result, they decide to approach P. J. Felstead and Associates, public relations consultants. They are given a brief to discover why the public image of the unions is so bad. The senior partner, Alwyn Griffiths, takes on the assignment himself in the first place, realizing that such a major brief may give the firm good publicity. The fee is likely to be quite modest, partly because Alwyn's father was a Labour MP in the early post-war years and Alwyn remains a supporter – if slightly less staunch these days. He calls in his team for preliminary discussions.

'Look,' he says, 'I see no point in undertaking any further surveys at this stage. Let's have a Think Tank session. I'll give you 24 hours' notice and we'll spend 2 hours together in this office from 3 o'clock tomorrow afternoon. Don't forget the question: 'Why have the unions generally got such a bad public image?'. And don't forget that we're supposed to be analysts. Let's be objective, shall we?' (from J. Chilver, *People Communication and Organization* (Pergamon, Oxford, 1984), pp. 155–6)

	Percentages		
	Yes	*No*	*Don't know*
Do the unions deliberately make trouble among work people?	60	29	11
Should people be obliged to join a union when they take a job?	27	71	2
Do the unions do more good than harm?	21	61	18
Do the high wages that unions get for their members cause unemployment elsewhere?	75	21	4

What ideas do you think might emerge from the Think Tank? Analyse industrial relations problems currently in the news. When the necessary information has been collected, students could form groups with a view to producing joint reports, *or* produce them individually.

Project 2

Examine the arguments for and against the proposition that the state is neutral in industrial relations.

1 Use current and past examples of the state being involved in disputes (the miners, printers etc.).
2 Examine the role of the media.
3 Analyse recent labour legislation in Britain and the USA.
4 Examine the relationship between the directors of large corporations and other members of the elite (see chapter 3).

Further Reading

P. J. Armstrong, *Ideology and Shop Floor Industrial Relations* (Croom Helm, London, 1981)

H. A. Clegg, *The Changing System of Industrial Relations in Great Britain* (Basil Blackwell, Oxford, 1979)

C. Crouch, *Trade Unions: The Logic of Collective Action* (Fontana, London, 1982)

W. W. Daniel and N. Millward, *Workplace Industrial Relations in Britain* (Policy Studies Institute, London, 1987)

D. Farnham and J. Pimlott, *Understanding Industrial Relations* (Holt, London, 1986)

A. Fox, *Man Mismanagement* (Hutchinson, London, 1985)

R. Hyman, *Industrial Relations: A Marxist Introduction* (Macmillan, London, 1975)

R. Hyman, *Strikes* (Fontana, London, 1984)

T. Kennoy, *Invitation to Industrial Relations* (Basil Blackwell, Oxford, 1985)

C. Littler and G. Salaman, *Class at Work* (Batsford, London, 1984)

M. Poole, *Industrial Relations in the Future* (Routledge and Kegan Paul, London, 1984)

B. Sherman, *The State of the Unions* (Wiley, Chichester, 1986)

T. J. Watson, *Management: Organisation and employment strategy* (Routledge and Kegan Paul, London, 1986)

Notes

1 D. Farnham and J. Pimlott, *Understanding Industrial Relations* (Holt, London, 1986).

2 Ibid.

3 A. Fox, *Man Mismanagement* (Hutchinson, London, 1985).

4 R. Hyman, *Industrial Relations: A Marxist Introduction* (Macmillan, London, 1975).

5 C. Littler and G. Salaman, *Class at Work* (Batsford, London, 1984).

6 P. J. Armstrong, *Ideology and Shop Floor Industrial Relations* (Croom Helm, London, 1981)

7 Farnham and Pimlott, *Understanding Industrial Relations*, p. 74.

8 J. Watson, *Institute of Personnel Management Digest*, 1985.

9 R. Taylor, 'The New Union Radicalism', *New Society*, 29 August 1986.

10 Ibid.

11 D. Thomas, 'New Ways of Working', *New Society*, 30 August 1985.

12 Ibid.

13 Ibid.

14 Based on research by J. Atkinson, Institute of Manpower Studies, Sussex University.

15 B. Sherman, *The State of the Unions* (Wiley, Chichester, 1986).

16 M. Beer et al., *Human Resource Management: A General Manager's Perspective* (Collier Macmillan, London, 1985), pp. 20–1.

17 Sherman, *The State of the Unions* (Wiley, Chichester, 1986).
18 Glasgow Media Group, *Bad News* (Routledge and Kegan Paul, London, 1976), p. 228.
19 B. Khei-Paz, *The Social and Political Thought of Leon Trotsky* (Clarendon Press, Oxford, 1979), pp. 187–9.
20 M. Mann, *Consciousness and Action Among the Western Working Class* (Macmillan, London, 1973).
21 Farnham and Pimlott, *Understanding Industrial Relations*, p. 347.
22 F. J. Roethlisberger and W. J. Dickson, *Management and the Worker* (Harvard University Press, Cambridge, 1939).
23 T. Nichols, 'The Sociology of Accidents and the Social Production of Industrial Injury', in G. Esland et al. (eds), *People and Work* (Open University Press, Milton Keynes, 1975) pp. 217–29.
24 Ibid., p. 227.
25 Ibid., p. 228.
26 M. Poole, *Industrial Relations in the Future* (Routledge and Kegan Paul, London, 1984).
27 A. Fox, *Man Mismanagement*, p. 32.
28 J. Goldthorpe, D. Lockwood, F. Bechoffer and J. Platt, *The Affluent Worker: Industrial Attitudes and Behaviour* (Cambridge University Press, Cambridge, 1969).

6   The Motivation to Work

1 Introduction

Richard Brown, in his 1984 presidential address to the British
Sociological Association, remarked that factories are private places
with their own language and rhythm. Yet there are surprisingly few
accounts of factory life by workers. How do you explain the daily
experience of boredom? 'A long, boring day' takes two seconds to
read. But, surprisingly perhaps, most people say they are satisfied
with their work. Brown suggested that sociology should investigate
this paradox; the results could lead to a new and better understanding
of work experience, upon which to base a critical debate with the
public about the way things are run.

Brown's remarks seem very sensible, and would probably be
acceptable to most sociologists. Yet, as mentioned, it is the sociologist's
task to question everything, however reasonable it might appear.
Thus, of Brown's remarks it might be asked:

- Is it being 'typically British' to assume that factory work is boring?
- Do managers and workers in large Japanese firms assume factory
  work is boring?
- Do we look down on factory work because it has low status?
- Do we notice that a decreasing number of people in Britain and
  the USA actually work in factories now, as a result of 'de-
  industrialization'?
- Is office work, sales work, catering and so on really less boring?
  Some sociologists believe such work can be just as alienating.[1]
- Is it really true that most people are dissatisfied with their work?
  How do you measure this?[2]

What can be done about boring jobs, low morale and poor productivity? Can anything be done? This chapter seeks to put the important questions and discuss the attempts various people have made, but it cannot always offer answers. First, then, the following attempts to improve the social quality of work are critically examined, namely:

- job enlargement – making the work less fragmented;
- job rotation – moving on to different types of work;
- job enrichment – giving people more control over their work.

The chapter then proceeds to examine commonly held views:

- that management can reduce alienation in office and factory work;
- that management can increase productivity by encouraging harmonious social relations at work;
- that management can enrich jobs and the work experience generally.

The chapter concludes by indicating the weaknesses of traditional organizational psychology in tackling such problems as low morale and lack of motivation to work, and in turn shows where sociology might have a keener perception (but you can judge for yourself). First, then, three practical attempts to tackle these work problems – job enlargement, job rotation and job enrichment.

Job enlargement

A job is enlarged when an employee carries out a wider range of jobs of approximately the same level, usually a low level of skill. Here are a few examples: a travelling salesperson who is given an additional area to cover; a typist/secretary who has to take on work from an additional manager; an assembly-line worker bolting on the bumpers of a car as well as the wheels, thus increasing the job cycle from 130 seconds to 300. The assumptions here are that the expanded job may be more interesting, because it is more varied, that it gives the operative more control over the job, or even that workers will feel that they are participating more in the firm.

The difficulties are that job enlargement often does not really make the job more interesting, as the examples given here and research indicate. Moreover, contrary to the principles of job enlargement, it may suit the logic of the production line, or the office routine, to have jobs broken down into small parts. Management may not want the operative to have more control over what is going on, as it means less control for management, and this may be important, as the discussion on scientific management and de-skilling in chapter 3 indicated. It is difficult to see any reason why workers doing two routine jobs should feel significantly more motivated than those doing one.

Job rotation

In job rotation, the individual changes jobs during the day, for example, from bolting on car wheels in the morning to bolting on bumpers in the afternoon. The aim is to avoid boredom. The limitations are the same as those to job enlargement. As will be argued later in this chapter, the roots of alienation lie not so much in the technology of work but rather in the social arrangements for the work, particularly when the individual has no real control over the situation.

Job enrichment

Job enlargement and job rotation could be criticized on the grounds that they merely add one boring job to another. One researcher, whose work is described later, has called this 'horizontal loading'. Job enrichment on the other hand means giving people more control over their work, having a whole job to do rather than a fragmented job, having the freedom to decide how to do the job, having full information about the job and having the opportunity to develop further, to grow with the job.

2   Job Enrichment Considered Further

Job enrichment (and job enlargement and rotation) are ideas that have emerged from management theorists. The aim of such schemes is, in the long run, to improve productivity. It has been known for many years that the attitudes of employees to work affect the effort they put in, and it has been felt by many that job satisfaction would lead to higher productivity and less conflict at work. Various approaches will be examined here, before the sociological approach is given.

A hierarchy of needs

Underlying most theories of job enrichment, job satisfaction and the motivation to work is the idea that individuals have needs, that they are not fulfilling their potential unless these needs are satisfied (and further, that in satisfying their own needs individuals will also be satisfying the needs of the organization of which they are members). (The concept of needs was discussed in chapter 4.) One of the best-known theories is A. H. Maslow's concept of the 'hierarchy of needs',[3] in which the individual is seen as seeking to satisfy basic needs first, leading in turn to the satisfaction of higher level needs and finally to the highest level needs, the need for *self-actualization* or fulfilling ones full potential, as shown in figure 6.1.

F. Herzberg, whose ideas are covered next, drew on Maslow's concept of needs for his theory of job enrichment and motivation.

Job enrichment and the motivation to work

The main aim in Herzberg's research was to find out how people could satisfy their higher needs in their work.[4] He believed that in

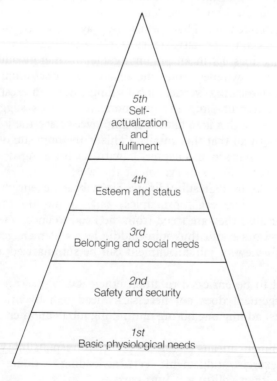

Figure 6.1 *The order of priority of human needs according to Maslow*

Source: A. Maslow, *Motivation and Personality* (Harper and Row, London, 1954).

many organizations people were not satisfying their highest needs, and this was because of the way in which business and industry (and public authorities) were organized. Three questions could be posed here. What are these higher needs? Why are they not satisfied? What can be done to satisfy them?

Herzberg conducted a survey of 200 accountants and engineers in the Pittsburgh area. He asked them to note those occasions when they felt particularly good about their jobs and give reasons for their feelings. He then asked them to note those occasions when they felt bad about their jobs, again giving reasons.

Herzberg apparently found that the factors that lead to job satisfaction were quite different from those factors that lead to job dissatisfaction. The main factors leading to job satisfaction were achievement, recognition, the work itself, responsibility and advancement. Those factors leading to job dissatisfaction mentioned by the respondents were not the opposite, but quite different factors, as figure 6.2 shows.

What should a manager or consultant employing Herzberg's theory do? First, the job should be 'cleaned up' – the 'hygiene' factors should be attended to. This means the pay, work conditions, job security, etc. should be satisfactory. Only after that can the job be *enriched*. This does *not* mean job enlargement – merely adding other similar jobs, or switches from one to another (horizontal loading). Herzberg is advocating 'vertical job loading'; more interesting, more responsible different work (as the motivator factors suggest). One way to achieve all this is to allow the employee to see the job through to the end, with all that this entails. (This is the opposite of scientific management discussed in chapter 3, with its breaking down of the task and its very close supervision of the worker.)

The theory goes that subordinates' jobs become enriched by the application of Herzberg's principles, but so too do the jobs of managers because they are freed from the need to check every detail. Some supervisors could thus join middle levels of management.

Herzberg's view of job enrichment can be summarized as follows:

- Jobs need to be enriched to attain efficiency.
- Job enlargement does not necessarily lead to job enrichment. It may be just adding one boring unfulfilling job to another (horizontal loading).
- Job enrichment means giving people more responsibility, allowing them to exercise judgement, 'vertical loading' – doing the whole job rather than splitting it into parts.
- Job enrichment as described here cannot take place unless the job has been 'cleaned up' first – unless the 'hygiene factors' have been satisfied, i.e. good working conditions, adequate pay, etc.

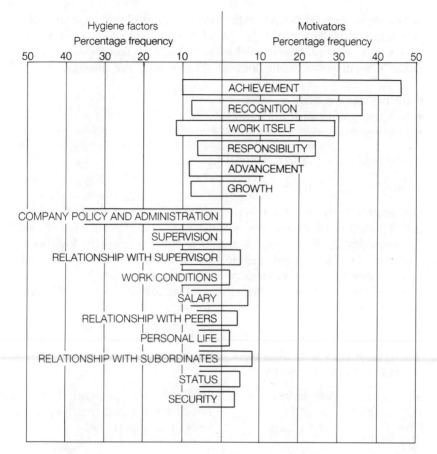

Figure 6.2 *'Hygiene' factors and 'motivator' factors in attitudes to work*

Source: based on F. Herzberg et al., *The Motivation to Work* (Wiley, New York, 1959), pp. 25–6.

One criticism that could be made of Herzberg's theory of job enrichment is that it seems to apply to white-collar, professional and managerial jobs. It is exceptional for people doing routine factory work to have much control over their work. Consider the following quotation.

A man can be coerced into performing routine physical movements with regularity and speed. But he cannot be coerced into making good judgements, exercising initiative or using his discretion creatively in the service of another person's objectives. Good judgements and creative initiatives spring from co-operative high-trust responses which involve his mind and spirit as well as his physical self.[5]

The argument presented in favour of job enrichment ignores the possibility that this could be an ideology. The 'real' reason for advocating job enrichment may be that it leads to greater productivity rather job satisfaction, but does it? What should the manager do?

- Go for more control at work?
- Increase profits and pay packets?
- Stress participation at work?

Theory X and theory Y

One approach to job enrichment implicitly based on the concept of the satisfaction of needs was advanced in *The Human Side of the Enterprise* by D. McGregor.[6] He argued that management had been ignoring the facts about people, following an out-moded set of assumptions about people because it adhered to 'Theory X' when the facts are that most people are closer to the assumptions of 'Theory Y'. The two theories are set out as follows.

Theory X	*Theory Y*
The typical person dislikes work and will avoid it if possible.	Work is as natural as play or rest.
The typical person lacks responsibility, has little ambition and seeks security above all.	People are not inherently lazy. They have become that way as a result of experience.
Most people must be coerced, controlled and threatened with punishment to get them to work.	People will exercise self-direction and self-control in the service of objectives to which they are committed. People have potential. Under proper conditions they learn to accept and seek responsibility. They have imagination, ingenuity and creativity that can be applied to work.
With these assumptions the managerial role is to coerce and control employees.	With these assumptions the managerial role is to develop the potential in employees and help them release that potential toward common objectives.

Of course, there are important differences among people, so a few may come closer to Theory X, but nearly all employees have some Theory Y potential for growth. Managers had failed to recognize this potential. Consequently their policies and practices failed to develop it. The result was that many people regarded work as a curse on humankind instead of an opportunity for growth and fulfilment. Management's need was to change to a whole new theory of working with people, Theory Y.

The criticism that can be made of McGregor's theory is similar to that made of Herzberg's ideas about job enrichment. It is much easier to see how it could be applied to professional, managerial and skilled clerical work than to unskilled or semi-skilled manual work.

The theory of maturity

This theory is also based on the satisfaction of needs – as are most psychological theories of motivation. The theory was put forward by C. Argyris, who believes that in modern society basic physiological needs are met, but because of the nature of work organizations, the higher-level needs cannot be satisfied. He implies that everyone has a need to grow or *mature*:

from infant passivity	to adult activity;
from infant dependence	to relative independence;
from limited behaviour	to different behaviour;
from erratic beliefs and interests	to more stable beliefs and interests;
from short time perspective	to longer time perspective;
from subordinate social position	to equal or superordinate social position;
from lack of self-awareness	to self-awareness and control.

The organization can be judged by the extent to which it permits or thwarts this progress from immaturity to maturity.[7]

The importance of work groups: the Hawthorne experiments

One very influential study, by Elton Mayo, seems to show that management can increase productivity by encouraging harmonious relations at work. His research could be seen as a leading example of the 'human relations' school of industrial relations.[8]

It could also be seen as a response to the excesses of scientific management, whose emphasis is purely on the task, not taking into account the needs of workers and of the work group. The leading writers in the human relations tradition have been social psychologists rather than business managers. They include Elton Mayo, who pointed out the importance of work groups in satisfying individual needs and maintaining output.

Mayo's main research was carried out at the Hawthorne plant of the Western Electric Company near Chicago, 1924–1940.[9] Here is a brief summary and assessment.

Studies of work groups were carried out in phases, as follows.

First phase: the relay assembly test room Six women workers assembling telephone relays were segregated in order that the experimenters could observe the effect of changes in the working conditions on output. These changes included:

- the introduction of rest and refreshment breaks of varying time and duration;
- a group bonus system (i.e. bonuses were related to the total output of the six women and not the whole factory).
- The intensity of the lighting was increased;
- Ventilation was improved.
  Under this system, output increased significantly.

Second phase The operatives then reverted to the original conditions – no extra incentives, no rest and refreshment pauses. The original lighting and ventilation conditions were restored. Output went up to the highest yet recorded. Mayo concluded that it was not changes in the *physical* conditions of work that had caused increased output. Rather, the explanation seemed to be that the women got greater work satisfaction because they had more freedom and control over their output. Apparently this work group set its own norms and built up greater friendliness and mutual co-operation. The relations between the group and their supervisors became more friendly.

Mayo concluded that where norms of co-operativeness and high output are established because of a feeling of importance, physical conditions of work have little impact. There was no evidence, the researchers felt, in favour of the hypothesis that the increase in output was due to the wage incentive factor alone.

Third phase: the bank wiring room In another attempt to monitor a work group it was found that work groups set their own output norms (irrespective of bonuses introduced by management). Those members who worked too hard were known as 'ratebusters' while those who did too little were known as 'chisellers'.

The interview programme The purpose of the interview programme was to ascertain the employees' attitudes to working conditions, their supervisors, and to their jobs generally. It was found that formal questionnaires were useless for this purpose, and that workers really wanted to talk freely about their work problems (once they were sure that their trust would not be abused). The informal (unstructured) interviews lasted about ninety minutes. Over 20,000 employees were interviewed.

Hawthorne experiment 'rules' for interviewing

1 Give your whole attention to the person interviewed, and make it evident that you are doing so.

2 Listen – don't talk.

3 Never argue; never give advice.

4 Listen to:
- what they want to say;
- what they do not want to say;
- what they cannot say without help.

5 As you listen, plot out tentatively and for subsequent correction the pattern that is being set before you. To test this, from time to time summarize what has been said and present it for comment (e.g. 'Is this what you are telling me?'). Always do this with the greatest caution; that is, clarify but do not add or distort.

6 Remember that everything said must be considered a personal confidence and not divulged to anyone. (This does not prevent discussion of a situation between professional colleagues. Nor does it prevent some form of public report when due precaution has been taken.)

These 'rules' might be useful for personnel managers. See the Further Reading list for books on methods of social research.

Mayo found that relationships with other people were very important to the interviewees. Also, working groups that were well established were attractive to newcomers, who fitted in easily. Newly formed working groups took a long time to develop close ties.

Of course, the trouble with informal unstructured interviews is that it is difficult to quantify (measure) the responses. The researchers' findings are based on their feeling and impression of what most respondents meant on a particular topic. However, the importance of the work group was clear in their findings.

Criticisms   One critic of the Hawthorne studies, Alex Carey, demonstrated from Mayo's own evidence that financial reward was in fact the principal influence on work, morale and behaviour – contrary to Mayo's own conclusions.[10]

For example, Carey showed that in phase one, where payment was based on the output of the experimental group and not the whole department, this resulted in an increase of 12.6 per cent in output and therefore the wages of this group increased. But the experiment caused so much discontent among the women in the rest of the department (who wanted the same payment conditions) that this part of the experiment was discontinued in nine weeks. The output of the experimental group promptly fell by 16 per cent.

At one point fairly early in the experiment, two of the women in the group were replaced; the new workers were urgently in need of money, and they led the way in increased output.

Carey argues that there is no real evidence that phase one output increased as a result of changed, 'friendly' supervision. Rather the supervisor had become friendlier because output had increased. Far from supporting the 'human relations' thesis, the results of these experiments tend to show the importance of money incentives.

It must also be mentioned that many of the Hawthorne workers were first generation immigrants *and* first generation factory workers trying to cope with Al Capone's Chicago – no wonder they said, to the interviewers at least, that they wanted to belong.

All this raises important questions about the teaching and practice of industrial relations and the possible ideological bias of the human relations school. How is it that teachers and textbook writers can find discrepancies between the evidence and the conclusions in this important study? How is it that such a broad school of thought, which forms the basis of so much theory and practice, could be based on the observation of only six operatives? Probably the answer is that this is what people *want* to believe. Mayo himself believed that the breakdown of traditional values in society could be countered by creating conditions in industry which encouraged co-operation. He thought it was the task of management to encourage this group affiliation, and that these informal group bonds would replace the traditional ties of family and community which appeared to be weakening.

> It would seem that one of the important problems discovered by the research division at Hawthorne – the failure of workers and supervisors to understand their work and working conditions, the widespread sense of personal futility – is general to the civilised world and not merely characteristic of Chicago. The belief of the individual in his social

function and solidarity with the group – his capacity for collaboration in work – these are disappearing, destroyed in part by rapid scientific and technical advance.[11]

There may be good sense in Mayo's argument (apart from the irrelevant remarks about 'scientific' advance), but the important question is 'did these views influence the Hawthorne experiments?' Were the researchers looking for what they wanted to find? Is this what managers, teachers and others want to believe? For example, as already mentioned, there is no evidence that increased output arose from friendlier supervision, although researchers believed that it did.

Despite all these serious criticisms, the human relations approach to industrial relations remains firmly entrenched in management's thinking. After the Second World War research, mainly in the USA, extended the human relations approach in three directions.[12] First it was shown that democratic styles of supervision lead to greater output and job satisfaction. Second, research showed that social relations within groups were important. Third, surveys showed that job satisfaction is related to social factors such as good relations with peers in the group, and that job satisfaction correlates with high productivity.

Do the criticisms made here of the 'human relations school' pose any difficulties for the case made for job enrichment earlier? Are *all* these theories essentially manipulative? What do you think? One moral of this seems to be that researchers must be careful that their values do not dictate their conclusions so that they fail to see what is really there. The same applies to managers and to everyone else too.

3   Can Good Leadership Motivate People to Work Harder?

> God help the country that needs heroes.
>
> > Bertolt Brecht
>
> Grown men do not need leaders.
>
> > H. G. Wells
>
> Leadership as a topic has rather a dated air about it. It smacks of trench warfare and imperial administration. It implies setting one man up above another, raises spectres of elites and privileged classes.
>
> > C. B. Handy
>
> Better to reign in hell than serve in heav'n.
>
> > John Milton

Much is made in the press of certain individuals, top managers or businessmen, whose qualities seem to help their businesses to prosper. Is leadership a motivating force? Charles Handy, who has studied leadership in organizations in depth, describes various approaches to the study of leadership; for example, the 'leadership trait' approach; the 'leadership style' approach and 'best fit' theories.[13] On the trait approach, Handy describes the attempts that have been made to ascertain the ideal traits a good leader should possess – decisiveness, courage, self-assurance, enthusiasm, sociability, integrity, imagination, determination, energy, faith and even virility. However, possession of all or even a few of the desirable traits may be an impossible ideal, and in any case researchers cannot agree on which traits are vital.

The same may be said of the style approach, which asks what style is the most suitable: for example, 'democratic' or 'supportive'? Handy favours a 'best fit' approach, as demonstrated in table 6.1 and explained below.

An example of a good fit would be one in which the task is routine and closely defined, the subordinates do not seek control over their work situation and the leader's style is structured and controlling, as the table shows. Another good fit would be the opposite situation, where the task requires initiative, where the subordinates want autonomy in their work and where the leader should not try to exercise close control. Basically it may be that leadership depends on the situation. The leader should perhaps be seen as a facilitator rather than a director in most situations.

Like most psychological theories of motivation to work, leadership theory mostly ignores people's beliefs, values and ideologies. This is where a sociological view is helpful. Rather than concentrate on what it is about leadership that motivates, this chapter will look deeper, and ask 'what *does* motivate people?'

4   The Motivation to Work: A Sociological View

While psychologists frequently use the concept of 'needs' to investigate the motivation to work, sociologists have often used the idea of

Table 6.1 *The 'best fit' approach*

	Tight	Flexible
Leader	x	
Subordinates	x	
Task	x	

alienation in order to try to see what is happening at work. 'Alienation' is used fairly loosely in everyday conversation: it may be to denote being fed up, put off, bored and so on. To the sociologist though, the term has a special meaning. Two writers will be examined here, Marx and Blauner.

Marx's view of alienation

Marx believed that humans were essentially creative and that people expressed creativity through their work. In so far as this was denied to them they were alienated. Marx saw four aspects of alienation.

- Workers are alienated (or separated) from the product of their labour – they have no control over their fate.
- Workers are alienated from the act of production. The work offers no intrinsic satisfaction; they only work for the money; they only work because they have to. Marx called this the 'cash nexus'. This depersonalizes employment arrangements by converting everything to money.
- Because of the 'cash nexus' workers are alienated from their own true nature.
- Workers are alienated from each other. People are judged by their position in the market rather than by their human qualities.

In brief then, Marx's view is that people express themselves through their work, and in so far as their labour is merely a commodity to be bought and sold by the hour then they are 'alienated', that is to say separated from their true selves.

Blauner's view of alienation

The other view of alienation, that of Robert Blauner, distinguishes four dimensions to alienation: powerlessness; meaninglessness; isolation; self-estrangement.[14]

- *Powerlessness* People are powerless when they become objects for other people and cannot assert themselves or change their condition.
- *Meaninglessness* Here the individual's acts bear no relationship to a broader life programme. Much routine work in factories and offices would fit this category.
- *Isolation* A feeling of not being *of* society, a sense of remoteness from the larger social order and an absence of group loyalty – not really belonging.

- *Self-estrangement* Activity is not self-expressive and self-actualizing, the person is not using his or her full potential. There is a separation between work life and other concerns. Work does not contribute to a personal identity.

Having defined alienation, Blauner then asks which technology is the most alienating – but this may be his mistake. Has he mixed the social arrangements around the use of technology with the effects of the technology itself? He suggests that there is a relationship between alienation and technology which differs between different types of labour process, as figure 6.3 depicts. He sees alienation as least in the craft technologies, at a maximum in assembly-line work, and in between in the continuous process technology of the oil refinery, chemical works and fertilizer factory. These findings are partly based on Blauner's analysis of statistics showing the proportion of skilled workers in the respective categories, labour turnover, the proportion of workers expressing satisfaction with their job, and so on.

It will be seen then that Marx and Blauner have in practice quite different views of alienation. For Marx, it is *social* conditions, particularly the social conditions at work, that are important, rather than the technology used at work. For Blauner it is the technology at work that is the important determinant of alienation. He believed that automation at work would lessen alienation, as figure 6.3 hints (automation involving continuous process technology, that is).

The following study compares these two different views of alienation. It tends to take a Marxist approach, but readers should be able to give different viewpoints.

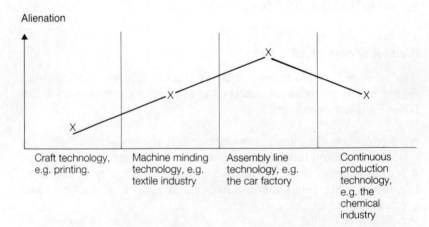

Figure *6.3 Alienation and technology according to Blauner*

Source: R. Blauner, *Alienation and Freedom* (University of Chicago Press, Chicago, 1964).

Alienation – a case study

Two researchers looked at a company where an 'enlightened management' was attempting to raise productivity, and studied the workforce's view of these attempts. The younger executives were keen to involve workers more, in line with Herzberg's theories. The factories produced chemicals and fertilizers, the sort of technology which, according to Blauner, is not the most alienating. In fact the researchers found a lot of disillusionment at the works.[15]

Much of the manual work was repetitive, boring, dirty and heavy. Management introduced job rotation. This meant that instead of loading *or* packing *or* sealing chemicals for the whole of an eight-hour shift, the men were permitted to work as a team, going from loading to packing to sealing. The men felt that the shift passed quicker, but they said that no man could load for eight hours solid anyway. To quote the authors: '"Rotation" then is necessary for survival, is part of the flexibility modern management want, but it did nothing for involvement. It does not make them feel involved in their work.' They then quote one worker whose views seem to summarize the position quite well. 'You move from one boring dirty monotonous job and then to another boring dirty monotonous job. And somehow you are supposed to come out of it all "enriched". But I never feel "enriched" – I just feel knackered.'[16]

Turning from the 'donkey' work to the technical work, it was found that much of this work was considered boring too. 'To be left alone in charge of millions of pounds of capital that could blow up in your hands involves a strain. "It is no game, being left alone with your thoughts and the noise of the plant", said one white-coated worker.'

There are many other frustrations for everyone – including the disruptions of shift work, job insecurity, a feeling of being trapped in the job because of the basic need for a job, any job. It is not the technology that causes the alienation at work. Rather it is the social arrangements for the work. As the authors put it:

This system, whatever the management 'style', and whether particular managers are good blokes 'personally' or not, was based on class relationships. Grasp these central facts and a lot of things being to fall into place – why men waste the product, why their lives are wasted, why managers play childish games, why they think 'their' workers 'childish', why though they sometimes say they want 'participation', they do not really want it, why some 'progressive' companies favour a policy of union incorporation, why, even for management, this is not enough, why it is that at Riverside's particular 'modern factory' there are so many respects in which everything remains essentially the same. And this despite ChemCo's 'change programme without parallel in British industry'.[17]

The alternatives to alienation

We tend to think that the work organization is designed for the highest productivity all round. Surely this is sensible. It leads to higher wages as well as higher profits. Some have argued, though (as mentioned before) that the origin and success of the factory lay not in its technical superiority but more in the fact that the factory owner rather than the worker could control the work process, the quality of output and so on.[18] Is this still true today? The persistence of Taylor's ideas and the resistance to workplace democracy suggest it may be. This in turn may help to explain why it is so difficult to enrich some jobs, particularly manual work, despite management's best efforts. Whatever one's political view is, these writers help to show why so many management initiatives to involve workers are ineffective.

Question

Do you accept this view? What (if anything) can be done by managers to lessen alienation within commercial firms?

Supposing it were accepted that the roots of alienation lie not so much in the technology employed but rather in the social system as a whole, what could be done? One answer may be more self-employment. Another possible solution to the sort of problems described in this section is the formation of workers' co-operatives – producer rather than retail co-operatives. Basically, each worker – each co-operator – holds a share in the equity of this venture. If they leave they must surrender their share. They are not allowed to own too large a proportion of the co-operative (otherwise it will be little different from the usual commercial firm). In effect co-operators are their own bosses. They run the enterprise, plan future policy and work for the enterprise. Labour hires the capital and not vice versa, as is the usual position. The co-operators can even employ their own manager. Even though the work itself may sometimes be boring, it may not be alienating because of the social circumstances under which it is done. In other words, those aspects of alienation described here – powerlessness, meaninglessness, isolation and self-estrangement are absent. It is not the technology which is the key factor affecting alienation; it is rather the social conditions under which the work is carried out.

There are many difficulties in establishing co-operatives and their history in Britain is not altogether a success story, but 'Co-operation appears to be at home among the new ideas of industrial democracy. Whatever its defects there can be no doubt that the co-operative way of life can do much to bring out the best social instincts in people.'[19] The most successful example of a producer co-operative is the Mondragon group in the Basque province of Spain.[20]

Perhaps what is striking in the British context is the extent to which management accountability, and alternatives to conventional management arrangements, are non-issues. Management is not seen as a social process at all, but rather as an uncontroversial technical function – 'It is just managing.'[21]

Mondragon

In the Mondragon group the worker–members own all the capital. The members must put in a substantive financial stake when they join and they cannot withdraw this until they retire. The co-operatives have minimum and maximum wages; they have their own welfare system. In 1960 there were four co-operatives with a total of 395 members. By 1985 this had risen to 111 co-operatives with 192000 members.

Source: H. Weiner and R. Oakeshott *Worker Owners, Mondragon Revisited* (Anglo-German Foundation London 1987).

---

5 Conclusion

As mentioned in chapter 3, behavioural science is an important component of courses in management schools in Britain and the United States and other developed countries. Why is this, and why is it called 'behavioural science' rather than 'industrial psychology' or 'industrial sociology'?

It is probably called 'behavioural science' because the name suggests that behaviour can be scientifically measured, controlled and modified in the interests of improved productivity. Look at some of the measuring instruments that a personnel officer could use:

- IQ tests;
- job evaluation;
- job analysis;
- work study;
- aptitude tests;
- attitude scales;
- sickness rates;
- absenteeism rates;
- turnover rates.

The aims of these various tests and measures seem self-evident; for example the success of a new shift system could be measured in terms of absenteeism and productivity. At a more abstract level, behavioural scientists use the concept of needs as their main analytical tool.

What needs does the individual possess? What are the needs of the organization? How can these two sets of needs be brought together? This theme can be seen in the writings of Mayo, Herzberg and Argyris outlined above, and in the rationale behind job enlargement, job rotation and job enrichment.

The approach of the sociologist to the question of morale and productivity in organizations is rather different, and may be summarized as follows.

- Most sociologists would not like to be labelled 'behavioural scientists' – it is too deterministic because, as mentioned, it implies behaviour can be controlled and measured.
- Sociologists prefer to try to understand what is really going on in an organization rather than primarily ascertain ways of raising output. For example, they may ask workers why they appear to be dissatisfied rather than how they can be motivated to produce more.
- Sociologists are as much concerned with what goes on outside the organization as inside; for example, analysing class-bound attitudes to work such as instrumentalism – the tendency of some workers, in this case 'affluent', semi-skilled workers, to work just for the money.[22]
- Some sociologists see organization theory as highly ideological, for example the work of Taylor and Mayo (as explained here). These ideologies tend to support managerial control. Sociologists' work leads them to the view that social arrangements for work that it is the root cause of alienation at work (and this keeps production levels down and costs up).
- Many sociologists question the concept of 'needs' as used by psychologists. While basic needs may be physiological in part, higher order needs are probably related to the culture to which the individual belongs.[23]

Of course, this does not mean that individual managers can do nothing until they have changed society. Rather it is important to be aware of what really limits work satisfaction and productivity (and a full life generally). Perhaps a helpful way to conclude this chapter would be to tabulate the non-sociological and sociological approaches to work motivation and productivity.

Non-sociological views of the motivation to work	*A sociological assessment*
• We need work to give ourselves a sense of fulfilment. Work satisfies our *higher needs* and gives us our self-esteem and our sense of identity and belonging. Work gives us a place, a role in society.	While most sociologists would acknowledge that there are basic physiological needs, whose satisfaction may be instinctive, they might argue that there is no intrinsic higher need. Instead they would argue that the need to work is a cultural (not biological) thing. It varies from culture to culture, as Max Weber showed in *The Protestant Ethic and the Spirit of Capitalism.*
• Management can and should enrich jobs, and allow greater participation and greater autonomy and work.	Many routine jobs cannot be enriched, but even if they could management often wants to retain control. Factories were originally set up not for reasons of technology or technical efficiency but rather to exercise greater control over a workforce.[24] This same desire to control, coupled with a lack of enthusiasm in the work by many employees, is rife in today's factory and office.
• Work can be made less alienating by changing the way the technology is used. For example, in Sweden some car assembly workers have been making the whole car rather than fitting parts as it proceeds along an assembly line. Many writers have sought to show a link between technology and alienation (or motivation) at work.	Sociologists try to show a link between alienation and the social arrangements at work. The key questions here are: • how much control over the work do employees have, and how much are they in fact controlled by management? • are they able to express themselves through their work or do they merely sell their labour by the hour as if it were like any other commodity?

- do workers (in factory or office) work just for the money?

Two further points worth considering are whether a person doing routine work in their own business or co-operative is less alienated than someone doing skilled work as a weekly paid employee? Secondly, will the new information technology (IT), with its control over the storage and transfer of information, take some of the chore out of some routine clerical work (like that of the ledger clerk), while, because IT also centralizes information resulting in greater central control at work and more 'alienation' in the sense that Marx uses the term?

- Mayo and others of the human relations school show that people like to work in groups. They like co-operating, and inter-group rivalry results in higher output. The model used is that of the social person (rather than the cumulative economic person used by scientific management (see chapter 3)). Groups establish group work norms.

The human relations approach and particularly the work of Mayo himself has been seriously criticized. Workers' main interest was in the money. Friendlier supervision was not leading to higher output (though the opposite might be true!). Mayo himself wished to promote co-operation at work, but his ideals and values might have influenced and perhaps distorted his findings. A basic objection to the human relations approach is that it involves manipulating employees for the purpose of raising productivity.

- Instead of constantly criticizing, sociologists should help managers in their difficult job of raising productivity and motivating

One of the main tasks of the sociologist is to show what is really going on in the workplace, and this means highlighting hidden discontent people to work, increasing job satisfaction and (eventually) promoting co-operation at work and the participation of all concerned.

(that management may prefer to remain hidden). Often sociologists show there is too much control at work, a lot of manipulation of lower-level workers, and a lack of genuine trust of these workers (who in turn lack trust in management). They find that the *whole system* works against co-operation and trust. What else can sociologists do?

Exercises

Self-examination questions

What is meant by:

- job enrichment
- co-operatives
- horizontal loading
- 'needs'
- hygiene factors
- motivator factors

- behavioural science
- aptitude tests
- human relations school
- deterministic
- leadership?

Essay or discussion questions

1 Discuss the view that sociology does not help managers in their work; it merely criticizes and undermines what they are trying to achieve.
2(a) Evaluate Herzberg's theory of job enrichment. What criticisms might a sociologist make of Herzberg's work?
(b) You are a personnel director in a firm of wholesalers dealing in a wide range of household goods. Recently sales have been falling. After careful consideration your Board feels the problem lies not with the products but with the staff, particularly the sales staff. You have been given the task of investigating this. Your preliminary enquiries reveal that the sales force is indeed demoralized, and it is not just a question of money. Sales people are not allowed to deal with customers' complaints, or make refunds, or deal with credit requests. These matters are dealt with by head office, and this gives rise to frustration on all sides. You feel this is a case where Herzberg's theory on the motivation to work may be applicable.

What enquiries would you make and what advice would you give to your Board? (Assume any further information necessary to answer this question, so long as it is not inconsistent with the factors already given.)

Set out your answer in the form of a report to the Board, including recommendations.

Suggestions: See how the job can be cleaned up first – deal with the 'hygiene' factors. Is the pay enough? Are working conditions good?, etc. Then deal with 'motivator' factors.

3(a) Critically assess the contribution of Elton Mayo's Hawthorne experiments to our knowledge of groups at work. How might the experiments be improved? How might they be made more interesting for the sociologist? (Use the summary in the book by Pugh et al. in the Further Reading list.)

(b) A large bank with headquarters in central London has a typing pool of forty shorthand-typists together with one supervisor and four assistant supervisors. The offices were built at a time when open-plan offices were in vogue.

A request for a typist goes through the supervisor or an assistant supervisor who then selects a typist who is free. Having typed the work the typist hands it in to the supervisor, who corrects it. The typist then awaits the next call.

What improvements would you suggest here? Support your views with the aid of the insights you have gained in this chapter, for example about work groups setting their own output norms.

4 Consider the following passage and assess its virtues and shortcomings as a theory of leadership.

One of the prime causes of the fury that crops up again and again in large organizations is leadership that does not listen. The decision to go ahead with a product without talking to the production manager, fixing the price without talking to the sales force, abandoning a development project without reference to the department doing the work on it – these are happening all the time and arouse emotions which have nothing to do with reason, logic or consideration of the facts. In cool retrospect many years later, I can see that my fury was often aroused by a decision which was substantially correct. I can think of other cases when I accepted an unpleasant decision philosophically because I had said my say, heard other people say theirs, and realized that the decision even if wrong had been reached in the light of all the available emotions and suggestions and information. It is the demand to be heard before the decision is taken which has operated in favour of survival, and the willingness to listen first and decide afterwards which has sorted out the successful leaders from the unsuccessful.

Most boards of directors and committees of executives understand two principles of group decision-making – listening before deciding, and building up a store of folk-wisdom by constant reviewing of causes and effects. What they seem to realize less often is the need for it, and the value of it, all the way down the organisation. The subject-matter may be different, but the process is the same. On the factory floor it will not be long-term expansion plans that people want consultation on: it will be design of parts, control of work flow, siting of machines, advance information of workload, as well as pay and conditions and holidays; and many factories are repositories of much ancient wisdom in these matters, as well as in ignoring instructions, concealing facts and thwarting the objectives of management. In the same way the sales force, the office staff, the transport staff and indeed every group in the corporation have these needs. (from A. Jay, *The Corporation Man* (Jonathan Cape, London, 1972), pp. 92–3)

Suggestions: Consult sections in this book on leadership, participation at work, and communications in organizations. If possible enrich your essay or report with actual examples from your own experience or from items currently or recently in the news.

Case study 1

As a labour relations consultant you have been asked by the Board of Novelties Limited to advise them on a number of employee relationship problems. The firm retails a wide variety of stationery, books, records and tapes and home computers. Recently sales of video cassettes of films, comedies and children's programmes have risen sharply. The firm has thirty branches throughout the country and a large headquarters store in central London. Despite a healthy market the firm has serious labour problems including lateness, absenteeism, pilferage by staff, and a high labour turnover. All these problems are worse in central London where it is most difficult to recruit staff.

Further investigation confirms that many of the staff work without enthusiasm. In the past schemes to motivate the staff (including 'job enrichment') have failed.

You feel that some of the blame at least lies with the branch managers who seem a bit 'heavy handed'; in particular, supervision is too close.

What might be wrong here? What would you suggest? What more information would you need to assess the situation?

Case study 2: Women on the line

Read the passage and attempt the questions that follow.

A tray took about twenty minutes to travel from the beginning of the line to the end. During that time, fifteen of us transformed two small basic mechanisms into complete UMOs (unidentified metal objects) ready to be put in a vehicle. The pressure to churn out hundreds of them was constant; it ensured a high level of production for the firm but it certainly took its toll on us. At the end of the day we were all 'jaded', but which limbs ached most depended on the particular job you'd been doing. The 'build up', modules, calibrating and all the checking jobs were hard on the eyes – concentrating so hard all the time and focusing on small holes and objects made your head buzz. Casing up, transistors, covers and packing were heavy work; in the one minute allowed for each UMO you were moving all the time – lifting boxes, changing over trays, throwing away bags and cases as well as doing the actual assembling. Unless you were well organised and knew exactly in which order to do the different movements, the work would get on top of you and you'd be up the wall with no chance of sorting yourself out. But however well you were organised and could keep up with the line, the speed and the amount of work tired you out. The jobs between calibrating and electrical checking were the central ones, controlled by the light; you felt part of a chain and had more contact with the other women. It was like being one large collective worker. Although we were more dominated by the light than the jobs at the front and back of the line we could also enjoy breakdowns more fully. We had nothing 'to be getting on with', like building up more basic mechanisms or assembling diodes, so if the line stopped we had a rest.

Differences between the jobs were minor in comparison with the speed and discipline which the line imposed on us all. We couldn't do the things you would normally not think twice about, like blowing your nose or flicking hair out of your eyes; that cost valuable seconds – it wasn't included in the layout so no time was allowed for it. In any case, your hands were usually full. We all found the repetition hard to take; once you were in command of your job, repeating the same operations over and over thousands of times a day made you even more aware of being controlled by the line. You couldn't take a break or swap with someone else for a change – you just had to carry on; resisting the light or the speed only made the work harder because the trays kept coming and eventually you would have to work your way through the pile-up. If you really couldn't keep up with the line, you were out. (from R. Cavendish, *Women on the Line* (Routledge and Kegan Paul, London, 1982), pp. 15–27, 40–1)

1   What is really wrong with this job?
2   As personnel officer what would you do improve the job?
3   What are the limits to what you could do?

Further Reading

P. D. Anthony, *The Ideology of Work* (Tavistock, London, 1977).

M. Argyle, *The Social Psychology of Work* (Penguin, Harmondsworth, 1974).

P. Cressey, J. Eldridge and J. MacInnes, *Just Managing: Authority and Democracy in Industry* (Open University Press, Milton Keynes, 1985).

A. Fox, *Man Mismanagement* (Hutchinson, London, 1985).

C. B. Handy, *Understanding Organisations* (Penguin, Harmondsworth, 1985) (for description of theories on leadership and on group behaviour).

F. Herzberg et al., *The Motivation to Work* (Staples Press, London, 1968).

J. E. Kelly, *Scientific Management, Job Redesign and Work Performance* (Academic Press, London, 1982).

P. McNeill, *Research Methods* (Tavistock, London, 1985).

D. S. Pugh, D. J. Hickson and C. R. Hinings (eds), *Writers on Organisation* (Penguin, Harmondsworth, 1983) (for short accounts of the work of Mayo, Herzberg, McGregor, Argyris and others).

D. S. Pugh (ed.), *Organisation Theory* (Penguin, Harmondsworth, 1984) (for extracts from key writers).

F. J. Roethlisberger and W. J. Dickson, *Management and the Worker* (Harvard University Press, Cambridge, Mass., 1967).

M. Rose, *Industrial Behaviour* (Penguin, Harmondsworth, 1985).

G. Salaman, *Class and the Corporation* (Fontana, London, 1981).

D. Silverman, *The Theory of Organisations* (Heinemann, London, 1970).

Notes

1 C. W. Mills, *White Collar* (Oxford University Press, Oxford, 1956).
2 I am indebted to Michael Kelly of Dundee College of Technology for these ideas.

3 A. H. Maslow, *Motivation and Personality* (Harper and Row, London, 1954).
4 F. Herzberg et al., *The Motivation to Work* (Wiley, New York, 1959), pp. 25–6.
5 A. Fox, *Man Mismanagement* (Hutchinson, London, 1985), p. 60.
6 D. McGregor, *The Human Side of the Enterprise* (McGraw Hill, London, 1960).
7 C. Argyris, *Integrating the Individual and the Organisation* (Wiley, London, 1964), pp. 32–3.
8 See D. S. Pugh et al., *Writers on Organisation* (Penguin, Harmondsworth, 1983), pp. 160–3 for an account of Mayo's work.
9 J. Child comments in S. R. Parker and M. A. Smith, *The Sociology of Industry* (Allen and Unwin, London, 1981), ch. 8, that the Hawthorne experiments have probably been more often discussed than any other piece of industrial research in Western society.
10 A. Carey, 'The Hawthorne Studies: A Radical Criticism', *American Sociological Review*, 1967.
11 E. Mayo, *The Human Problems in an Industrial Civilisation* (Macmillan, London, 1933), p. 159.
12 M. Argyle, *The Social Psychology of Work* (Penguin, Harmondsworth, 1974), pp. 187–9.
13 This section is based on C. Handy, *Understanding Organisations* (Penguin, Harmondsworth, 1985).
14 R. Blauner, *Alienation and Freedom* (University of Chicago Press, London, 1964), p. 32. Blauner acknowledges his debt for these ideas to M. Seeman, *American Sociological Review*, 1959.
15 T. Nichols and H. Beynon, *Living with Capitalism* (Routledge and Kegan Paul, London, 1977).
16 Ibid., p. 16. For criticisms of Blauner and Horton, see *British Journal of Sociology*, 1964.
17 Ibid., p. 204.
18 S. A. Marglin, 'What do Bosses Do?' in A. Gorz (ed.), *The Division of Labour* (Harvester Press, Hassocks, 1976).
19 J. Thornley, *Workers Co-operatives, Jobs and Dreams* (Heinemann, London, 1981), p. 178.
20 M. Poole, *Towards a New Industrial Worker: Participation in Industry* (Routledge and Kegan Paul, 1986), pp. 100–3.
21 P. Cressey, J. Eldridge and J. MacInnes, *Just Managing: Authority and Democracy in Industry* (Open University Press, Milton Keynes, 1985).
22 J. Goldthorpe et al., *The Affluent Worker: Industrial Attitudes and Behaviour* (Cambridge University Press, Cambridge, 1969).
23 D. Silverman, *The Theory of Organisations* (Heinemann, London, 1970), p. 77.
24 Marglin, 'What Do Bosses Do?'; E. P. Thompson, 'Time, Work-discipline and Industrial Capitalism', *Past and Present*, 36 (1967), 56–97.

7 Prejudice at Work: Sexism and Racism

1 Introduction

This chapter seeks to show briefly that there is widespread inequality at work – between men and women, and whites and blacks (differences between classes have already been discussed). In both cases, there has been legislation in the UK outlawing discrimination in employment, yet in terms of the unemployment figures and relative wages, women and blacks are still disadvantaged. The chapter aims to indicate some of the reasons for such inequalities (such as the ideologies of racism and sexism). It then poses the question: what can the manager do?

Why does inequality persist at work? How do some kinds of work get labelled as 'men's work' or 'women's work'? Why are so few women in top careers? Why do we have such strong expectations about women's roles at home and at work (to be a good housewife and a docile employee)? Do men also have roles laid down for them? Why do black people get the worst jobs? How do prejudices become institutionalized?

2 Women at Work

What jobs will women do?

Women can do any job now done by a man, except perhaps some requiring great physical strength. But if that is the case, why are so few women in top jobs? Here it may be useful to distinguish between *sex* and *gender*. 'Sex' refers to the obvious biological differences between men and women. The term 'gender' is used by sociologists to denote the *roles* played by women and men. These roles are *learned*,

not innate, for example the role of wife and mother, nurse and so
on. Women and men are socialized to take on a particular role.
Because these roles are learned they can be modified or changed
completely. It is important to remember that men's role too are the
result of socialization. For example, male aggression may not be an
innate characteristic – it is learnt.

The roles that women and men play vary from society to society;
from culture to culture. Culture here can be seen as incorporating
the widespread beliefs about women and men and their respective
places in that society. In Western society:

- Women are ascribed specific 'feminine' personalities and a gender
  identity. In other words, culture says more or less what a woman
  is to be. (So it does of men, of course.)
- Women are often excluded from public life and relegated to the
  home.
- Women are allocated the more menial work.
- Women are stereotyped – and seen as dependent on men.[1]

If the culture lays down what a woman's role is, it also lays down
what is women's work; thus because you are of a certain sex you
have certain tasks to perform.

We all have assumptions about what are men's jobs and what are
women's. These have been classified by their qualities by C. Aldred.

Men's work	Women's work
Dirty	Needs ability to concentrate on monotonous work
Requires physical strength	Requires dexterity
Involves night work	Uses domestic skills
Technical skill	Semi-skilled only

But, she then asks, does this sort of classification really work? Is
driving a lorry any more dirty than driving a van – is it any heavier?
No! If we look deeper into our assumptions, we may find that the
key factor in defining women's work is that it is lower-paid. But what
came first, the low pay or the kind of job? Take typewriting as an
example. In its early days it was considered a man's work and highly
skilled – and well paid. Now it is regarded as women's work and
poorly paid and not very skilled. Others jobs have also 'changed sex'.
Computer work was formerly a woman's job, but as this expanded
it came to be regarded as men's work and was paid better. In some
fishing areas filleting is regarded as men's work (and is therefore

better paid). In other ports it is regarded as women's work, and wages are lower.

Why do women do 'women's work'? Various reasons (beliefs) have been put forward.[2]

- tradition
- the belief that certain jobs are more suitable either for women or for men;
- employers prefer women or men for particular kinds of work;
- women or men are the only ones prepared to work at certain jobs;
- women are prepared to work for lower wages than men;
- women are not interested in a career or promotion prospects;
- women don't really want skilled or responsible jobs because they know they will have to give up to have children;
- our education and training systems make boys and girls go into different jobs;
- women work in those jobs which fit in with domestic responsibilities.

Can you think of any other reasons? Which reasons do you think help to make sense of the situation? Do they make sense of the examples – typing, computer work and filleting fish?

Aldred concludes that in looking at such examples we must decide first if the skills women use at work are being given proper recognition, and secondly if the women concerned have the trade union strength to be able to fight for the improved pay and conditions that go with the skilled status.[3]

Table 7.1 shows the proportion of women in the higher professions.

Some more facts about women and employment

More than half the population of Britain is female, yet only two-fifths of the workforce is female. In 1984, 15.5 million men and 10.9 million women had jobs; 1.1 million more than in 1975 (despite an *overall* increase in unemployment) but most of these women workers were part-timers. Women are more likely to be in temporary, seasonal or casual jobs than men. Only a quarter of women with children under four were at work.[4]

Women are concentrated in 'caring' occupations such as nursing, social work and domestic work or cleaning. This is seen as more 'natural' because of their association with caring in families, yet it limits women who are capable of and might enjoy work that is seen as more masculine.

Table 7.1 *Female membership of selected professional institutes/ associations, 1985*

Professional institute	Women members (%)
Hotel, Catering and Institutional Management Association	48.3
Institute of Personnel Management	37.8
Institute of Health Service Administrators	37.4
British Medical Association	24.8
Institute of Bankers	16.5
Royal Town Planning Institute	13.5
Chartered Insurance Institute	12.6
The Law Society (solicitors)	12.2
The Rating and Valuation Association	7.1
Institute of Chartered Accountants of England and Wales	6.5
Institute of Marketing	5.0
Institute of Chemical Engineers	4.3
Royal Institute of Chartered Surveyors	3.3
British Institute of Management	2.5
Institute of Mechanical Engineers	0.7
Institute of Production Engineers	0.7
Chartered Institute of Building	0.6

Source: Equal Opportunities Commission, *Women and Men in Britain* (1986), p. 37.

Question

What do you think table 7.1 highlights? What is women's work?

Why are women still unequal at work?

Personnel officers interested in developing the full potential of their staff may see the underachievement of women at work as a waste, both for the women themselves and for the employing organization. Why has there been so little success in combating sexual inequality at work?

Sociologists seeking to answer this type of question may use two concepts in particular. First, there is the ideology of sexism, concentrating on the person's sex rather than seeing her as a whole person. Second, there is the concept of socialization to the female gender role, a role handed on from mother and daughter and confirmed by the rest of society, fathers, friends and teachers. Women, once socialized, do not expect to achieve much in the world of work. Figure 7.1 seeks to chart these processes.

As mentioned, women may have a low view of themselves and their work as a result of earlier socialization (upbringing) in the home and school. Thus they do not apply for higher jobs, or undertake training for them. Of course, many other 'explanations' (excuses) for the low status accorded to women and their work are put forward. The most common one is that women bear children. It is assumed that therefore they must be the ones who stay at home to take care of them, or cannot take a very responsible job because they have too much to do in looking after them. Many prejudices about women at work relate to this question. If a woman applying for a job is not married, the employer may wonder if she might get married (and leave); if she is married, the employer wonders if she will have

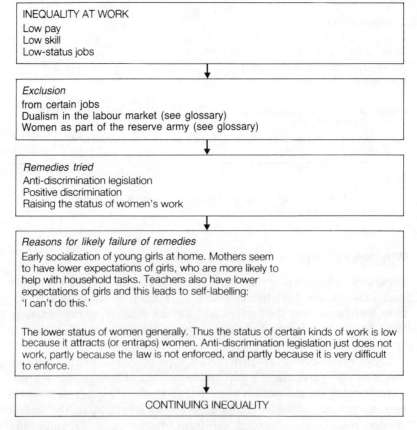

Figure 7.1 *Reasons for continuing inequality at work*

children (and leave or take long maternity leave). But is the problem actually with the women, or with the social arrangements for work and child-care which surround us?

We know from the example of the Scandinavian countries that where crèche facilities are provided, where allowance is made for interruptions in women's careers for child-bearing, where fathers are allowed paternity leave, the labour market adjusts.

Question

Is the idea that women must take the larger share of responsibility for children an ideology?

The status of women and expectations about the kinds of work they do do sometimes change. A film called *Lives and Times of Rosie the Riveter* shows women doing allegedly 'male' jobs alongside men in the shipyards in war-time America. But after the war such women were expected to resume the conventional female role of doing the housework and swapping recipes which took all day to prepare. Women could do 'men's work' when the men were away fighting, but not once they had returned!

Why do so few women attain top positions in management and the professions?

What are the obstacles in the way of women aspiring to the board? Two researchers investigated a large insurance company. The manager, as an ex-salesperson himself, had internalized the middle-class male values associated with selling, and consequently tended to reproduce job segregation and therefore discrimination against women. One danger of this sort of segregation is that what would normally be seen as a problem of controlling subordinates is interpreted as the difficulties *women* present in the running of a successful enterprise. The women clerks at the receiving end of such ideas (or ideologies) responded by showing discontent, which the manager saw as confirming his original beliefs. When there is no experience of women performing managerial or even sales roles, these tasks are already pre-defined as *male* – promoting a woman is seen as a risky business.[5]

The researchers concluded that the segregation of jobs is based on gender. Identity comes to be based on this segregation ('the institutionalisation of gendered job segregation'). The authors avoid blaming the manager for sexual prejudice. Rather, gendered job segregation reflects *patriarchy* (the rule of the male) both in the organization and in the wider society.

Some of the problems facing women trying to succeed in management may be set out as follows.

- The number of women in top jobs has not really increased in recent years. This in itself is an obstacle since there is still little experience of women in higher management.
- Although recruitment of women for potentially managerial posts is widening, discrimination often occurs after the 'entry gate'. Thus women graduates may be taken on, but tend not to be promoted as far or as fast as male graduates.
- The major problem seems to be progress in mid-career. Here there seems to be indirect discrimination because of the fact that women bear children, and still take most of the reponsibility for their care. Problems occur in inflexibility of working time, lack of procedures for reinstatement and progression after a career break, stereotyped ideas of the 'right' age for promotion, lack of child-care facilities and so on.
- There has been a general lack of momentum towards equal opportunities at work. A relaunch of the campaign is needed, involving trade unions, women's groups and the Equal Opportunities Commission.[6]

Summary

The following list may help to clarify some of the points covered in this chapter so far.

Commonly held views

- More women are working away from home. This must surely widen horizons.

- Paid work brings independence and will eventually bring equality with men.

Likely reality

Most women still see their main job as caring for the home and family.

Much of the work women do is poorly paid and not much more exciting than housework.
There is little evidence of increasing equality. Women's wages are about two-thirds of men's. The 1981 census showed women workers concentrated in three main areas:

Clerical work	33%
Service sector jobs	23%

Semi-professional jobs (mainly teaching, nursing and social work)   14%

Even where women are in the same occupation, such as teaching, it is much more likely that men will reach the top posts.

- The Equal Pay Act 1970, the Sex Discrimination Act 1975 and the establishment of the Equal Opportunities Commission should give women a chance to get into higher positions in the long run.

This legislation is difficult to enforce and has not had a major impact.

- The traditional 'housewife' image of women depicted in advertising is disappearing, as more married women enter the labour force.

Married women still have to perform housewife duties, *in addition to* paid work. Also, much of the paid work women do is traditional women's work – cleaning, caring and helping, as the figures quoted above indicate.

- A woman's place is in the home.

Historically this is not true. More women were solely housewives in the late nineteenth and early twentieth centuries than ever before. Before that the whole family may have worked together (see chapter 8).

- In times of unemployment, working women are taking away men's job.

As shown here, there are some jobs that only a woman will do. If women usually only do women's work they cannot be taking jobs away from men. Alternatively, why should jobs be seen as more of a right for men than for women?

Question

Do you agree with the views in the second column? Is there anything you would like to add? What can we do with this knowledge?

What can the manager do?

1 Watch your own thinking and behaviour. Do you expect women to behave differently from men? Do you treat women differently? Do you take differences in behaviour as evidence of inferiority? Would you think a woman who cried in private when the job got her down less capable than a man who didn't? Often women themselves have adopted prejudiced views about their own sex, so this advice applies to women too!

2 Try to ensure a career structure for women working in the organization. Consider employing more part-timers. Be flexible about working hours and maternity leave. If or when a mother returns, consider promoting her to that post she would have reached had she not left temporarily. In large companies, schemes can be set up allowing women to have a break of several years before returning.

3 Strive to enforce equality of pay for men and for women, not just where both are doing the same work, but where work of similar skill level is being done. This is easier said than done, since competitors may well be paying much less to women (perhaps personnel managers, through their Institute, could provide a code of practice).

4 Try to ensure that men and women are spread equally throughout the grading structure.

5 Provide good crèche facilities.

6 Offer training courses aimed particularly at women, such as assertiveness training. Encourage women to take up training opportunities.

Question

What are the chances of these managerial practices working?
Suggestion: Some are easier than others. Look at the obstacles here – particularly the socialization to gender roles described earlier in this chapter.

3   Race and Jobs

Why do blacks get the worst jobs?

The position of blacks (including Asians) in the labour market is in many respects similar to that of women.

- Both groups are discriminated against.
- Both form part of the *reserve army* of the unemployed during a recession. They can be taken on again when the economy improves.
- Both are the victims of *dualism* in the labour market; they tend to work in the poorest-paid jobs of the secondary sector. They work mainly in the *periphery*, rather than the *core*, jobs (see chapter 5).
- In general, both groups form part of an *underclass* because they share the above-mentioned characteristics.
- Legislation against discrimination has proved to be largely ineffective for both blacks and women.

Both groups suffer from the effects of ideologies believed by the dominant group in the population, that is to say *sexism* and *racism*. In both these ideologies the sex of a person, or their race, becomes more important than the person themselves; they are perceived as being of lower status and therefore only fit for the lower-status jobs which are the poorest paid, least secure, least skilled jobs, having poorest career prospects. Because women and blacks fill these jobs, this tends to confirm the assumption that those are the jobs that suit them, so the pattern is reinforced. These arrangements in the labour market are of course to the advantage of the more fortunate and more powerful in society, who keep the best, most rewarded work for themselves. Sexism and racism are ideologies because they are

---

Dual labour markets
The concept of dual labour markets may be useful in alalysing what is really happening. The idea is that an economy consists of at least two sub-labour markets which, though related, do not compete with each other. The *primary labour markets* are where the well-paid jobs are, jobs that offer a good career and the chance to acquire a skill. *Secondary labour markets* offer only low wages, few prospects and lack of job security. It seems that blacks and women are largely confined to secondary labour markets.

distortions of the truth that serve the interests of the powerful, in this case white males.

Some more facts about black people and employment

Black people also suffer higher unemployment than whites, as table 7.3 shows.

- Black people in Britain are twice as likely to be out of work as whites.
- In 1984 their rate of male unemployment reached 20.4 per cent compared with 10.6 per cent among their white counterparts.
- A large proportion of Asian men work for themselves (and their families work with them).
- Many black people can only get semi-skilled or unskilled jobs in engineering and manufacturing industry, the areas most hard hit by job-cuts.
- 29 per cent of West Indians and 28 per cent of Asians have no qualifications, compared with only 17 per cent of whites.[7]

Table 7.2 *The proportions of UK black and white people in different kinds of job, 1983 (percentages)*

Type of work	Asian	West Indian	White
Professional, managerial and capitalist	13	5	19
Unskilled, semi-skilled and manual	40	35	16

Source: Adapted from D. Thomas, 'The Job Bias against Blacks', *New Society*, 1 November 1984, pp. 167–9.

Table 7.3 *Unemployment rates among UK blacks and whites, 1983 (percentages)*

	Men	Women[a]
Asian	20	20
West Indian	25	16
White	13	10

[a] These figures may be too low because many women cannot claim benefit and are not registered as unemployed, though they want work.
Source: as for table 7.2 above.

Of course racial discrimination is an important factor in not getting a job. One survey found that 82 per cent of West Indians thought that employers discriminated racially in recruitment, compared to 59 per cent of Asians and 65 per cent of whites.[8] Another factor is the fact that over 40 per cent of West Indians and 20 per cent of Asians live in inner-city areas, compared with 6 per cent of whites, and these are generally areas of high unemployment.

Black people are more likely to suffer from long-term unemployment. Five per cent of whites are unemployed for more than a year, compared with 13 per cent of blacks.

What are racial prejudice and racial discrimination?

The real nature of racial prejudice and racial discrimination should be recognized. *Prejudice* means a preconceived opinion or bias, normally against a person or group – prejudgement. The victim is then *stereotyped*. How does prejudice arise? Perhaps the most famous research on this was done by Theodor Adorno. He and his colleagues showed that some people have certain character traits which lead them to adopt prejudiced attitudes. The 'authoritarian personality' adheres to and stresses respectability, is submissive to authority, is domineering to subordinates, is pre-occupied with status and hostile to 'outgroupers' in general and to members of different races in particular.[9]

The trouble with prejudice is that it seems to be self-confirming. If black people are forced to take inferior jobs, then seeing them in these jobs confirms the prejudice – this is the only kind of job they can do! This leads to *discrimination* – the active result of prejudice. Because of the interviewer's prejudice a black person does not get the job; this means he or she has been discriminated against. Prejudice and discrimination reinforce each other. Three types of discrimination can be distinguished here.

- *Direct discrimination* – a black person is not offered a job because he or she is black.
- *Indirect discrimination* – for example an employer has devised a test which a black person is likely to fail, and passing the test is not justifiable as a necessity for getting the job.
- *Institutionalized discrimination* – for example a political party dedicated to racial discrimination.

What can the manager do?

1   As with sexism, start with yourself. Know your own prejudices, and don't let them cloud your judgement.
2   Find out the scale of discrimination in the organization. Bear in mind that this may involve a loss to the firm or organization, in that the best people are not being selected for the job, or, if already employed, the black people are not using their full potential in their work. (This applies to women too, of course.)
3   The organization should declare itself an Equal Opportunities Employer. The Confederation of British Industry is supporting this policy, and some 250 organizations have declared themselves to be equal opportunity employers, including the Civil Service, many large local authorities, British Rail, the Post Office, six London clearing banks, Marks and Spencer plc, Littlewoods plc, Mars plc and Ford.[10] A similar picture emerges from the USA. Of course, it must then prove that it *is* open equally to blacks and whites.
4   The organization could adopt ethnic monitoring to determine what percentage of a particular workforce belongs to ethnic minorities and to what extent they are represented at various levels.[11] (Some people, including blacks, might oppose this especially if it led to positive discrimination – deliberately choosing applicants because they are black.)
5   Encourage those whose English is poor to attend language classes (there is a strong correlation between lack of fluency in English and unemployment).[12]

There are some hopeful signs. There is evidence that more personnel officers are taking their anti-discrimination duties seriously. In addition, outside large organizations there has been a rise in the number of small black-owned businesses. Unfortunately high unemployment makes improvement difficult.

Exercises

Self-examination question

What is meant by:

- prejudice
- discrimination
- positive discrimination

- equal opportunities
- gender
- indirect discrimination

- reserve army
- dualism
- underclass

- sexism
- racism

Essay or discussion questions

1   How would you account for continuing sexual inequality at work?
2   Analyse the findings of table 7.4. For example:
    (a) Try to relate the 'female' occupations to the supposed feminine qualities (such as caring and attention to detail).
    (b) Do the same for the 'male' occupations.
    (c) Why do you think people think as they do?
3   What does table 7.5 indicate?
4   What sociological explanation would you offer for the continuing inequality between blacks and whites in the labour market?
5   As personnel director in a large organization, what steps would you take to eradicate racial discrimination at work?
    Suggestion: Consult literature on personnel management and journals such as *The Personnel Manager*. See also D. Thomas, 'The Job Bias Against Blacks', *New Society*, 1 November 1984.
6   Who gains and who loses from racial discrimination?
    Suggestion: No one really gains in the long run and everyone loses. Do you agree?

Case study 1

'Better Print' is a small to medium-sized firm of general printers producing all types of printing, including specialized printing for the top end of the market. It employs 80 people in its print room, including 35 skilled printers. Twenty people are employed in the office, and 12 more on sundry jobs such as salespersons, drivers and storekeepers.

Wendy Smith has been working for the firm for 15 years. She could be described as a career woman, and aims to get on to the Board. She has been acting temporarily as office manager for the past eight months because of the absence through illness of Tom Webster. However, she has not been paid for taking on the extra duty. The personnel officer, Jim Morgan, has now been informed that Tom, who is 59, is going to take early retirement at virtually a full pension, under the company's pension scheme.

At the same time another important change is taking place: the office is to be re-equipped and all records, including accounts, are to be put on to computer. The problem here is that few of the staff have had experience of the latest equipment. Changes will be required in the pattern of work, and in addition there may be some redundancies.

1   Should Wendy Smith be offered the job of office manager?
2   What are the obstacles in her way?
3   How should Jim Morgan deal with this situation in general?

Table 7.4 *British attitudes to women and work (percentages)*

Attitude statements	Agree	Neither agree nor disagree	Disagree
Traditional attitudes to home and work			
A woman's place is in the home.	25	18	57
A husband's job is to earn the money; a wife's job is to look after the home and family.	46	21	33
In times of high unemployment married women should stay at home.	35	16	49
A job is all right, but what most women really want is a home and children.	41	25	34
Women can't combine a career and children.	29	16	55
Most working women with families want jobs with no worries or responsibilities.	49	17	34
Most married women only work for pin money.	20	14	66
Attitudes to the benefits of work to women and family			
If her children are well looked after it's good for a woman to work.	71	17	12
Having a job is the best way for a woman to be an independent person.	67	17	16
A woman and her family will all be happier if she goes out to work.	29	32	39
Other statements			
If a woman takes several years off to look after her children she should expect her career to suffer.	44	20	36

Table 7.4 *British attitudes to women and work (percentages) cont.*

Attitude statements	Agree	Neither agree nor disagree	Disagree
Married women have a right to work if they want to, whatever their family situation.	71	12	17

Base (= 100%): 5,588.
Source: Department of Employment, *Women and Employment* HMSO, London, 1984.

Table 7.5 *The proportions of working women and working men in different kinds of work in the UK (percentages)*

Occupational order	Working women	Working men
Managerial general	—	1
Professionals supporting management	1	6
Professionals in health, education, welfare	13	5
Literary, artistic and sports	1	1
Professionals in engineering and science	1	5
Other managerial	4	12
Clerical	33	6
Selling	9	4
Security	0	2
Catering, cleaning and hairdressing	23	3
Farming and fishing	1	2
Material processing, excluding metal	1	3
Making and repairing, excluding metal	5	6
Metal processing, making, repairing	2	20
Painting, assembling, packing	5	5
Construction and mining	0	6
Transport	1	11
Miscellaneous	0	1

Base (= 100%): 3,354 women; 8,024 men.
Source: *General Household Survey*, 1987.

Case studies 2 and 3

What do these two case studies tell us about the employment of women today, especially at managerial level? Examine the assumptions that appear to be made by parents, colleagues, husbands and children, clients and customers. What are the main obstacles to acceptance and promotion of women at work?

Sarah Blackburn – Area Catering Manager, Head of Food Services

Curriculum vitae

Date of birth	5.11.1954
Marital status	Married
Education	
–1972	Junior/Middle/Upper School to 'O' Level (comprehensive throughout)
1972–73	College of Further Education for Ordinary National Diploma in Business Studies – gained with Distinction
1973–76	University – gained BA in Hotel Management
Career	
1975–6 (6 months)	Industrial Release, 'Swiss Hoteliers Association', spent at hotel in Liestal, Basle, Switzerland
Sept. 1976–Sept. 1977	Graduate Management Trainee for large Limited Hotel Company – involved working in many different hotels throughout the UK (residential)
Sept. 1977–Feb. 1978	Junior Assistant Food and Beverage Manager with same hotel company at tourist spot in the Midlands (residential)
Feb. 1978	Promoted to Assistant Food and Beverage manager at large four-star hotel at tourist spot in the north, with same company (residential)
July 1978 (6 weeks)	Period as Relief General Manager at a small hotel with the same company in a city centre (residential)
Aug.–Dec. 1978	Personnel Manager at a medium-sized hotel with same company, at a tourist spot in the Midlands (residential)
Dec. 1978–Dec. 1979	Food and Beverage/Deputy Hotel Manager at a large Airport Hotel with same company (residential)
Jan. 1980	Appointed Unit Catering Manager in large industrial firm
Sept. 1980–Oct. 1983	Assistant Area Catering Manager with same firm
Oct. 1983–present	Area Catering Manager, Head of Food Services for twelve units (6,000 meals daily, in charge of 140 personnel), same firm.

Family background

I am second of four daughters. My father is a headmaster and my mother a lecturer, so I was brought up with every opportunity to take advantage of the educational system. Indeed, both my parents always encouraged me to make the most of myself and of my future. For instance, at one time I was interested in nursing and my parents obtained details of degrees in nursing which would lead to a more 'rewarding' career.

As it happened, though, 'Hotel and Catering' became my chosen career path. As a teenager I spent a week at a park centre which involved working as a

General Assistant on a cafeteria counter. I really enjoyed the job and enjoyed the social interactions and the variety of work involved. I also felt that if I went to University, I wanted to train for something that had a purpose, so to speak, and that would increase my chances of getting a job at the end!

Undoubtedly, being a woman, the challenge was much greater than it would have been for any male. The expression on some people's faces when I turned up at their request to see the manager was often quite comical! Occasionally, people inferred that as a woman I couldn't possibly do the job of an hotel manager as well as a man, as it involved having to be physically strong. My reply would always be that if the men were doing their jobs properly, then as managers they should not be physically lifting barrels of beer from the cellar but do as I did and get the labourer(s) to do the work. I also pointed out that I was quite capable of changing a beer barrel, although (like many men) I was unable to lift a full one containing 22 gallons.

My present job involves supervising and controlling 12 different catering units. The work involves a lot of travelling and no day is ever the same. I have direct input to policy decisions and I feel most comfortable in this job, having encountered no serious difficulties related to the fact that I am a woman. In fact I was the first female to attend a monthly meeting, and since my appointment two other women have been taken on from outside the firm, at a similar status to mine.

Handling home/work conflicts

I think that it's social attitudes, as well as those held by people I work with, which are the hardest to ignore. These can exert considerable pressure upon you as an individual. For example, many people still like to think you hold the traditional belief that 'a woman's place is in the home'! The way I handle comments such as: 'How does your husband cope when you are away on a course?' is by answering, 'very well; he's been well trained!' I find the best thing is to invite humour without creating conflict.

Another common potential conflict comment involves the reference to the rights and wrongs of being a working wife or mother. The best way I've found for dealing with this is to stress that what is right for you is not necessarily right for another individual and that every case is different. This type of approach doesn't put you in conflict with someone like the Managing Director, for example, whose wife probably gave up work when she had her first baby!

Having been married for some years I can honestly say that I have no home/work conflicts. The household jobs are shared with my husband and we support each other in every way. Actually, any home conflicts are created by OTHER PEOPLE who may think, for example, that I should do all the ironing – which is out of the question, as it is shared.

Advice to other women

Don't squash your own capabilities because those above you don't think you are worth developing and assume that you are not interested in career progression, merely because you are a woman. They are labelling you in accordance with their own beliefs. What is important is what you BELIEVE and WANT.

Always let your employer know if you are interested in promotion. If you don't get it, then move firms. Sometimes just applying for other jobs lets everyone realise you are serious and not just the 'token woman'. You must do whatever you feel is right for you, and don't let people you work with, or family or friends, influence your decisions as far as the type of job you do, your domestic duties, whether you should take maternity leave, and so on.

Maureen Jones – Film Producer – Head of Production

Curriculum vitae

Date of birth	10 August 1953
Education	Kindergarten/Prep School/Grammar School to 'O' Level
May/June 1971	Sixth Form College, 'A' Levels
July 1971–Aug. 1972	Travelled abroad
Sept. 1972–June 1974	Studied at College of Further Education for Diploma in Business Studies, Economics and Marketing

Career

July 1974– Jan. 1980	Worked for advertising agency as writer/producer, rising to position of Creative Director/Producer
March 1980	Joined Film Production Company as Producer
Jan. 1981	Left work to have baby
May 1981	Gave birth to baby boy
March 1982	Returned to work full-time – having in the interim done some freelance work at home
Jan. 1983	Joined present company of Film Producers
Feb. 1984	Appointed Head of Production with Film Production Company

Family background

My father owns a business so I grew up in a 'business' family. I'm the only girl. My five brothers regularly helped in the business during school holidays and there was never any suggestion that I couldn't also be involved. In fact all the men who featured strongly in my childhood – i.e. uncles, family friends and the like – were their own bosses!

The idea of running a business or being my own boss was therefore a very natural aspiration. I was never treated any differently by my father, in a working context, because I was female but I do know that my mother felt there was something 'slightly unfeminine' about a young woman who 'too actively' pursued a business career. Mummy had many friends in professional theatre – that was all right – but business was to her a masculine pursuit.

Work and life profile

The only things I was ever really sure I enjoyed were writing and language, so my first job was with an advertising agency as a junior copywriter. I stayed with the company for five years and was promoted during that time, first to senior copywriter, shortly afterwards to the Board of Directors and finally to Creative Director. Within months of joining the agency I was involved in the production of television work, so I was learning the craft of production almost from the word go. I knew immediately that it was this area of the industry on which I wanted to concentrate and so I worked hard and learned quickly.

My aim now is to be the best producer I can be. I am a woman working in a male-dominated environment but I'm not aware that my being female creates any particular problem. I don't expect any advantages because I'm female nor do I expect any disadvantages! I like being female and I like being feminine but when I'm working surely the fact that my body is a different shape is irrelevant . . . my brain is just as good.

I certainly wouldn't resent any other female producers coming to work for the company and capable, ambitious secretaries would be encouraged by me to seek advancement. I find myself dealing with women more frequently, both as clients and suppliers, as time passes. I must admit I do like working with men. Many of my friends are men and I'm used to working with men – maybe it has something to do with having five brothers.

Handling home/work conflicts

To strike a balance, be good at my job and be a successful wife and mother, can be difficult. For the first few months back at work I fully expected to walk in one evening and hear my son say 'Go away, you don't care for me.' I now realise that it's quality of time and not quantity that counts with children. When I get home I try to be consistent. We talk, play, read stories, sing songs all very much to an established pattern. Sometimes all I want to do is put my feet up and have a drink but that will just have to wait until my son is a little older. On the advice of my brother, who is a child psychiatrist, we have a 'private time' each day. Evening has proved better than morning, and our private time consists of spending about an hour together in his room before my son goes to bed. No-else is allowed to join in at this time – it is strictly a time when he and I can work at our relationship. He calls his bedroom his 'safe place' so this is where the hour is normally spent.

Advice to other women

When you start work, find good teachers and watch and listen to them. Forget that you're female, don't expect favours because you're female, and don't expect to get away with things. Be determined, work hard and pay attention to how you sound and look – in other words behave like any normal young executive.

Postscript

I've never referred to myself as a 'career woman'; it is just a label. I enjoy my home and my family but I also need the stimulation of work to feel that I'm getting as much out of my life as I can. (from M. Davidson, *Reach for the Top* (Piatkus, London, 1985), pp. 161–73.)

Case study 4

What are the problems facing young blacks in the labour market? In the following passage, what do the authors mean when they say 'racial inequality is then a *three dimensional phenomenon*'?

The important point is that these inner areas do not have high unemployment rates BECAUSE so many blacks live there; the rates are high for everyone. It is the areas themselves that have declined. In the outercity areas, unemployment rates are lower, but BLACKS do relatively badly. Therefore, campaigns against racism in recruitment will deliver more to blacks who live or work in areas of the city where employment is POSSIBLE. Moreover, unemployment rates for ethnic minorities are much nearer those of whites when they live in parts of the country that have not been subject to economic decline on the same scale. For example, the unemployment rate for blacks is 11 per cent in East Anglia and

19 per cent in Scotland, but for whites it is 8 per cent and 14 per cent respectively.

These differences are not because racism is more entrenched in London or the West Midlands, but are the result of living and trying to work in areas where the demand for unskilled or semi-skilled labour has been dramatically reduced.

Racial inequality is then a THREE DIMENSIONAL PHENOMENON. In addition to the struggle to overcome racism itself, there is a need to ensure that blacks have the qualifications to get the new jobs, and that they have access to the labour markets in which these jobs are situated. If we are content to try to overcome the effects of racism alone, then Afro-Caribbean and Asian minorities will simply find themselves achieving equal access with impoverished whites to second-class schools, welfare housing and crumbling health and social services. If racism in access to those services were overcome tomorrow, it would still leave Britain's black population on the margins of society and denied an opportunity to participate in the new zones of affluence and success. (from M. Cross, 'The Black Economy', *New Society*, 24 July 1987)

Further Reading

C. Aldred, *Woman and Work* (Pan, London, 1981)

C. Brown, *Black and White Britain: The Third PSI Survey* (Gower, Aldershot, 1985)

E. E. Cashmore and B. Troyna, *Introduction to Race Relations* (Routledge and Kegan Paul, London, 1981)

R. Cavendish, *Women on the Line* (Routledge and Kegan Paul, London, 1982)

S. Delamont, *The Sociology of Women* (Allen and Unwin, London, 1980)

S. Dex, *The Sexual Divisions of Work* (Wheatsheaf, Brighton, 1985)

E. Gamarnikow, D. Morgan, J. Purvis and D. Taylorson (eds), *Gender, Class and Work* (Heinemann, London, 1983)

R. Goffe and R. Scase, *Women in Charge: The Experience of Female Entrepreneurs* (Allen and Unwin, London, 1985)

F. Klug, *Different Worlds: Racism and Discrimination in Britain* (Runnymede Trust, London, 1983)

Ann Newham, *Employment, Unemployment and Black People* (Runnymede Trust, London, 1986)

V. Novarra, *Women's Work, Men's Work: The Ambivalence of Equality* (Boyars, London, 1980)

A. Oakley, *Subject Women* (Martin Robertson, Oxford, 1981)

A. Pilkington, *Race Relations to Britain* (University Tutorial, Slough, 1984)

A. Pollert, *Girls, Wives and Factory Lives* (Macmillan, London, 1981)

TUC, *TUC Workbook on Racism* (London, 1983)

Notes

1 Adapted from 'Stereotypes' in the *Penguin Dictionary of Sociology*, 1984.

2 C. Aldred, *Women and Work* (Pan, London, 1981), pp. 20, 22.

3 Ibid., p. 37.

4 New Society Database: 'Women and Employment', *New Society*, 3 October 1986, p. 44.

5 '"Men Only" Theories and Practices of Job Segregation in Insurance', in D. Knights and H. W. Willmott (eds), *Gender and the Labour Process* (Gower, Aldershot, 1986), p. 150.

6 M. Fogarty, I. Allen and P. Waters, *Women in Top Jobs* (Heinemann, London, 1981).

7 New Society Database, 'Black People and Employment', *New Society*, 17 October 1986, p. 44.

8 D. Smith, *Unemployment and Racial Minorities* (Policy Studies Institute, London, 1981), p. 194.

9 T. Adorno et al., *The Authoritarian Personality* (Harper and Row, New York, 1950).

10 Central Office of Information, *Britain's Ethnic Minorities* (HMSO, London, 1982).

11 Ibid.

12 D. Thomas, 'The Job Bias against Blacks', *New Society*, 1 November 1984.

8 The Changing Occupational Structure

1 Introduction

The 'occupational structure' indicates who is employed to do what. It is constantly changing; a change in demand may cause one occupation to flourish and another to decline. For example, consider the general increase in employment in the motor industry until recently, compared with the decline in employment on the railways. Changes may be the result of an industry's decline, or productivity changes. For example, the number of workers in agriculture is declining, especially in continental Europe, through higher productivity (despite food mountains). This chapter begins by setting out some of the main recent changes in the occupational structure. It then attempts to offer possible sociological explanations for these changes, particularly for unemployment, and the effects of new technology. (The last chapter touched on the effects of the changing occupational structure on women and black people.)

Employment changes

It may be interesting first to consider what sectors of the British economy have declined, and why, and what the consequences will be. Table 8.1 summarizes some of the main changes in the occupational structure. Before reading it, try to identify the changes yourself, and then consider their causes and consequences before proceeding with the rest of the text.

The table shows some of the large-scale changes in the occupational structure of Britain. These include:

- A steady move away from employment in agriculture and other areas of the primary sector such as mining, fishing and forestry.

Table 8.1   *Numbers of people in employment, by industry, in the UK, 1971 and 1985*

A selection of sectors	1971 (thousands)	1985 (thousands)
Agriculture, forestry, fishing	432	338
Energy and water supply industries	797	613
Extraction of minerals and ores other than fuels, manufacture of metal, mineral products and chemicals	1,278	799
Metal goods, engineering and vehicle industries	3,705	2,612
Other manufacturing industries	3,102	2,122
Construction	1,207	970
Distribution, hotels, catering, repairs	3,678	4,470
Transport and communication	1,550	1,304
Banking, finance, insurance, business services, leasing	1,336	1,972
Other services	5,036	6,266
All industries and services	22,121	21,466

Source: Social Trends 1987.

- A reduction in the number of those employed in the manufacturing (or secondary) sector.
- An enlarged service (or tertiary) sector, especially in distribution and finance.

Other noteworthy changes, not seen from the table, are as follows.

- An increase in professionalization – about 15 per cent of the working population are professionals.
- A large increase in white-collar work.
- A decrease in trade union membership, which reflects the changing occupational structure. The exception to this trend is the increase in the membership of white-collar unions.
- The ageing of the workforce.
- An increase in married women at work.
- Increasing unemployment, partly as a result of changes in the occupational structure.
- Increasing concentration; that is to say the larger firms are getting larger. This trend has slackened in recent years, while at the other end the number of small businesses has increased.

- The taking up of new technology, resulting in an increase in 'sunrise' industries. At the same time many traditional ('smoke stack') industries, such as steel-making, coal-mining and shipbuilding, have declined.
- A rise in employment in the public sector in the long term (though this rise has slowed down in recent years).

A few further points on the economy and employment can be made. First, even though the British economy is now employing more people this is not yet enough to reduce unemployment to an acceptable level.[1] Secondly, the apparent increase in the employed labour force is a product of rising employment in services (for example, cleaners and waiters).[2] Thirdly, many of those who have recently obtained jobs are female part-timers previously unregistered as employed or unemployed.

The theme throughout this chapter is that appearances are deceptive: that for example unemployment may have a different meaning for the unemployed person than for the employed; that new technology may be the result of, rather than the cause of, changes in society; that there are subtle and hidden social factors preventing sexual and racial equality in the labour market. The sociologist must always look behind appearances; try to explain the inexplicable and to question the obvious.

More facts about the future of work

- By 1986 non-manual jobs grew from 43 per cent to 54 per cent of all jobs; i.e. there are now more white-collar jobs than blue-collar (manual) jobs for men and women.
- Roughly one in ten of the workforce is now self-employed, the highest figure since 1921.
- There has been a large increase in flexible working (i.e. not set hours every day).
- There has been a large increase in the *grey economy*. The grey economy includes housework, voluntary work and DIY. The *black economy* covers work done for cash to avoid tax.

Source: Social Trends 1988 (adapted), *New Society* 25 July 1986.

The changing nature of work

Some of our views about the social nature of work, employment and unemployment have been challenged by sociological research. Ray

Pahl, for example, suggests that the nature of work has changed in the past and will do so again.[3] For example, in the eighteenth century most working women worked in agriculture; by the mid-nineteenth century they were overwhelmingly in domestic service. We are now experiencing a fall in demand for waged workers, especially manual workers, but Pahl argues that there is no sign of a 'collapse of work'. The notion that people should want to be waged labourers shows a failure to recognize the importance of other kinds of work.[4] As mentioned before, work discipline had to be especially instituted in the mills and factories of the eighteenth and nineteenth centuries.[5] Until that time many wage labourers were considered outcasts, likely to be conscripted into the army or navy. Nowadays, we have a one-sided emphasis on employment and on the individual wage-earner, rather than considering the household as a unit in which work (paid and unpaid) and income are organized to look after the interests of the household.[6] Overall, the following changes may be taking place.[7]

- There seems to be a shift from production to consumption in determining consciousness, resulting in a more home-centred family. For many people, it has been argued, 'real life' begins outside work. Work is becoming a 'temporary occupation by which individuals acquire the possibility of pursuing their main activities'.[8]
- Centralization has been reversed by micro-technology and auto-mation as much as by the recognition of the evils of bureaucrati-zation.[9]
- Industry is becoming more capital-intensive, leading to more job losses and a weakening of the unions.

Pahl believes that English individualism and the tendency to provide for themselves (self-provisioning) will re-assert themselves, based on a tradition of radical independence.[10]

One view of the economy would be to see recessions as temporary, with a return to full employment when better times come, as happened in the 1950s and 1960s. Realistically, though, this seems unlikely, since too many 'traditional' jobs have gone forever and many of the new jobs seem to be capital-intensive rather than labour-intensive.

Another view would be to see the current changes as a return to a more rural and stable past system, with greater individualism and self-provisioning and less formal employment for wages. This view has been criticized as being too romantic (a yearning for a rustic past).[11] Some suggest that advocates of pre-technological primitivism are but a small vocal fringe, wanting a return to a world most of us would hate.[12]

Question

What kind of future society do you foresee?

Summarizing so far, it has been argued that:

- The occupational structure is constantly changing; for example, the decline of the agriculture and manufacturing sectors and the growth of services.
- Although jobs are being created there are not enough at present to offset those lost through new technology and changes in demand.
- Many of the traditional jobs lost are not particularly attractive.
- We should not regard the existing employment structure as permanent. We tend to over-emphasize waged employment of individuals rather than looking at the work done by the whole household.
- Perhaps the emphasis should be more on all work rather than on paid jobs – including work we do for ourselves, for each other, home work, housework, DIY and so on.

Sociological explanations could be offered for many of the changes in the economy, but it is not possible to analyse all of them in detail here. Therefore only two kinds of change, of particular interest to sociologists, have been selected for deeper examination. They are high unemployment and the effects of the new technology.

2   High Unemployment

This section begins by asking 'What groups in the population are most likely to be unemployed?' It then compares present-day studies of unemployment with a famour pre-war study of unemployment carried out in Austria. This comparison shows that though there is apathy now among the long-term unemployed, it is less than that during the 1930s. A sociological view of unemployment is then attempted, showing that for some people unemployment becomes part of a way of life. The section concludes with a case study which indicates that the experience of unemployment appears to have little effect on the values and attitudes of the victims. First, then – who loses from unemployment?

Unemployment – who loses?

Unemployment is an important feature of the changing occupational structure of Western developed economies (though in Japan and some countries of the Pacific basin there is a shortage of labour). Who does it affect?

- Unemployment hits most harshly those who are likely to be the poorest and least powerful in the labour force, especially unskilled manual workers. Statistics consistently show that the highest incidence of unemployment is among general labourers.
- Those who were repeatedly unemployed in the past are the most likely to be unemployed in the future. The repeated recurrence of unemployment makes such people particularly liable to poverty.[13]
- The long-term unemployed are hard hit first because they are less likely to be re-employed and secondly because welfare benefits are geared to the short-term unemployed; hence long-term poverty is likely to be harsher.
- As mentioned in the previous chapter, women are hard hit by unemployment. They form part of what Marx called the 'reserve army'. In good times their services are sought by employers; in recession they are among the first to be made redundant. The hiring and firing of women in this way minimizes employers' costs and allows them to adjust to market pressures with little loss to the firm. Between 1961 and 1985 the number of unemployed male claimants has increased tenfold, but the number of unemployed female claimants has increased *sixteen-fold* (and probably more, because many women do not register as unemployed).
- Young workers, particularly those under 18, are more likely to be unemployed. The true extent of youth unemployment is hidden by the Youth Training Scheme. (Cynics suggest this may be the real reason for the scheme, rather than to prepare the young for work.)
- Older workers, over 50, are more likely to be unemployed. The extent of their unemployment is hidden by the fact that many of them opt for early retirement knowing that their chances of finding a job at their age are remote.
- Black workers are hard hit by unemployment. This is partly owing to employers' prejudices, and this is well documented, but it is also a result of the fact that they are likely to be unskilled workers,

Table 8.2   *UK unemployed claimants (thousands)*

	Male	Female
1961	231	61
1985	2286	1003

Source: Social Trends, 1986.

and it is unskilled workers in general who have the highest rates of unemployment. They cannot get work because they are unskilled, and because they cannot get work they stay unskilled.

- Some areas suffer more than others. In Britain the north of the country fares worst (see table 8.4); so too do the inner-city areas. This is more than just a geographical phenomenon; the worst affected areas are those containing the highest proportion of working-class people.

Unemployment past and present

How does the experience of unemployment in the 1980s differ from that of the 1930s? The psychologist Marie Jahoda carried out research on the effects of unemployment in both periods.[14] In the thirties physical deprivation in food and clothing were the rule rather than the exception in Britain, and it was worse in many continental countries. In her study of Marienthal in pre-war Austria she distinguished four types of unemployed: those whose morale was unbroken; the resigned; those in despair; the apathetic. Her findings

Table 8.3   *The proportion of UK males in employment, by ethnic origin, 1985 (percentages)*

	White	West Indian	Indian/Pakistani/ Bangladeshi
In full or part-time employment	66.3	56.4	48.8

Source: Social Trends, 1987.

Table 8.4   *Unemployment by selected UK regions, 1987*

	Percentage of working population	
Selected regions	*Male*	*Female*
South East	9.2	6.1
Greater London	10.3	6.6
West Midlands	14.3	9.5
North	19.0	10.4
Scotland	17.4	10.8
Northern Ireland	22.4	12.6

Source: Employment Gazette, June 1987.

showed that those in least despair gained most assistance; that people reacted with shock to the onset of unemployment; that women panicked about household management and some got into debt, but most learned to manage on reduced resources later on.

She concluded from her study that the process of adaptation to long-term unemployment has several stages: an immediate shock reaction which may be followed by a slight recovery when people learn to manage somehow, but adaptation may be threatened as economic hardship increases. With the aid of several other studies Jahoda showed that this process is common to many cultures.

Jahoda recorded that unemployment results in the destruction of a habitual time structure. Most employment has a fixed working day; when this structure is removed boredom and waste of time settle in. Part of the appeal of leisure is its comparative scarcity. In addition, the unemployed feel a sense of purposelessness; they feel they are on the scrap heap. Unemployment leads to apathy, loss of status and loss of personal identity.

Looking at the 1980s Jahoda believes that even though physical conditions have improved considerably in the last fifty years, people's psychological needs are the same and the burden of unemployment is similar. Even though there is less absolute deprivation (deprivation measured against an unchanging standard) now, relative deprivation (deprivation measured against the average standard of living in the society) is still important, for example, compared with those still in work. In the thirties many 'adjusted' to unemployment by giving up, but Jahoda concludes that:

> Resignation and apathy as the result of suppressing one's needs will be less dominant among the unemployed of the eighties than it was among those of the thirties, even though it will still be the response of many. Giving up comes less automatically to people in better health, with a higher standard of living and a higher level of education and aspiration than was the case then.[15]

Will unemployment disrupt our society?

Behind this question is the common view that unemployment will somehow rot the social fabric of our society: that there will be more street riots, that youth will lose the will to work, that there will be more suicides and mental illness, that older people made redundant will 'go to pieces' and so on.

Research shows that there may be some truth in all these propositions (see the project at the end of this chapter), but there is another way of looking at the problem. We tend to have stereotypes of the unemployed, for example the 'solid respectable not very skilled working-class man made redundant through no fault of his own', becoming increasingly depressed and hopeless. Ray Pahl suggests that there is a fallacy in stereotyping like this.[16] It lies in seeking the unemployed as a separate category, or type of person, from the employed. Rather there is a flow of workers moving through the status of being unemployed, later becoming employed, then perhaps unemployed again for a time. Even in times of fairly full employment closures and redundancies are part of every day life in many working-class areas.

Again, 'the idea that workers should be utterly committed to industrial employment that is boring, dirty, noisy and dangerous is not a widely shared idea' – among the workpeople concerned. From this viewpoint, being unemployed is not such a catastrophe, since being employed is not all that marvellous either. In addition, the casual nature of the labour market is a kind of support for the unemployed.[17]

None of this is meant to make light of unemployment. There remains, for example, the increasing incidence of structural (long-term) unemployment due to dying industries etc. Overall, however, the views advanced here indicate that the problem of working-class unemployment should be seen as part of the problem of poverty, which includes the problem of low pay.

Unemployment, low pay, depressing work, poor education, casual labour are all part of the same problem – poverty.

The 'message' for the personnel officer may be not to be deceived if the labour force seems compliant for the moment. This could be mainly a result of unemployment which many feel is hanging over their heads. While many managements may feel this is a good time to press on with introducing new technology and new ways of working, one should be considerate. It may be that when the economy recovers and there is less unemployment the workforce, feeling less threatened, will think this is a time to become more militant.

3   New Technology

What is 'new technology'?

The 'new technology' is most often thought of as the improvement in the storage, analysis and transmission of information. Computers are becoming increasingly efficient at storing information, filing it (database), and manipulating it. One example of this would be keeping accounts, noting payments, and raising invoices which used to be done by ledger clerks but is now largely done by computers in big organizations. These improvements arise from the advances in electronics. Electronic machinery used to be based on the vacuum tube valve, which meant it was very bulky. In the 1970s this was replaced by the transistor, which was much smaller. The transistor in turn has been replaced by the microchip, which essentially is a miniature electric circuit. A circuit of 100,000 components can be contained in a chip measuring only 5 mm across. The decrease in costs has been dramatic.

The other part of the revolution is the improvement in telecommunications. Not only can information be stored and analysed more efficiently, but it can flow more quickly and be acted upon more rapidly – money can be transmitted from London to New York in seconds. Is information technology just another technology? Some have argued that the microprocessor is truly revolutionary in that it possesses an intelligence function. Just as the steam engine transformed the limited strength of a person in the production of goods, so too the new technology will enable people to extend their mental capacity to an unprecedented degree. There is no field to which it cannot be applied.[18]

So far the emphasis has been on improvements in computers and telecommunications, but there have been many other technological improvements, in quality control, process control (in the chemical industry), for machine tools, in the office, in defence systems, in automation in factories, etc. Whatever form technology takes, sociologists will ask the same type of question – why is this technology being introduced now; who will benefit; what changes will come with it?

Who benefits from the new technology?

Some fear that while the advent of the 'new information age' will bring great opportunities for raising the quality of life, there is a danger that in the end social inequalities could be extended. Centralizing of information into databases stored by sophisticated computers, plus improvements in telecommunications through the linking of computers, and improvements in the monitoring systems of computers, will of course increase the power of those controlling the technology. If past experience is anything to go by, the benefits from all these developments will go to those who have invested most heavily in the new technology, in other words, large and powerful organizations, successful multinational enterprises and so on. So Third World countries will be at a disadvantage compared with the West. In answer to the question 'who benefits?', the following suggestions have been advanced.

- Projects concerned with social need will take second place to military development.
- The most educationally advantaged will benefit more than the least educated.
- The research efforts of the large corporations will receive more government support than universities.
- Those with greater resources will derive more from the new technology than those who are economically weak (for example, it will enable very large firms to centralize information and control their staff and their sophisticated technology, analyse their business environment, and so on).
- Information systems will be designed to meet the needs of a small group of privileged special users.
- All this will widen the gap between the privileged and the less privileged, for example the skills difference.
- The new technology may result in more freedom for some and less for others. Thus there may be more centralized control in the hands of those at the top of the organization and more surveillance of those lower down in the hierarchy. But there may also be more freedom for the individual computer operator in some organizations.[19]

What effect will the new technology have on the quality of work? It will be recalled that scientific management (see chapter 3) implied de-skilling, fragmentation of the task, with control and planning in the hands of the management. While such developments on the shop floor have proceeded apace for two centuries or more, in the office they have attracted little sociological comment.[20] Some believe that there will be formalization of office routines, with clerks and secretaries spending more time on monitoring and supervising processes being carried out by computer-based devices.[21] The new skills required will be the ability to use the computer efficiently and to get the most out of it; traditional skills such as calculating and typing will be less important. Certainly there will be de-skilling of the typist's job.

Another 'Taylorist' development may be the shift of assembly-line work, and skilled specialized tasks, to the office, where they can be controlled and monitored, while within the office itself there may be increasing impersonalization.[22]

On the other hand, perhaps computers will give their operators more power and freedom, as others have argued:

> Computers are now becoming integrated totally into the very fabric of the manufacturing, commercial, service and government sectors. Where once they were used to handle payrolls and invoices they now handle almost all – on occasion all – of an organisation's information, as well

as being used for control functions. As both employers and society as a whole becomes ever more dependent upon computer operations, so their vulnerability increases.

Stop the computers at Heathrow Airport and not only would you not get a single flight into or out of Heathrow but the Customs and Excise Department would halt and even a cup of tea would be difficult to come by. Stop the computer at the Prudential Assurance Company or the organisation that clears bank cheques (CHAPS) and financial chaos will not be far behind, with public panic a mere step further back. As we transfer more of our knowledge and information onto them, as production becomes that much more based on, integrated and controlled by them, and as transport, medicine, government, benefits, the military and defence, indeed almost all of life, is affected by them, so the possibility of strikes, or even worse, by computer people, will have to be considered very seriously.[23]

Naturally sociologists are interested in the cultural reasons for introducing, or not introducing, new technology. Gill has noted that in large Japanese enterprises employees are adaptable to new technology because their employment is secure. Also, a much larger proportion of their pay (up to half) is in the form of bonuses; hence again they are more willing to use more efficient technology. In contrast, many British and American managers seem conservative, reluctant for example to relinquish the status of having their own personal secretaries or to use a computer keyboard.[24]

Question

On balance, do you think the new technology will be enslaving or liberating for office and factory workers?

How will the new technology affect employment?

It might be thought that office and factory workers would resist the new technology on the grounds that it would threaten their jobs. However, the Policy Studies Institute, in a study of a cross-section of British firms, came to the conclusion that acceptance of new technology is not a problem, although there are exceptions, notably in some newspapers.[25] Indeed, trade union opposition is twice as common in France and Germany as it is in Britain. There have been other obstacles to the introduction of new technology, in particular the recession and the shortage of key new skills in workers. Another difficulty is that the original capital cost of new technology is very high even though subsequent running costs are low. Managerial opposition to new technology has not been particularly strong. Here the problem is managers' lack of awareness of the possibilities of the new technology. Having found this out, the researchers then reformulated their question to ask 'Why has new technology been accepted?'

They found that new technology has been accepted where unions have been able to negotiate benefits for their members in the past. Generally, where new systems have been introduced gradually, there has not been much opposition. Nor has there been much sign of 'big brother' depersonalization of work.

Another reason for the lack of opposition to the new technology is that, whatever the fears, it has caused little job loss so far in Britain: 0.5 per cent of the total employment in industry. The main problem is not loss of jobs but lack of new skills. However, a lot of industry and commerce still needs modernizing and further job losses could occur, for example when the fully electronic office is introduced. Some argue that the computer revolution is still only in its infancy.

One idea of the changes – now and in the future – has been put forward by Charles Handy.

- The full-employment society is becoming the part-time employment society.
- Labour and manual skills are yielding to 'knowledge' as the basis for new businesses and new work.
- Industry is declining and services are growing in importance.
- Hierarchies and bureaucracies are going out and partnerships are coming in.
- The one-organization career is becoming rarer, job mobility and career changes more fashionable.
- The third stage of life, beyond growing up and employment, is becoming more important.
- Sexual stereotypes are being challenged and sexual roles are less rigid.
- Work is shifting southward; this applies to Britain (to the south-east) and to the USA (to the 'sun-belt').[26]

Handy poses, and offers historical answers to, some key questions.

Common questions	Possible answers
• Will there be enough jobs in the economy with the growing population?	Between 1932 and 1937 in the UK we increased the number of jobs by 2.25 million and reduced unemployment by 1.25 million.

• Will the growth in the labour force outstrip the number of jobs available?	Between 1860 and 1960 the labour force doubled, but so did employment.
• Will workers be able to transfer from declining sectors to ascendant areas of the economy?	Between 1860 and 1960 agricultural jobs fell from 25 per cent of the labour force to 3 per cent. The former agricultural workers were absorbed into new industries and occupations.
• Will workers be able to adjust to technological change?	We have seen technological change before. In the same period 1860 to 1960 capital per worker employed dropped, but output trebled. The car industry and many others were born.
• Will there be sufficient flexibility in the economy generally to allow changes to take place?	Yes. This will come from short-term contracts, subcontracting by large firms, more personal pensions, better education and training to enable and encourage adaptability in the labour force.[27]

A final question could be asked here – is the above too optimistic? Probably the answer is 'Yes'. For example, although the nineteenth century can be depicted as a time of economic expansion in Britain and the USA, it was also an era of great hardship for ordinary people. Handy gives the impression that everything will be all right in the end – but is this an ideology too? Might not those who have invested in new technology put forward a similar case to that on the right hand side of the table?

One suggestion for developing new technology – specifically information technology (IT) without the disruption and waste of competition is the Department of Trade and Industry Alvey Programme in Britain.[28] By 1988 the programme had spent £350 million on research into information technology, in four years. The Alvey Committee decided that the best way to develop IT in Britain would be to choose a programme of 'pre-competitive research', i.e. 'any work on which people [large firms and universities] will collaborate'. The Alvey Programme also emphasizes industrial exploitation of the research at all stages. Virtually all British universities are participating. One example is the Flagship Project which has allowed ICL to carry out work at Manchester University and Imperial College. ICL means to develop the project to involve major computer firms on the continent and to create new ranges of European machines in the 1990s for the expanding field of inference computing (inferring answers from incomplete knowledge).

It is too early to say if the Alvey Programme will succeed, and so whether its approach to the development of new technology will be adopted in other areas. Although it represents an attempt to introduce co-operation between firms and universities, it is not concerned with the wider issues of the social effects of IT's introduction.

Will the new technology disrupt our society?

We speak about the industrial revolution, and assume new technologies will cause fundamental changes in our society. We believe that the latest advances in micro-electronics will cause a 'collapse of work', or herald the entry of the robots to our factories, or do away with the need to commute to the office.

In general this assumes that technological changes are going to bring about great social changes. Underpinning this kind of thinking is 'technological determinism', the idea that the technology determines the social structure (rather than the reverse). Technology is seen as having a life of its own which proceeds almost naturally along a single path.[29]

Perhaps the most famous example of resistance to new technology was that of the Luddites, British textile workers in the nineteenth century whose skills were made obsolete by the introduction of new machinery. In doing so, they were also defending a way of life.[30] Today new technology is represented as a development to be adopted regardless of its effects on any social problems which simply have to be coped with.[31] New technology is represented as beyond choice – every sensible person is supposed to be in favour of it. Nevertheless, some people will be hurt by it: the poorest, the de-skilled and the unemployed – and their viewpoint is worth considering.

It has been suggested that instead of asking 'how will the new technology affect society?', it might be more profitable to ask 'what kind of society produces new technology?' This avoids the trap of technological determinism and concentrates on the *social* conditions that give rise to inventions and innovatons, and their adoption (see glossary).

Another kind of simplistic thinking is that indulged in by futurists who project present trends as a straight line into the future, but fail to take account of changes in the *conditions* of change. What we can say is that new technology will be strongly resisted by the *powerful* interest groups badly affected by it. Most people – trade unions, firms, the public services – have a vested interest in the status quo. For example, the social structure of the office depends on managers having a certain number of secretarial staff; they give status to the manager. It is possible that the comparatively slow take-up of the word processors (whose technology has been around some years now) may be due to this factor. This question needs examination.

The new technology is here already; why is it not being introduced far more widely? The cash dispenser at a bank is a piece of quite advanced technology which could probably replace many cashiers. The word processor, if employed wherever it would be more 'efficient', would make many people redundant. The weaponry on a modern fighter plane is extremely sophisticated but this technology has not been widely applied. The quite understandable opposition of various interested groups has already been mentioned, but on the 'positive' side we should ask 'what encourages the introduction of new technology?' It is, of course, mainly market forces, which means that people want and are prepared to pay for. What consumers seem to want are sophisticated toys, more reliable cars and dishwashers, home computers and video equipment.

There have been many examples in the past of new technology being available but not introduced. The technology for the practice of birth control was known about fifty years or so before its widespread introduction. Vulcanized rubber could be produced in the 1820s, but the practice of birth control by the middle classes was not generally used till after 1870; the reasons were social. The rearing of middle-class children was becoming more expensive owing to the long period of education. The cost of maintaining middle-class status was increasing; the extra servants, carriages – what has been called 'the paraphernalia of gentility' – all seemed to lead to the acceptance of birth control where previously it had been socially unacceptable.[32]

The most sophisticated uses of new technology are currently restricted to comparatively small sectors, such as defence, because of the lack of demand in other areas. In the past it has been mainly war and revolution that have wrought changes in society rather than new technology by itself. Technology has often been implemented only under pressure of war. (Think of radar, the jet engine, antibiotics, computers, nuclear power, where the technology was known (or virtually known) before the Second World War, yet was only developed in war-time).

There may be a lesson here for politicians and scientists who wish to denigrate sociology as impractical, unscientific and useless. What is needed is not necessarily more research on new technology but a deeper appreciation of the social causes and consequences of the introduction of new technology.

4   Concluding Remarks

Earlier it was said that appearances are deceptive. This chapter has shown this is true. We can easily recognize some economic changes of the type shown in the first table of this chapter (the decline of employment in industry, the rise of employment in banking and financial services), but not necessarily see the social effects of some of these changes. Managers may want to know:

- How can we improve productivity and profitability?
- How can we speed up the introduction of new technology?
- What will be the effect of the new technology on society?

But sociologists may ask a different kind of question. Rather than ask 'how can we improve profitability?', sociologists may ask 'For whom is new technology profitable?' Certainly the Luddites did not think new technology was profitable for them – they were losing their income completely. Rather than ask 'What will be the effect of the new technology?', the sociologists asks: 'What kind of society produces new technology?'. Early in this century Max Weber was asking this sort of question: 'In what kind of society does industrialization take place?' (see chapter 1).

We could also ask 'What kind of society tolerates widespread poverty and unemployment, the unfair treatment of women, racial discrimination, and so on?'. It may be answered that we have to put up with poverty and unemployment. It is too costly to eradicate it – the country cannot afford it! To this the sociologist would respond that what we can 'afford' depends on our values; we can afford anything if we want it enough to make it a high priority. In time of war, for example, expense is of no account. Winning is top priority. In the lease-lend arrangements made during the Second World War between the USA and Britain, the USA sent warships and other armaments to Britain at no immediate cost – 'take it now and pay for it after the war.'

Another argument of the 'we cannot afford it' variety is that the economy cannot afford expensive welfare provision including good housing, health facilities, good education and so on. It is only a strong economy that can produce the wealth that makes these welfare benefits possible. However, it might be argued that we should reverse this order and say that when the citizens are well cared for, healthy and well educated, genuine advance in the economy can take place.

It is asking the right questions that yields the true sociological insights. Try this for yourself; question the assumptions you live with every day.

Exercises

Self-examination questions

What is meant by:

- the occupational structure
- IT
- primary, secondary and tertiary sectors
- concentration (see also chapter 2)
- 'self-provisioning'

- the grey economy
- the black economy
- absolute deprivation
- relative deprivation
- technological determinism

Essay or discussion questions

1   What contribution can sociologists make to the study of unemployment?
    Suggestion: The sociologist should see unemployment in its wider perspective, not just as an economic or personal problem. What are its costs to society as a whole?
2   It has been suggested that many of the long-term unemployed seem apathetic. Do you agree? If so, can you suggest reasons? If not, why is this viewpoint advanced by some writers?
    Suggestion: You could put the case for and against the proposition.
3   Who benefits from the new technology? Who loses?
    Suggestion: You could do the case studies below before answering this question.
4   What is the 'best' technology in the following cases:
    (a) the word processor;
    (b) a new automated car factory;
    (c) sophisticated machinery in the newspaper industry;
    (d) sophisticated systems in the defence industry;
    (e) more cures for cancer and heart disease.
    Suggestion: Ask 'best for whom?'. The atomic bomb dropped on Japan seemed the best technology at the time, but was it? 'Yes' for the Allies in terms of winning the war quickly; but what about in the longer term?

Case study 1

Read the passage and answer the questions that follow.

The experience of unemployment

This is a study of the experience of unemployment for two contrasting groups – executives and working class youth. The samples are drawn firstly from the unemployed executives who have participated in the Job and Career Change Programme at Oxford Polytechnic, and secondly from a group of young unemployed, many of them school leavers, who met at the UB40 Club in Oxford.

The unemployed executives

The Job and Career Change Programme is a mutual help programme for unemployed managers, executives and professionals, run by Oxford Polytechnic and other colleges under the auspices of the Manpower Services Commission. There were about 1,000 unemployed executives in the Oxford area in 1984. The aim of the course is to help participants to find a new job by improving self-presentation. It also covers job search, career development and career change and employment counselling. In a typical day's programme new participants give a brief account of past career and future plans, practise at interviews, improve their curricula vitae, have group discussions of each individual's employment problem, and so on.

Here are some of the verbal comments of the unemployed executives in reply to a series of *open questions*.

'I don't think the government has much to do with it (unemployment). I am a firm believer in – if you haven't got a job you shouldn't be doing it.' (professional engineer).

'Firms are using the government's stance to rid themselves of bad working practices of the past. But really nothing has changed – the government has not changed anything.' (professional mechanical engineer)

'Unfortunately my firm was taken over by an asset stripper, and that is why I am out of work. I am still shaken from it.' (laboratory technician)

'We are paying now for past wage claims by the trade unions.' (ex-marketing executive)

'I only wish I had been a member of a union.' (ex-pilot)

'It is good to be back in an exporting job and helping the country again instead of drawing dole.' (extract from a letter from a salesman who had found employment after the course)

The following are a representative selection of *written statements* made by the 'redundant executive' group on a self-administered questionnaire.

'Employment legislation seems to be hindering small employers taking on staff for fear of not being able to dismiss them . . . there should be fewer trade unions per industry and "no strike" contracts should be encouraged.'

'The efficiency of industry is the first priority – employment will then follow.'

'Talent is being wasted . . . mobility of labour must be encouraged. Pension schemes must be national to encourage movement.'

'I feel there is a very wide opportunity for a new breed of expert to guide and advise the unemployed on a fee basis.'

Most of the unemployed executives do not seem to blame the government or their former employers for their plight. Compare this with the second group, unemployed teenagers.

The UB40 group

The second group whose experience of unemployment was studied, the UB40 group, gets its name from the form claimants present at DHSS offices when collecting benefit. The group meet in a former furniture shop converted to provide a large lounge/refreshment room, a workshop, snooker/table tennis room, a video, tv, etc. I seemed to be the centre of some merriment ('hey you, baldy!') and when I explained the purpose of the form there was general hilarity. Nevertheless, the form was treated seriously, all but two of the fourteen present on the first occasion agreeing to complete it. In addition, the comments (see below) were very much fuller than those of the unemployed executives. Three people asked me what the form was *really* for. One man asked me if I would comment on his comments. Surprise and pleasure at this positive response is perhaps a comment on my own stereotyped expectations. (I had expected to have to read out the form item by item or to administer the questionnaire myself.) The content of the questionnaire gave rise to anti-Thatcher comments, but I felt that any radicalism in the group was not so much leftist as anarchistic; this comes over on the written comments. While I was present a woman came in with friends and announced she had just been fined £50. This was treated as a joke. Many present had been arrested at some time: two had gone to prison.

Here is a representative sample of comments on the *open questionnaire*.

'I am unemployed becuase I do not want a job. I do not know if I could get one because I have never tried.'

'When employers in this country pay proper wages maybe I'll look for a job.'

'As soon as we have a government that truly represents the people there would be lots of things to add (to this questionnaire) — but as it is now anything I had to add would probably be just ignored.'

'Out with Maggie and maybe a better future could be gained for those that feel when leaving school that there is only a life on the dole. Also get rid of the present YOPs unless they make a change of present wages.'

'I am unemployed because I do not want to work as long as Maggie Thatcher is at the top. LU7 skins Oi!'

'I never want a job — Oxford Prison would miss me.'

The table contrasting the two groups is based on answers to a *formal questionnaire*. (adapted from M. Joseph, 'The Experience of Unemployment in Oxford', in *Industrial Tutor*, vol. 4, no. 2, Autumn 1985, pp. 60–8)

1   What would you say are the main values or beliefs of each group?
2   What do the members of each group really want?
3   What are the main differences between the groups?
4   Does the experience of unemployment cause people to change fundamentally?

The experience of unemployment in two contrasting groups

	% agreeing with the statement	
Statement	Unemployed executives	Unemployed young people (UB40 group)
1 I am unemployed now mainly because the employers are going through difficult times.	67	12
2 I am unemployed now mainly because I was not up to the job.	0	6
3 Unemployment is generally the fault of government policies.	33	47
4 Unemployment is caused by the activities of trade unions (for example in pressing for wages that are too high).	33	12
5 Unemployment in Britain is no worse than in many other countries.	56	35
6 I have tried hard to get a job.	73	60
7 I could have tried harder to get a job.	56	71
8 I have lost some friends through being unemployed.	11	29
9 To a large extent unemployment is the fault of the employers.	17	24
10 The government should make the reduction of unemployment its first priority.	67	60
11 I believe I am unemployed now mainly because I have no formal qualifications.	6	12
12 I wish I had stayed longer in education.	56	35
13 I do not like telling people that I am unemployed.	28	24
14 On the whole I disliked school.	0	50

The number in each group was 18 executives, 16/17 young people.

5   Do the groups blame the government for their predicament?
6   Do the groups suffer from 'false consciousness' or a distorted picture of social reality? Does one group know more of 'what is really going on' than the other? If so, why?

Case study 2

Read the passage and then attempt the questions that follow.

THE ROVER MANAGEMENT SEEM TO HAVE BROKEN THE BACK OF SHOP FLOOR OPPOSITION. WAS TECHNOLOGY MORE CRUCIAL THAN THE NEW UNION LAWS?

Many old type manual jobs have been eliminated and robots have been taught to carry out repetitive tasks at Rover's factory at Longbridge, Birmingham. New technology often takes away a worker's discretion and this even applies at management levels where junior managers spend much of their time on routine monitoring. Longbridge has a long history of poor industrial relations, of 'entrenched' shop stewards and autocratic management.

At Longbridge, management were faced with an entrenched and purposeful union organisation. How could the unions be discouraged from using the changes in technology as a weapon against the new management policy? Clearly, whatever the political and economic background, the potential for disruptive actions was there, as the powertrain workers had indicated. That such actions did not take place on a much wider scale seems to be due in part to the new technology itself. Not its control and monitoring capability, but its IDEOLOGICAL POWER.

With so much government and industry propaganda urging us to love the microchip, new technology enjoys an important ideological status as an inherently progressive force in society. Few if any trade unions, for example, are willing to risk the accusation of being 'Luddites' in relation to changing technology.

The car industry, in particular – though it has seen successive waves of technological change undercutting union power – has had little concerted opposition to technology itself. Even in the 1920s, when the assembly line was brought into Europe and broke the craft workers' stranglehold on production by introducing unskilled labour, the craft unions did not oppose it. It was, they said, a 'finding of science' and therefore not negotiable.

In the 1980s management at Longbridge were still able to exploit the mystique of technology for overcoming labour resistance. On a number of occasions, changes in work practice which had little to do with technology but a lot with raising productivity, were introduced under the banner of 'technical necessity' or the 'needs of production'. Even the shop stewards on the Works Committee – notable for their communist sympathies – far from using new technology as a bargaining lever, actually sought to protect it from the plant's industrial relations problem. Derek Robinson's successor, Jack Adams, said at the time of the Metro's launch: 'Whatever problems we have in the plant, we recognise the priority of the Metro. We have done everything possible to accommodate the Metro.'

There were sound economic reasons for the unions' attitude. But some of the reasoning can be traced back to the 'alternative plan', put forward by the shop stewards' combine in the 1970s. This had made massive investment in new production facilities the centrepiece of its approach. When the investment actually materialised at the plant in 1980, the unions could hardly stand on their heads and oppose its introduction. Even their politically radical proposals only served as a means of bolstering technology's ideological halo.

Four years on from the launch of the Metro, it is clear that installation of new technology – though it did not directly bring about the radical shift in the company's industrial relations – did help to provide a 'window of opportunity' for such a shift. In the future, the balance of power may shift back towards the unions, but many of the changes introduced in that period are now firmly embedded and unlikely to be changed. All this suggests that, insofar as unions' shopfloor activity can be likened to guerrilla warfare – aggression on the margins, hit and run tactics, sometimes having to withdraw to the hills – the real danger of new technology for trade unionists is that it gradually but irretrievably changes the terrain on which shopfloor battles are fought. And always of course in management's favour.

If and when shop stewards in many companies, not just Austin Rover, come back down from the hills, they may find that what was once friendly territory has been lost forever to the onward march of the microchip and the robot. (from H. Scarborough and P. Moran, 'How the New Tech won at Longbridge', *New Society*, 7 February 1985, pp. 207–9)

1   How do you account for the fact that Rover was able to introduce the new technology comparatively easily?
2   How would you account for the comparative weakness of the unions?
3   What advice would you offer to:
   (a) management;
   (b) the unions?

Suggestions: Frank Webster investigated the introduction of new technology at Longbridge. He suggests that few unions are willing to risk being labelled as Luddites. He argues that the unions were so ensnared in the ideology of technological progress that even shop stewards noted for communist sympathies sought to protect the new technology from the plant's industrial relations problems. According to Webster technology is not neutral, nor is it a liberating force. New technology is at the forefront of the strategy of increasing competition and restoring profitability and from an industrialist's viewpoint is a major reason why the unions with their restrictive practices must be broken.[33]

Webster goes on to write of the politicization of technology. He believes we should concentrate less on what technology *can* do and more on what it *is* doing (note the use of the present tense). We should see how technology serves powerful interests – how it displaces employees, speeds up work, de-skills labour and increases the national and international dominance over labour. Do you agree?

Case study 3

Read the passage and answer the questions that follow.

Company background

This optical company is concerned mainly with the manufacture of lenses and the making of spectacles to prescription (a prescription comes from the optician, and a pair of spectacles is returned from the factory to the practice). About 1,600 to 2,000 pairs per week are produced. A small but expanding section of the company is the Instrument Division, which designs and manufactures industrial profile projectors for inspection functions in a range of industries. This section, however, has only two or three employees, and will not be a concern of this case study. Recently the recession has begun to affect even this company, and although the slight drop in sales is unlikely to be seriously damaging to the firm in any way, its expected expansion will now be delayed for the foreseeable future.

The company belongs to a group of companies which altogether employ about 350 people, with total sales of around £4m. The optical company itself employs 45, and its own sales are about £1m. The group includes a chain of Midlands optical practices, and although the optical company is closely connected to them, a customer–supplier relationship is maintained. Operating very autonomously from the group – the directors rarely being seen even by the general manager – there is a good deal of room for internal manipulation. A capital sanction scheme is operated by the group, but 'once the capital is approved, we can swap and change our investments.'

Including foremen, the internal management team consists of seven people, and is represented in the diagram.

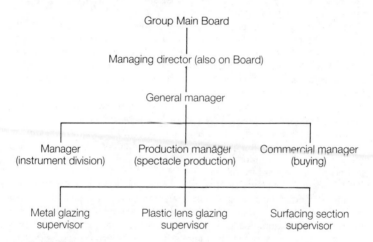

Group Main Board
|
Managing director (also on Board)
|
General manager
|
Manager (instrument division) — Production manager (spectacle production) — Commercial manager (buying)
|
Metal glazing supervisor — Plastic lens glazing supervisor — Surfacing section supervisor

The changes

Since 1988 the whole factory has been rationalised, reorganised, and modernised – under the direction of a new general manager who was appointed just prior to that by the group main board. Before his arrival all production was in one room, which he described as a 'maze'. The surfacing and glazing sections were segregated, production 'lines' were straightened up, and a computing room was created. At the same time the general manager set up the system for the collection of data on internal trends – rejection rates, maintenance requirements for machinery, and so on – so that remedial action could be taken on more easily identified problems and bottlenecks. Also, the group bonus system was reorganised so that workers could understand its mechanics more easily, and so that bonus pay was related more directly to output.

The most interesting changes for our purposes are the new pieces of machinery and equipment which have been introduced over the last few years. The firm now prides itself as 'one of the most advanced producers of spectacles in the UK'.

New equipment

In the surfacing section the firm has for some time used automatic machinery – rather than hand controlled machinery – whereby the machine is set, switched on, and the rest is automatic. (Hand controlled machinery still has to be used for some jobs.) The task of setting has recently been simplified through the introduction of a computer. Previously a skilled worker would receive a prescription for the lens to be made from the optician (every lens is unique) and from this would make 'rule of thumb' guesses as to which blank to use, and which tools and settings to apply. Before being made perfect, the lens may have to be 'recut' several times – surfacers would tend to underestimate their initial calculations because more can always be taken off the lens, but not put back on. Blank selection, tool selection, and machine settings can now, however, be predetermined by use of a computer, which is programmed to translate that information into which machine settings, etc., to use. The woman who does this 'computing' sends the information from the computer room upstairs to the surfacing room. The surfacers can then simply follow the instructions on the ticket to select tools and set up machines. An accurate lens is then produced in one cut, meaning faster production runs; and the elimination of guesswork means a far lower scrap rate.

The de-skilling implications of the new methods are their most important feature, and these will be discussed below. However, it is worth mentioning the implications for the group bonus scheme. The surfacers' bonus pay is separate from that of the rest of the factory – their bonus being related to the number of lenses they turn out each week as a group. Traditionally, through varying their effort, they have been able to control between them the amount of work they turned out, and thus their bonus. But now, especially with the current slight shortage of work, the amount they can do depends on the amount of lenses 'computed' by 'the woman downstairs', and sent up by her to the surfacing room. Control of bonus pay by surfacers is now dependent on her co-operation, and so far this has been forthcoming – the surfacing section supervisor himself carrying out the necessary liaison.

In the glazing section the firm has over the last few years introduced a variety of automatic equipment. This includes automatic edging machines – which shape the lens to fit the frame, and put the 'V' on the lens which allows it to be held by the frame, and electronic focimeters – which make the task of lining up the lens for an accurate fit in the frame far simpler. There is a small production line in the glazing section, and the various tasks involved are rationally segregated.

Taken together, the new machinery and the division of labour on production line principles take a good deal of the skill out of the work, and this aspect of innovation for both surfacing and glazing sections will now be discussed.

De-skilling

The firm's policy towards production machinery is to buy the best and the most modern. The general manager and the production manager make the choices of particular machines and pieces of equipment, spending a good deal of time visiting exhibitions in Europe to ensure that they are up to date with the latest. They try to replace most machinery 'every five years' in any case, and as innovative machinery comes on the market they buy it.

The de-skilling which most of this modern equipment entails is seen as an unfortunate side effect which management themselves would not have chosen.

The production manager and the metal glazing supervisor are particularly articulate on this matter, both having been in business most of their lives, and both still considering themselves to be craftsmen. They talk about the change from highly skilled craftsmen to semi-skilled machine operators, and this transformation is perhaps most clearly seen in the case of surfacing, where the surfacer's work is largely reduced to carrying out instructions on a ticket which comes from a computer. The extent of the de-skilling is perhaps best displayed by reference to the new surfacing supervisor, who is in fact a master glazer. He has been in the surfacing section for several months only, but by working to computer print-outs his work is as good as anyone's, and he is quite capable of supervising the section.

Job rotation

The general manager and his supervisors talk enthusiastically about the technical advantages of the new machinery, and spend a good deal of time keeping up with the latest developments in Europe. As we have already mentioned, the production manager as well as the general manager try to visit other companies in Europe, and often travel to the exhibitions. In fact to hear them talk, one suspects the interest to be as much a hobby as a simple concern to improve the company's efficiency. But they are unhappy about the effects the new machinery has on the workforce. For instance, after describing at length what a 'remarkable device' the new focimeter was, the production manager complained that:

'There's no training needed to operate this, so it's de-skilling the job and I don't like that, I like to train somebody . . . All you need to know is about four different movements, whereas on a focimeter (of the old type) you have to know what you're doing – you have to know the plus and minus aspect of the lenses.'

It was the general manager, however, who was responsible for actually introducing a system of job rotation. Arriving only three or four years ago, and bringing with him a strong philosophy of participation and involvement, he has now managed to establish job rotation as an institutionalised (and compulsory) practice, so that workers now rotate automatically and regularly from job to job, and so that any new recruits are given training in a range of functions. Job rotation is not generally practised *between* surfacing and glazing sections – only within them. This is mainly because surfacers have wished to hang on to their traditional position within the firm: most of the surfacers are long-serving and highly skilled in their craft, and would object to job changes between sections.

To summarise, we might characterise the firm as being the recipients of a Tayloristic technology designed to de-skill what is traditionally a craftsman's domain. To alleviate the worst psychological effects, and to ensure a responsible and flexible workforce, the management have introduced an extensive and very serious system of job rotation. This does not mean that craft skills are retained – on the contrary, the tasks involved are very different and the processes are more resembling 'a science rather than a black art'. But it does mean a very different way of working than would otherwise be the case, and this is reflected in the large amount of time and attention paid to training. The importance of the firm's management, then, in shaping the social and technical organisation of work around the latest spectacle producing machinery, should not be underestimated. (from B. Wilkinson, *The Shop Floor Politics of New Technology* (Heinemann, London, 1983), pp. 41–7)

1 What is meant by 'segregated production'?
2 In what ways have the surfacers lost their control over their work since the introduction of a computer?
3 What is the firm's attitude towards de-skilling?
4 Will job rotation solve the problems of workforce and management? (See chapter 6.)
5 What is meant by 'Tayloristic technology'? (See chapter 3.)
6 What are the interests and values of the people implicated in the technical change (engineers, managers, groups of workers, etc.)?
7 How do they perceive the change and what do they expect to gain or lose from it?
8 At what stage of technical change do powerful people affected attempt to impose their own aims (design, trial, implementation, etc.)?
9 Does the technology act, or is it perceived to act, as a determinant of, or constraint upon, the form of work organization which has evolved?
10 How is technology chosen?

Suggestions: There is a short answer straight from the text, as well as a longer, more general answer to most of these questions. Thus the short answer to question 3 is that management saw de-skilling as an unfortunate side-effect of the introduction of new machinery. A longer answer might mention that de-skilling means a loss of control over the job by the craftsperson. This loss of control (and correspondingly increased control by management) may result in lack of interest and lower productivity, thus defeating management's aims. This could lead on to a discussion of alienation and the labour process.

Case study 4

Read the passage and answer the questions that follow.

Unemployment and health

A study in Edinburgh during 1978–82 found that the unemployed had a much greater risk of attempted suicide than employed men; of the order of 11:1. The risk ratio increased sharply with the length of the spell of unemployment as follows:

Duration of unemployment (men)	Ratio of risk of attempted suicide of unemployed to the employed
Less than 6 months	6:1
6–12 months	10:1
Over 12 months	19:1

Hawton and Rose, in a study in Oxford in 1979–82, found that the attempted suicide rates for unemployed men were 12 to 15 times higher than those for employed men, and again were particularly high for the long-term unemployed. Brenner's studies of national economies and national health statistics have also shown consistent correlations between indicators of recession and mortality in several countries.

The unemployed experience higher levels of illness too. For example in the General Household Survey of 1984, 28% of unemployed men report long-standing illness compared to 25% of working men. Similarly, 29% of unemployed women compared to 25% of working women had some long-standing illness. For women there is the added dimension of the housewife role. Arber found that women classified as housewives had even higher rates of limiting long-standing illness than those who were classified as unemployed.

Poorer health and development have also been found in the children of the unemployed. Using data from the 1981 census Maclure and Stewart found that children living in deprived districts of Glasgow were 9 times more likely to be admitted to hospital than children in non-deprived districts. Overcrowding and parental unemployment were the aspects of deprivation most strongly correlated with hospital admission rates. A study of births in the Greater Dublin area found a higher incidence of low birthweight in babies with unemployed fathers than in those whose fathers were employed. The National Survey of Health and Growth found that children with unemployed fathers, especially the long-term unemployed, tended to be shorter than those with employed fathers. (from M. Whitehead, *The Health Divide* (Health Education Council, London, 1987), pp. 20 ff.)

1   Are people who are in poor health more likely to become unemployed or does the experience of unemployment itself have an adverse effect on health?
2   Discuss the relationship between poverty, unemployment and ill health.

Project:

Referring to table 8.1 on p. 199, how would you explain each item in the table, bearing in mind the following:

* You should attempt to show both the causes and the consequences of each item.
* Try to offer a sociological explanation in each case.
* Show how a sociological analysis of these items might differ from that offered by, say, an accountant, an economist and a manager.

Suggestions: Take the fourth and fifth items in table 8.1 as examples. Many of these industries are old and cannot compete. It may seem sensible to cut costs and close them down. But there is a cost to society (not shown in the profit and loss accounts) in terms of unemployment pay to the unemployed, their loss of income, status and opportunity.

Further Reading

E. Batson, *New Technology and the Process of Labour Regulation* (Clarendon Press, Oxford, 1987)

W. W. Daniel, *The Nature of Current Unemployment* (British/North American Research Association, London, 1985)

A. Friend and A. Metcalfe, *Slump City* (Pluto, London, 1981)

T. Forester, *High-Tech Society* (Basil Blackwell, Oxford, 1987)

C. Gill, *Work, Unemployment and the New Technology* (Polity Press, Cambridge, 1985)

M. Jahoda, *Employment and Unemployment: A Social Psychological Analysis* (Cambridge University Press, Cambridge, 1982)

B. Sherman, *Working at Leisure* (Methuen, London, 1985)

K. Thompson (ed.), *Work, Employment and Unemployment* (Open University Press, Milton Keynes, 1984)

P. Warr, *Work, Unemployment and Mental Health* (Clarendon Press, Oxford, 1987)

Notes

1. National Institute Economic Review, 113, August, 1987, pp. 15–16.
2. Ibid.
3. R. E. Pahl, *Divisions of Labour* (Basil Blackwell, Oxford, 1984).
4. Ibid., p. 41.
5. E. P. Thompson, 'Time, Work-discipline and Industrial Capitalism', *Past and Present*, 36 (1967), pp. 56–97.
6. Pahl, *Divisions of Labour*, pp. 84–6.o
7. Ibid., pp. 319 ff.
8. A. Gorz, *Farewell to the Working Class* (Pluto Press, London, 1982), pp. 80–8.
9. Pahl, *Divisions of Labour*, p. 334.
10. Ibid., p. 326.
11. F. Webster and K. Lambe, 'Information Technology – Who Needs It?', in J. Weston (ed.), *Red and Green* (Pluto Press, London, 1986), p. 59.
12. A. Toffler, *The Third Wave* (Collins, London, 1980), p. 167.
13. B. Showler and A. Sinfield (eds), *The Workless State* (Martin Robertson, Oxford, 1981), pp. 11–12.
14. M. Jahoda, *Employment and Unemployment: A Social Psychological Analysis* (Cambridge University Press, Cambridge, 1982).
15. Ibid., p. 98.
16. R. E. Pahl, 'Family, Community and Unemployment', *New Society*, 21 January 1982.
17. Ibid.
18. C. Gill, *Work, Unemployment and the New Technology* (Polity Press, Cambridge, 1985), p. 5.
19. Gill, *Work*, pp. 7, 8.
20. But see C. W. Mills, *White Collar* (Oxford University Press, Oxford, 1956), referred to in ch. 3 above.

21. Gill, *Work*, p. 43.
22. Ibid., p. 51.
23. B. Sherman, *The State of the Unions* (Wiley, London, 1986), p. 157.
24. Gill, *Work*, pp. 32, 40.
25. J. Northcott, *Chips and Jobs* (Policy Studies Institute, London, 1985).
26. C. Handy, *The Future of Work* (Penguin, Harmondsworth, 1986).
27. Ibid.
28. B. Oakley, 'Industry has Lessons for Academics', *New Scientist*, 2 July 1987.
29. D. F. Noble, *The Forces of Production* (Alfred A. Knopf, New York, 1984).
30. F. Webster and K. Robins, *Information Technology: A Luddite Analysis* (Able Publishing Corporation, Norword, NJ, 1986), p. 3.
31. Ibid., p. 31.
32. J. A. and O. Banks, *Feminism and Family Planning in Victorian England* (Liverpool University Press, Liverpool, 1965), pp. 82–4.
33. F. Webster, 'The Politics of the New Technology', in R. Milliband et al. (eds), *Socialist Register 1985/6* (Merlin Press, London, 1986), pp. 385–413.

9 Conclusions

The introductory chapter indicated the questioning nature of sociology as a discipline: that it seeks to look behind appearances to investigate what is really going on; that it queries the 'official' interpretations of events; that it studies individuals in their social surroundings, relating their behaviour to class, sex, race and religion (rather than analysing individual behaviour on its own). Sociology stresses that we are what we have learnt rather than what we have inherited, that is to say we are *socialized* to our roles in society – woman, man, middle class, working class, old, young, mechanic, professional, and so on.

Chapter 2 demonstrated the different ways business developed in the West and then showed how Western economies dominate the world through, for example, multinational enterprises. It compared American business values (with their stress on individual success) with Japanese business values (with their stress on the group and their apparent need first to catch up with and then to surpass the West). An attempt was then made to analyse the 'British disease'.

Chapter 3 sought to demonstrate the social nature of work – that work is more than a job; it is a way of life. The sociologist is interested in occupational and professional ideologies. These insights are useful to the manager too in revealing the ideologies (including managerial ideologies) with which he or she works, and in revealing the alienating nature of much routine work.

Chapter 4 contrasts our everyday view of organizations with a sociological approach which shows that organizations tend to:

- have ideologies about themselves and their work;
- have a tendency towards oligarchy (rule by the few);
- allow the means to become more important than the end;
- suffer from tight control;
- over-centralize;
- suffer from breakdowns in communications.

Commonly accepted views on industrial relations were contrasted with a sociological approach to industrial relations in chapter 5. The sociologist concentrates on power and control and asks 'What is the result of excessive control in the office, shop and factory?' The response to over-zealous control may be subtle – not strikes, but absenteeism and lack of enthusiasm. Many sociological studies chronicle this phenomenon.

What motivates people to work is the theme of chapter 6. How can profitability and productivity be increased? This is the main reason for managers' interest in motivation. But sociologists prefer to ask different questions, such as 'What is really happening in this organization?' and 'Why are employees dissatisfied?' The roots of alienation at work may be in the social arrangements for work (e.g. not being your own master), rather than in the kind of technology used.

Finally, chapters 7 and 8 uncover underlying facts about the changing occupational structure. All is not what it seems. The roles of women and blacks are not the product of rationally made decisions; they are not treated equally with men and whites. Changes wrought by unemployment and new technology are not as great as they appear. It seems that it is society that determines the economy and the invention and use of new technology, and not the other way around.

The book ends with a reminder of what we have learnt, distinguishing between some 'apparent' realities, and the alternative view.

Appearance	*Possible Reality*
• The new technology is revolutionary, leading to greater efficiency all round and changes in society.	Society changes slowly. The crucial question is not 'how much will the new technology affect society?', but rather 'what kind of society produces this kind of new technology?' Society decides what research is done, whether it is implemented, and how it is used. The effect of its introduction is the result of social acts.
• The new technology will bring greater efficiency.	Efficiency for whom? Those made redundant and unemployed? Those whose skills are now outdated? The unskilled?

- Work is a job, a task to be performed and paid for at the appropriate rate (a fair day's pay for a fair day's work).

Sociologists stress the social nature of work. Work is more than a job; it forms part of a way of life. This is most obvious in the professions. A profession is like a community whose members share similar values and a similar life-style. Middle-class people tend to have careers, rather than just 'jobs'.

- Sociology is useless. It does not help the manager decide what to do; it does not cultivate managerial skills; it does not help to raise productivity or motivate people to work.

Sociology is (among other things) an assessment of society. It aims to find out what is happening, first and foremost; it did not set out to help any particular group in society. It asks questions rather always giving answers. Many attempts to give answers to managers have proved to be misguided (e.g. so-called scientific management). As mentioned in chapter 1, if all the powerful figures in the land were to say what a useful subject sociology is, there would be a fair chance that sociology was not doing its job properly, since sociology often undermines the validity of ideologies believed and promoted by the powerful. Sociology *is* useful to managers in showing them how to ask questions, and how to think clearly, rather than accepting the assumptions on which much thinking is based.

- Enlightened management tries to enhance work; to cut out boring work; to give incentives; to improve surroundings.

On the other hand, many jobs have become de-skilled, and broken up into little parts. Ultimately management controls the work situation and this may be resented.

- Management is more flexible now. Horror stories of the past do not apply now. Most personnel managers seem very reasonable and understanding.

There have been improvements, but the basic fact of management control and employee powerlessness has not changed; perhaps it just has a more human face. Profit for the firm remains the only fundamental aim.

- We have better industrial relations in Britain and the USA now than we used to.

Perhaps it is the threat of unemployment that makes workforces more compliant.

- But there are fewer strikes now; surely that is a good thing? There has been more peace in industrial relations in the eighties.

Strikes are the most obvious but arguably the least important aspect of industrial relations. The USA and Australia have had far higher strike rates than Britain, yet their productivity is much better.

- Striving to raise productivity must be a good thing – it benefits everyone.

How is higher productivity achieved? If it is through greater control by management this may be self-defeating, resulting in more absenteeism, higher labour turnover and low morale. How do people made redundant because more goods can be made with fewer people benefit?

- The Sex Discrimination Act in Britain and the establishment of the Equal Opportunities Commission should result in greater sexual equality at work. Similarly the establishment of the Commission for Racial Equality should help to ease racial discrimination at work.

In reality sexual and racial discrimination in Britain and most other countries abounds. Women's wage rates are still only two-thirds of those of men doing similar work and their promotion prospects are poor. Blacks suffer greater unemployment than whites and when they do get work it is usually unskilled. The ideologies of sexism and racism are widespread. People are judged on the basis of their sex and colour rather than as persons in their own right.

- Organizations in modern society are rational bodies using logical means to achieve rational ends; for example, cutting costs to achieve higher profits.

Organizations are permeated by ideologies such as those mentioned in chapter 4: structuralism, psychologism, consensualism, welfareism and legalism. Often the means become more important than the ends. For example, some organizations seem to be run for the benefit of the staff rather than the customers. Frequently there are breakdowns of communication between the various levels. This may be due to people having different goals rather than any technical fault in the organization.

Where do I Go from Here?

Possibly the best advice, whether to managers or to anyone else, is to try to develop what C. Wright Mills called 'the sociological imagination'.[1]

Do not accept things at their face value. There is a constant need to examine and re-interpret experience, says Mills. Keep a notebook and try to capture fringe thoughts; write down instances of ideologies at work; insights into the behaviour of organizations, speeches of politicians and managers, etc. Do not put too much trust in 'practicality' and apparent 'common sense'. There is a constant need to re-examine common assumptions – the chapter on industrial relations perhaps showed the need for this most clearly. Mills suggests that we try to view what is going on from a variety of perspectives. Whether in a workplace dispute, a court of law or indeed any social occasion, there will be a variety of viewpoints, and a variety of 'truths'. The sociological task is to detect these and not to make hasty judgement.

Avoid stereotyping and avoid rigid procedures. Remember that individuals are socialized individuals, not isolated actors. It is likely that persons from similar social backgrounds (e.g. similar social class) will act in similar ways.

Make the distinction between private troubles and public issues. One person's unemployment is a private trouble. When half the working population in a city of 300,000 are unemployed then this is a public issue, leading to sociological questions such as 'What are the values of this sort of society?'

Certainly a knowledge of sociology will help the decision-maker at work – it will enable clearer thinking, clearer perception and clearer analysis. It should also prove to be an enjoyable lifelong experience.

Note

1. C. W. Mills, *The Sociological Imagination* (Oxford University Press, Oxford, 1959).

Glossary

Ageism	Discrimination or prejudice against a person on the grounds of age.
Alienation	Marx held that we are basically creative animals and we need to express ourselves through our work. In so far as we cannot do this we are alienated – separated from our true selves. It has been argued that modern capitalism leads to alienation among workers.
Authority	The *legitimate* use of power. The government has authority because it was elected. This legitimates its rule.
Bureaucracy	In everyday usage this is associated with red tape. To Weber it meant a large organization with a hierarchy of office, and 'official' rules and systems. He thought this would be the most efficient kind of organization.
Class	This is very difficult to define, although everyone knows the concept! In sociology it is usually used to refer to socio-economic differences which create variations between the material wealth and power of large groups within one society.
Concentration	The term used for the development by which large firms buy up rivals and so fewer and fewer firms come to own more and more of the production in a country (or the world). Power comes to be concentrated in fewer and fewer hands.
Consensualism	This ideology assumes that all members of the organization, high or low, share the same goals.

Culture	The norms, values and material goods of a group or society; its ways of thinking and behaving.
Culturism	The assumption that a society is shaped (or determined) by its culture – that, for example, the American stress on success has shaped a society which includes great luxury and enterprise at the top but great poverty and crime at the bottom. This might be considered to be too simple a view of society; what shaped the culture?
Division of labour	The specialization of work tasks, by which different occupations are combined within a production system. For example, in the home certain tasks are performed by each member of the family; the same process applies in organizations.
Dualism (in the labour market)	There are at least two general nationwide labour markets. In the *primary labour market* there are good jobs involving careers. In the secondary market there are poorly paid, poorly regarded jobs. Each individual is employed in one market or the other; there is hardly any movement between them. Disadvantaged groups cannot enter the primary labour market.
Embourgeoisement	Working-class people adopting middle-class life-styles and values. This can happen both to individuals and to groups.
Globalization	The development of the international economy in the interests of the wealthier countries of the North (see chapter 2).
Ideology	Shared ideas or beliefs that usually serve to justify the interests of the powerful. Often the beliefs are wrong or an exaggeration. Sexism and racism are ideologies.
Labour process	The process by which labour is transformed into goods and services. In this process, it has been argued, management seeks to maximize its control over the workforce.
Laissez-faire	The idea that the government should not intervene in society, particularly applied to the economy. *Laissez-faire* economists would argue against price or wage controls, believing that the market should be left to determine supply and demand. It could be taken as an ideology supporting the wealthy and powerful.

Legalism	An ideology which assumes that employer and employee have freely entered into a binding contract of employment (ignoring the fact that the employer is considerably stronger).
Nepotism	The practice of passing power or privilege to members of one's own family; for example the managing director appointing her son to an important job in the company.
Norms	The usual and approved ways of doing things; what is seen to be 'normal' in a society or group.
Paternalism	A term used of firms which look after their employees well, providing good working conditions and benefits where the primary objective is really just to raise productivity. The idea is that of a father looking after children, so it can be criticized as patronizing – not giving workers equal status.
Prejudice	The holding of preconceived ideas about an individual or group, ideas that are resistant to change even when new information is provided. Prejudices cloud our judgement, preventing us seeing people as they really are. The ideologies of racism, sexism and ageism work in favour of the more powerful.
Profession	One of several occupations devoted to particular tasks, requiring high-level educational qualifications usually subject to codes of conduct laid down by central bodies, for example law or medicine. Professions involve high status. Some jobs can become professionalized (e.g. personnel management) while others lose status (e.g. nursing or teaching).
Proletarianization	Middle-class people becoming absorbed into the working class. This can happen to groups as well as individuals.
Psychologism	An ideology which assumes that the individual must adjust to the organization rather than vice versa.
Racism	The attributing of characteristics of superiority or inferiority to a population sharing certain physically inherited characteristics.
Reserve army (of the unemployed)	Those unemployed people who are only sought for work by employers when times are good (especially women).

Role	This refers to the part we play in society. We all have several roles, such as father/ mother/child, teacher/doctor/factory worker/ housewife, voter/peace campaigner, patient, church-goer. The concept of roles is important in sociology as it links the individual and society. Society defines what the 'correct' roles are, and how they should be performed, and we all expect people to conform. We have definite expectations as to how a priest, nurse, manager, lawyer, etc. should behave.
Scientific management ('Taylorism')	A set of ideas about industrial management put forward by Frederick Taylor. It involves separation of management functions (thinking) from actual production; each worker's job is to be as simple as possible. Management must say not only *what* is to be done but also *how* it is to be done. It has become a widely accepted ideology used to justify firm (even oppressive) rule by management.
Sexism	Discrimination or prejudice against a person on grounds of their sex.
Social mobility	The movement of individuals or groups between different social positions. Upward social mobility is where a person moves to a higher social class than that of his or her parents. Downward social mobility involves moving to a lower social position, e.g. the son of a lawyer who becomes a plumber.
Socialization	The process by which people acquire the norms and values of the society they have entered. Examples include children who watch and copy their parents and thereby learn the role of man or woman, father or mother, and so on; and immigrants who have to learn the norms and values of their new country.
Society	A group of people who live in a particular territory, are subject to a common system of political authority and are aware of having a distinct identity and of sharing the same values.
Status	The social prestige or honour which a person or group is accorded by other members of a society. Status normally goes with particular life-styles.

Structuralism (*in organizations*)	This is an ideology which assumes the way an organization is structured cannot be changed; that the current structure is the most 'efficient'.
Technological determinism	This denotes that it is the technology that determines our society. (Against this view sociologists show that society itself creates the conditions in which new technology occurs.) See chapter 8.
Values	Ideas held by individuals or groups about what is desirable, proper, good or bad. What individuals value is strongly influenced by the society in which they live.
Welfareism	This is similar to paternalism (above).
Work ethic (*Protestant ethic*)	The idea that work is valuable in itself; that one should work hard and aim to succeed. Early Protestants believed that material success in this world might be a sign of fitness for the next.

Index

Index by Elizabeth Clutton